D1528563

Democracy in Question

Democracy in Question

Democratic Openness in a Time of Political Closure

Alan Keenan

STANFORD UNIVERSITY PRESS

Stanford, California

Stanford University Press
Stanford, California

© 2003 by the Board of Trustees of the
Leland Stanford Junior University.
All rights reserved.

Printed in the United States of America
on acid-free, archival-quality paper.

Library of Congress Cataloging-in-Publication Data
Keenan, Alan.

Democracy in question : democratic openness in a
time of political closure / Alan Keenan.
    p.   cm.
Includes index.
ISBN 0-8047-3747-9 (cloth : alk. paper) —
ISBN 0-8047-3865-3 (pbk. : alk. paper)
1. Democracy. I. Title.
JC423 .K363 2002
321.8 — dc21 2002005862

Original Printing 2003

Last figure below indicates year of this printing:
12   11   10   09   08   07   06   05   04   03

Typeset by BookMatters in 10/12 Sabon

To my parents & to my friends
Maria, Cathy, Jon, Ira, Jane, and Hawley

Contents

Acknowledgments

The ideas and arguments in these chapters have been developed over a number of years at a variety of institutions and within various intellectual contexts. It is my pleasure to publicly express my appreciation for the institutional support, the intellectual exchanges and advice, and the friendship that have made this book possible. Although writing the book hasn't quite been a democratic process, it has taught me the democratic lesson of just how much I owe to all those others who help make "my" work possible.

I have written and rewritten much of the book while being paid to teach, so it bears the traces of the courses I have taught and the many students who have freely shared with me their reactions to my ideas in the making. From the handful of patient students in my first seminar in the Humanities Center at the Johns Hopkins University, to the much more crowded classrooms of the Department of Rhetoric at the University of California at Berkeley and the Politics Board at the University of California at Santa Cruz, and finally to the cozy freshman seminars and sophomore and junior tutorials in Social Studies at Harvard University, my students, through their intelligence, enthusiasm for political life, intellectual curiosity, and critical responses, have strengthened my arguments immeasurably and have helped keep alive my own intellectual enthusiasm. I thank them all for sharing their talents with me.

I am also thankful for the support and criticism of my teachers and colleagues at all four institutions. In roughly chronological order, my thanks go to the following readers for all their critical insights and helpful suggestions: Neil Hertz, Kirstie McClure, Vincent Descombes, Suzette Hemberger, Fred Dolan, Marianne Constable, Ken Cmiel, Peter Euben, Jeremy Elkins, Pratap Mehta, Glyn Morgan, April Flakne, David Peritz, Sayres Rudy, Peter Lindsay, David Kahane, Lawrie Balfour, Patchen Markell, Jill Frank, and all the members of the Social Studies political and social theory reading group.

Special thanks go to Judith Butler, Richard Flathman, Bonnie Honig, and most especially William Connolly. For their years of encouragement, intelligence, gentle criticisms, and continuing support, I will always be grateful.

Others who have kindly taken the trouble to read various chapters and offer valuable comments include Wendy Brown, Jane Bennett, Michael Shapiro, Jeff Tulis, David Braybrooke, Tom Dumm, Anne Norton, Mark Warren, Tracy Strong, Melissa Williams, Rein de Wilde, Kostas Economou, Per-Anders Forstorp, Sissel Myklebust, Mikel Hard, and anonymous readers at *Political Theory* and Stanford University Press. Thanks also to Carrie Mullen for her enthusiasm and hard work on my behalf and to Helen Tartar for patiently allowing the manuscript to turn into a book.

I have also benefited enormously from a group of friends, now scattered across the world, whose encouragement, advice, critical acumen, sense of humor, and kindness have helped sustain me and helped improve the book. This work would not have been possible without their spirited support. I thank Zarin Ahmad, John Barry, Emily Berg, Chip Bradish, Francesca Bremner, Barbara Brown, Jennifer Culbert, Ori Dasberg, Tanya Elder, Liz Goodstein, Vanessa Gosselin, Samantha Hammond, Thich Nhat Hanh, Beatrice Hanssen, Elke Heckner, Beatrice Juaregui, Priscilla Lee, Jennifer Lindstrom, Sid Maskit, Prasannan Parthasarathi, Tom Quinn, Steve Rubenstein, Bill Taylor, and Karen Werner. Thanks also to Maria Poulos for generously opening her doors, and to Minel Perera for her care and hospitality, at the last stages of the book's coming into being.

Finally, I thank my family, and a group of friends who have been like a second family to me. Thanks to my brother, Tom Keenan, without whose example and inspiration I would never have been crazy enough to begin such a project, for all the support he has shown me in my intellectual endeavors over the years. From my parents, Joan Swenson Keenan and Francis Keenan, I have received the love of books, politics, and ideas, together with the confidence to try to express my own; I have also received much love, financial support, and encouragement along the way. I am particularly delighted that the cover displays the latest talent of my late-bloomer father. For almost two decades now, I have also been blessed with a very special set of friends who have shared the ups and downs of my intellectual pursuits and whose many talents have helped make this book possible. For all the pages of mine they have read and commented on, the conversations and arguments we have shared, the dinners they have cooked for me and eaten with me, for the long walks together, for believing in the book even when I doubted it, and for the love and encouragement that has kept me going in a million other ways, I dedicate the book to all of them, too: Maria Farland, Cathy Kerr, Jon Kranes, Ira Paneth, Jane Thrailkill, and Hawley Truax.

I thank the following journals for permission to reprint material originally published in their pages: An earlier version of Chapter 2 was published as "Promises, Promises: The Abyss of Freedom and the Loss of the Political in the Work of Hannah Arendt," *Political Theory* 22, 1 (May 1994). A section of Chapter 3 was published originally as "The Difficult Politics of Democracy: Freedom, Openness, and Contingency in the Recent Work of Ernesto Laclau," *Political and Legal Anthropology Review* 18, 1 (May 1995). Finally, small sections of Chapter 4 were originally published as part of "The Twilight of the Political? A Contribution to the Democratic Critique of Cynicism," in the electronic journal *Theory and Event* 2, 1 (February 1998), http://muse.jhu.edu/journals/theory_&_event.

The Master views the parts with compassion,
because he understands the whole.

— *Tao Te Ching*

Introduction

Democratic Openness and the Difficult Experience of Political Freedom

Those who met together with intention to erect a city, were almost in the very act of meeting, a democracy. For in that they willingly met, they are supposed obliged to the observation of what shall be determined by the major part; which while that convent lasts, or is adjourned to some certain days and places, is a clear democracy. For that convent, whose will is the will of all the citizens, hath the supreme authority; and because in this convent every man is supposed to have a right to give his voice, it follows that it is a democracy.

— Thomas Hobbes, *De Cive: or, The Citizen*

It goes without saying that all forms of the state have democracy for their truth and that they are therefore untrue insofar as they are not democracy.

— Karl Marx, "Contribution to the Critique of Hegel's Philosophy of Right"

Democracy, Now?

This study of democratic politics begins from, and attempts to make sense of, the radical premise — and promise — that in a democracy it is the people who rule. In a democracy it is not a special class of citizens who rule over the rest, but the citizens themselves, coming together as political equals to give themselves their own laws and run their own governing institutions, guided by their respect for the common welfare and the equal freedom of all. Or in Abraham Lincoln's felicitous phrase, democracy means "a government of the people, by the people, and for the people."

What can these ideals mean today, though? And how precisely are they radical? For although *democracy* was once a word both scorned and feared by those in power and by those whose privileges rested on entrenched hierarchies removed from popular scrutiny and control, today it would seem that the language and ideals of democracy are spoken and accepted everywhere, by rulers, elites, and commoners alike.[1]

When one looks more closely, however, it seems as though the ubiquity, even the banality, of the democratic idea today has been bought at the cost of fully respecting its central principles.[2] Indeed, to be engaged in a study of the radical nature of democracy has often seemed a quixotic task, especially given the particular vantage point from which it has been written — that of the United States in the last few years of the twentieth century and the very beginning of the twenty-first. For any attempt to take seriously the radical impulse behind democratic politics is immediately confronted with a daunting, apparently paradoxical, challenge. In the name of democracy itself, a particular form of political society — one of formal liberal freedoms, constitutional norms, regular elections, and increasingly deregulated economic markets — has been enshrined across the globe as the only legitimate, even imaginable, form of political society. So much so, in fact, that it seems at times as if debates about political legitimacy and the meaning of democracy have already been decided, with little or no room left for other, more participatory and egalitarian interpretations of democracy's central principles.

Yet even as this particular form of liberal democracy has largely triumphed institutionally and ideologically, its deep limitations are increasingly apparent.[3] For the reigning understandings and practices of democracy, both in the United States and elsewhere, increasingly offer only a limited and symbolic role to citizen participation and power.[4] Not only has the scope of democratic rule been reduced almost entirely to the election of, and then governance by, public officials, but even within this sphere, average citizens have an ever more limited role to play. Doubts about whether the people can really be said to rule in the United States were raised with unusual vigor and visibility after the presidential election of 2000, when the results of the undemocratic Electoral College trumped those of the majority of voters. Doubts about the people's rule were warranted even before this election, however, by the steady decline in voting rates over the past forty years, which now means that victorious candidates to national office frequently win after receiving barely a quarter of the votes of adult citizens.[5] The shrinking percentage of those eligible voters who choose to vote no doubt has something to do with the fact that elections today, both in the United States and increasingly in the rest of the world, are dominated by massively expensive private television and radio advertisements. With campaigns largely limited to the airwaves and increasingly oriented toward small segments of the electorate rather than toward mass mobilization, there is less room than ever for average citizens to be active participants, much less candidates for office themselves.[6] And with the expenses of political campaigns paid for by the rich and by large, powerful institutions, citizens largely find themselves reduced to spectator-voters, unable to influence the political agenda except in sporadic and marginal ways.[7] This, in turn, convinces ever greater numbers of citizens that politicians care only for themselves and their wealthy contributors, that political issues are thus of little concern to them, and that citizens' votes don't count.[8] As the percentage of those who vote shrinks further, laws and public policies come to reflect ever more clearly the interests and influence of the wealthy and powerful few, rather than the needs and interests of average citizens, thus explaining in part the large and disturbing increase in economic inequality in the United States over the past thirty years.[9]

Although the central principles of democracy — citizen participation, accountable government, equal treatment, and institutions that are open to revision according to the needs of the people themselves — may thus still be formally enshrined in the laws and political institutions, the people themselves are increasingly locked out of their own political system. Such closures are both procedural — taking the form of barriers to a wider range of people having their voices heard about a larger range of ideas and political possibilities — and substantive, in the sense that many of the options most difficult to have heard and seriously considered are those in which citizens would have greater control over their collective lives and in which policies and institutions would be more egalitarian and more oriented to common concerns and needs. With more accountable, participatory, and egalitarian alternatives to the political and social status quo largely excluded from the political agenda, any active project of democratic renewal would necessarily be radical, challenging the basic political relationships and institutions of today's society.

To give up on democracy meaning anything more than the existence of "free" markets and regular elections would seem, then, to condemn ourselves to the most depressing form of cynical resignation. We would be left to go through the motions of a system whose legitimating principles had largely been rendered meaningless. Yet whether we are political theorists or democratic citizens, we would seem in danger of provoking cynicism whichever direction we turned. For simply to press on in the face of such obstacles and democratic deficits for the achievement of a radical interpretation of democracy's principles of equal power, active participation, and radical questioning would risk generating even more disappointment and public disenchantment when such strong interpretations of democratic principles prove, as they have in the past, to be less than fully realizable.[10] This would be especially true if, as many have argued, modern democracy itself is defined by the very absence of a clear identity or direct experience of the people themselves. Even if one chooses not to accept the pessimism of Max Weber's "Caesarean democracy" or the apparent realism of Joseph Schumpeter, both of which in their different ways reduce the role of the people to convenient fictions at the disposal of nondemocratic leaders, much evidence suggests that the people's present "eclipse" is more than a contingent, and in theory reversible, setback to democratic progress.[11] Indeed, a strong argument can be made that the uncertain, ghostly character of the people today is in some ways in the nature of modern democracy, perhaps even of democracy as such. To the extent that this is true, and the rule of the people is always open to question, the central issue for those who wish to take seriously democracy's radical promise of popular power and participation would then become how to resist today's democratic closures without demanding an impossibly direct or transparent rule of the people. What, in other words, is the relation between the politics of opening and openness characteristic of radical democracy and the particular form of democratic openness that emerges when there is no clear people who would rule? Are these forms of democratic openness at odds with each other, or is there a more complicated, potentially fruitful relationship between them? What are the various meanings of democratic "openness" and how do they relate to what I have begun to suggest is the *radical* nature of democratic politics?

These questions are at the heart of this book. In it I offer no new definition of democracy or radical democracy. Nor do I propose a normative defense or justification of any particular practice of democratic politics. Instead, I attempt to excavate and make sense of the radical impulses within the democratic ideal and by doing so reveal the central role that the concept and practice of openness — in various and complex forms — play in democratic politics. I argue that an awareness of these forms of openness can illuminate a number of crucial — and difficult — aspects of democratic politics, ones that any theory or practice of democracy will encounter, most especially those that seek to take its central principles as seriously, and radically, as possible. Respecting democratic openness, I argue, presents basic challenges to both democratic theory and practice. Yet as I argue in the final chapter, it can also suggest the possibility of modest but important resources for creating more sustainable forms of democratic politics, ones that might more successfully negotiate the tensions between democracy's radical promise and the people's uncertain, ghostly presence today.

Radical Democracy and the Uncertain People

An initial sense of the deep connections between modern democracy and the uncertain, questionable status of the people — and of political and social foundations more generally — can be glimpsed in Alexis de Tocqueville's discussion of the "democratic revolution" in the introduction to *Democracy in America*.[12] For Tocqueville, the democratic revolution refers not to any particular historical event but rather to the gradual but inevitable trend toward "equality of condition" for all classes of society (5), a trend that had already been long under way by the time he was writing in the early eighteenth century. Democracy, in this interpretation, is born with the slow but "irresistible" collapse of social and political hierarchies previously believed to be grounded in the nature of things, and ultimately in God's will. Democracy, Tocqueville explains, comes into being when "the noble" can no longer simply assume "the privileges which he believed to be legitimate" and the serf no longer "looks upon his own inferiority as a consequence of the immutable order of nature" (8–9). The image of society as a natural, hierarchical order is slowly and through much struggle replaced by the ideal of equal freedom, of "a society in which all men would feel an equal love and respect for the laws of which they consider themselves the authors," and where each "perceive[s] that his personal interest is identified with the interests of the whole community" (9–10). As the grounds of the aristocratic order give way, there emerges "the people," both as the name for all those who remain in the absence of that order and as the ideal of a community to which all belong equally and which acts as its own self-constituting foundation.

According to the terms of such a definition, however, it remains quite uncertain what it actually means for the people to rule. Democracy is defined instead primarily by the *absence* of the previous foundations undermined by the corrosive logic of social and political equality. In a sense, then, the people rule by default, through lack of any other suitable or effective foundation, but without being a terribly clear principle of authority themselves. Born of the process of questioning previous forms of hierarchical authority, democracy and the people would themselves be essentially questionable. Democracy would thus be that regime in which there are no other grounds for legitimate authority than the community members themselves, governed by the principle of equality, yet without any clear guide as to what that means: When and where are they equal, and in what ways? What does it mean to "share" power and to be together as equals? How and when are the people to rule?

Explicitly following in this Tocquevillean line of argument, the contemporary French political philosopher Claude Lefort expands on and radicalizes the open nature of democracy and the questionable status of the people. For Lefort, the democratic revolution takes place when the king's body ceases to function as the ideal image and anchor of society's unity, "when the body politic was decapitated and when, at the same time, the corporeality of the social was dissolved."[13] Democracy arrives with "the disappearance of the natural or supernatural basis which . . . gave . . . authority an unassailable legitimacy and an understanding both of the ultimate ends of society and of the behavior of the people it assigned to specific stations and functions."[14] With the birth of the people as sovereign, and the symbolic beheading of the king, power is no longer understood as grounded in a body. Instead, "the locus of power becomes an empty place": "it cannot be occupied — it is such that no individual and no group can be consubstantial with it — and it cannot be represented."[15] The openness that accompanies the disincorporation of society produces a fundamental transformation in the status of "grounds" of all sorts, not just in how power is used and understood. Democracy, for Lefort, is "instituted and sustained" by the general "*dissolution of the markers of certainty*" and brings with it the experience of "a fundamental indeterminacy as to the basis of power, law and knowledge, and as to the basis of relations between *self* and *other*, at every level of social life" (QD 19, emphases in original). The generalization of uncertainty that comes with the absence of natural and/or divine foundations makes all aspects of society fundamentally questionable:

There is no law that can be fixed, whose articles cannot be contested, whose foundations are not susceptible of being called into question. . . . There is no representation of a center and of the contours of society: unity cannot now efface social division. Democracy inaugurates the experience of an ungraspable, uncontrollable society in which the people will be said to be sovereign, of course, but whose identity will constantly be open to question, whose identity will remain latent. (BT 303–4)

In Lefort's narrative, what replaces the people's common body, grounded in that of the king and in God, is the "public space." Writing of the freedom of thought and opinion established by the French "Declaration of the Rights of Man and Citizen" of 1791, Lefort argues that

as everyone acquires the right to address others and to listen to them, a symbolic space is established; it has no definite frontiers, and no authority can claim to control it or to decide what can and what cannot be thought, what can and cannot be said. Speech as such and thought as such prove to exist independently of any given individual and belong to no one. (HR 33)

This public space is the space of freedom: it is called into being through the declaration and the continual exercise of certain freedoms (of speech, assembly, and so forth), which exist beyond the control of any authority; it forms the "location" in which the other rights so essential to democracy are formulated, questioned, debated, and accepted.

What democratic citizens have in common, then, according to Lefort's analysis, is not a substantive common good or shared collective identity but an ever-changing set of rights, a public space, and a commitment to the process of argument about those rights, a process that takes place within that space. Rights thus constitute a primary discourse through which the community continuously names and renames itself, through which it tries to define what it is that all share as its equal members. And given that it is only in the declaration of specific rights that the "ground" of those rights — humanity, or the people — itself comes into being, rights are never established once and for all. They emerge out of the community's continuous debate in the public sphere over "who" it is, as part of its "constant search for a basis" (HR 34). If democracy has a ground, then, or anything like an "absolute," it is this debate itself. "Modern democracy," Lefort writes, "invites us to replace the notion of a regime governed by laws, of a legitimate power, by the notion of a regime founded upon *the legitimacy of a debate as to what is legitimate and what is illegitimate* — a debate which is necessarily without any guarantor and without any end" (HR 39).

In this understanding of democracy, then, a fundamental uncertainty would necessarily haunt any legitimately democratic society. Indeed, the radicality of democracy on this reading would lie in the way in which the people form not so much a clear ground as the open site and object of permanent debate and contestation. Yet it is hard to see how the other, stronger, vision of democratic rule can ever simply disappear without democracy itself disappearing. In Sheldon Wolin's words, democracy would be "a project concerned with the political potentialities of ordinary citizens, that is, with their possibilities for becoming political beings through the self-discovery of *common* concerns and of modes of action for *realizing* them."[16] For *democratic* to be a meaningful description of a political society, then, there needs to be more than simply debate and the public space and rights that enable it. We must also be able to make a plausible case that the community as a whole in fact manages its own affairs, both in the sense of actively caring about and participating in collective decision-making and in terms of the quality of the decisions made — that is, in their respecting the basic equality of all citizens and in their orientation toward the common needs and concerns of the people themselves. Indeed, to a degree that Lefort does not always recognize,

there must be a significant degree of equality and commonality established between citizens simply for political conflict and debate to be effectively and sustainably institutionalized, that is, for the conflict to be about
the people's shared rights rather than taking the form of oppression or
civil war.

One of the basic concerns of this book is to investigate the precise relationship between these two different "radical" strands and visions of
democracy and the different senses of openness and community they
involve. The radical promise of democracy would lie, in one sense, in the
possibility of a community of equals, bound together in the common
project of ruling themselves and maintaining the equality and commonality necessary to that rule and to achieving their shared ends. Yet the radical nature of democracy would simultaneously reside in the experience of
the basic uncertainty and questioning that comes with this "being-
together-as-equals" with no ground other than that which the community
members themselves determine. Whereas the radical nature of democracy
on the first vision aims, at least in part, at the achievement of something
like a shared identity — if only in a set of rights that all would equally
enjoy — the radicality of democratic politics would, from the other angle,
amount to the impossibility of ever achieving a people who could be said
or seen to rule clearly. The people and democratic politics would thus
have this constitutive openness — Lefort's "empty place" of power — at
their very "center," or "ground."

It is one of the central claims of the chapters that follow that these two
strands of democratic politics and their apparently opposed forms of radicality are, in fact, deeply intertwined. This connection has already been
implied in certain of the passages quoted from Lefort, when he suggests
that it is precisely *because* the people are sovereign and must therefore
give themselves their own law and foundation that their identity is rendered deeply questionable and democratic politics comes to be characterized by fundamental openness (of various sorts). It is through what is best
if somewhat inadequately called a deconstructive reading of the most
basic definition of democracy — the rule of the people — that I initially
explore this relationship, and the complex meanings of democratic openness, in greater depth. By *deconstructive* I refer to a mode of critical
analysis that works to reveal the inherently unstable, internally inconsis-
tent logic of self-identity. In this particular case, the analysis centers on the
collective self-identity of the political community — or "the people" — and
the moment, or rather process, of their supposed self-constitution or self-
foundation. It aims to reveal the *non*simultaneity and essentially rhetorical nature of the process whereby the people must call itself into being as
a political community of equals. Such an analysis thus works to show

how the very logic of collective autonomy at the heart of the ideal of democratic self-rule renders uncertain and questionable the "self," or collective subject, of "the people." Oddly enough, that is, through a close analysis of the logic of democratic autonomy, which promises a collective political entity in charge and in control of itself, we end up at something very much like Lefort's democratic *un*certainty, openness, and questioning. My analysis aims not only to show the instability and uncertainty of democratic identity and subjectivity, however; in an attempt to move beyond earlier deconstructive political analyses, it also aims to investigate the complicated and difficult effects this uncertainty has on the theory and practice of democratic politics and the need to formulate productive responses to its effects. An underlying theme of the book, then, is a consideration of the often heated topic of the political implications of deconstructive critique.[17] Although this theme is only explicitly raised in the final two chapters, I nonetheless offer the book in part as a modest contribution to such debates, in hope of suggesting the important aspects of democratic politics that can be illuminated through such an approach, as well as the serious limits that such analyses encounter when trying to come to terms with the actual experience of democratic political judgment and action.

Democratic Openness and the Paradoxes of Collective Autonomy

The central arguments of this book about the nature and difficulty of democratic openness, then, grow out of a consideration of the logic of collective autonomy embedded in the ideal of democracy as the rule of the people. Through an initial engagement with the radically democratic portrait that Cornelius Castoriadis paints of the ancient Athenian polis, I argue that democratic politics is animated — in the sense of both enlivened and haunted — by the ideal of a fully open community. Such openness would be twofold. First, in order for it to be the people who rule, rather than some faction or special class of the people, the process of making decisions must be open to all members of the community affected by them. For the same reason, decisions and arguments must be oriented toward the concerns and needs shared by the community as a whole; it must be the general interest that motivates collective decisions, not the personal interests of only some. It is through respecting such general concerns and commonality that the people becomes a "people" and not just a collection, or, in the favored language of the social contract tradition, a "multitude" of individuals. In this sense, then, democratic politics is first of all characterized by the openness of *inclusion* and *generality* that is needed for the people's rule.

Democratic self-rule also requires that it be the people or community of *today* who rule, not that of yesterday, or of tradition. For the people to be free and to give themselves their own law, they must be able to revise their decisions, institutions, and practices as they wish or need.[18] Thus the centrality to democratic politics of a second kind of openness that is institutionalized in habits and rights of debate, argumentation, questioning, and revisability. As both Castoriadis and Lefort argue at length, the democratic spirit or imaginary is fundamentally one of questioning. For the community's rules to be their own, nothing can be taken for granted or closed off from critique and revision. Thus democratic politics in principle renders everything provisional and open to question. Such debate and argument, of course, are required not only for purposes of revisability and resistance to entrenched institutionalization. They are also necessary aspects of the openness of inclusion and generality. For what members of the political community are included "within" is precisely the debate about, and ultimate formation of, what it is that holds them together as a community of equals.

In practice, however, and in order to respect the very same principle of the rule of the people, it turns out that the people cannot be fully open, either in the sense of fully inclusive and general, or in the sense of fully open to question. As I argue in the first chapter, in a critical reading of Castoriadis, in order to be the kind of entity able to have and to regulate its own collective life, "the people" must take on an identity whose relative clarity and stability depend on *particular* foundations, traditions, and institutional forms that cannot be fully general or fully open to question. It is only through the widespread attachment to or identification with such forms and markers of collective identity — whether constitutions, the stories of particular political histories, or specific procedures of inclusion and participation — that the community takes on enough form to be and to rule itself. These less than perfectly open practices, institutions, and markers of identity function, in fact, as the necessary background to the activity of questioning, contestation, and revision. It is only when such practices, and the assumptions and habits that go with them, are in place that other things can be called into question in properly democratic fashion. As I argue first with respect to the radical democratic ideal of Castoriadis and later in response to the "deliberative" model of democratic legitimacy offered by Seyla Benhabib, the *procedural* openness of an inclusive debate, oriented toward general concerns and always open to revision, inevitably encounters limits, ultimately taking on particular, less than open, and *substantive* forms.

The closures necessary to the people's identity and rule, then, in a paradox typical of democratic self-rule, mean that the people never in fact completely closes in on itself, never reaches completion or achievement. I argue that this nonclosure can, in turn, be understood to constitute a third form of democratic openness: the openness of *incompletion* and *imperfection*. This is so for the paradoxical reason that the democratic ideals of openness characteristic of collective autonomy — both the openness of inclusion and generality and that of collective self-revisability — are in another sense equally ideals of closure: of the people knowing, controlling, and being present to itself in and through its equality and collective identifications. In this sense, then, the limits on democratic openness sketched out above, and argued for at length in the first three chapters, produce their own more chastening and difficult form of democratic openness, with the people themselves rendered more fully questionable — in the sense of doubtful, uncertain, open to challenge — than even Castoriadis, with his equation of democracy and questioning, is able to accept.

If the political community is never fully achieved *as* "a people" — as a general and open entity — it is instead constantly in formation, continually in the process of calling itself, and being called, into being. To better understand the complexities of the process through which the people is formed and reformed, I turn to Rousseau's famous discussion of the people's self-foundation in *On the Social Contract*. Through a close reading that focuses on the paradox of foundation that Rousseau himself locates, according to which "the effect would have to become the cause," I argue that the very fact of the people's autonomy — that they themselves must form themselves into a people, yet without natural or external rules for what they share that makes them a people — renders their identity and legitimacy forever open to question. The very absence of authoritative grounds other than those affirmed by the people themselves means that some element prior to or other than the people will always be necessary to the people's coming into existence. As I argue in the first chapter and then in different ways throughout the book, despite the best efforts of Rousseau (and the tradition of political theory as a whole) to solve or avoid the paradox, it remains ineradicable, posing both practical and theoretical problems that are constitutive of democratic politics as a whole.

In the particular version found in Rousseau's text, the paradox concerns how the people, in the process of self-foundation, can find or create the laws that would guarantee the equal treatment and general norms necessary to their legitimate authority (and thus their existence as a people). Rousseau's answer is that they would be able to create, or recognize, such general laws only if they had already developed the social spirit — the orientation toward generality and attachment to the common good — which it is precisely the job of the general laws to create. The people need to form themselves — in their generality and social spirit — through common identifications with a particular vision of equality and commonality. But where will this vision of commonality and the common attachment to it come from? How will people be able to look beyond their individual interest to recognize the interest they share as members of the community until such a communal interest and norms are already established in practice?

Rousseau's "solution" to this problem is to recommend that his hypothetical founding legislator, or lawgiver, invoke the powers and authority of "the gods" in order to persuade or threaten the people into accepting his laws for their own good. Although this is obviously neither a practical, nor a democratic, solution to the problem, I argue that the paradox, and the role Rousseau gives to the legislator, nonetheless points to the need for various non-autonomous rhetorical and political interventions to construct the people's autonomy. For the freedom and openness of the people's foundation, which means that "they" must call themselves into being before they exist and thus from a point that is not yet "the people" themselves, rule out the possibility of there being any politically neutral source of generality, or definition of who the people are. One must therefore speak and act in the name of the people before receiving the people's own sanction, in an attempt to call the people into being and form their generality from a not-yet-fully-democratic position. Indeed, as I show in a reading of Rousseau's own suggestions for negotiating these difficulties, as well as through a critique of Seyla Benhabib's deliberative model of democratic legitimacy, one is often forced to use less than fully democratic or open procedures precisely in the hopes of making things more democratic and more open. Democratic politics, I argue, is in this and other ways forever torn between the demands of openness — in the form of inclusion or in the form of contestation and revisability — and those of closure — of limiting participation, or of more or less forcefully closing down debate so as to defend or institutionalize a particular vision of the people and of equality. Yet without any external, nonpolitical, non-self-generated standards for judging the "correct" vision of the people — without, that is, anything beyond what our always imperfect and incompletely open deliberations and negotiations can produce — one can never be certain of what the most democratic course of action is. Although I argue that there are ways of bringing the people into (partial) being that are more democratic than others, whatever legitimacy such action and its end results have can only be determined retroactively.

Democratic politics is thus caught in a perpetual state of transition, with democracy never fully, or once and for all, achieved, and with the democratic "we" always uncertain, the site of perpetual contestation. This, then, constitutes from a different angle the third form of democratic openness mentioned above: that of the fundamental incompletion of the democratic "we" and the uncertainty of democratic action, grounded as it is in principles and demands that have no necessary coherence. Torn between openness and closure, and between different forms of openness, the experience of democratic politics frequently requires one to risk, or even violate, some democratic principles in order to respect others. Democracy must, in short, always remain a *question*, for no theory of democracy can ever be adequate to the experience of democratic politics. Rather than offering answers, democracy presents citizens and theorists alike with a set of questions: Who are the people? What is it that they have in common? How should they rule? How best can the need to establish their rule be weighed against the need to make that rule effectively questionable? These are questions whose "solutions," I argue, can only be generated out of a process of situated, practical, judgment and through which one can never be certain to have gotten closer to the democratic ideal "itself."

Responding to Democracy's Radical Incompletion

My argument thus amounts to a challenge to two other traditions of theorizing the radical nature of democracy. It challenges, first, the very ideal of radical democracy as unmediated popular power, arguing that the vision of the people ruling itself clearly and directly is an impossible one — for the very ideal of democratic openness and freedom is at odds with itself, torn between the closure necessary for the people's identity and rule, and the openness of contestation and revisability. What's more, in the face of such deep democratic uncertainty, the demand for the clear rule of the people can take on dangerous dimensions, as the drive to closure built into the ideal of collective autonomy threatens to take more forceful, even violent, forms. To limit such dangers (for I argue that such force can only be limited, never simply ruled out), sustainable democratic politics requires the institutionalized *affirmation* of the impossibility of ever completing the democratic community or of achieving democratic legitimacy once and for all.

The more complex and chastened vision of radical democracy sketched out in the following chapters is thus a challenge to both the overoptimism and the hyperpessimism of much of the radical democratic tradition. Although my argument cautions against attempts to realize democratic community and popular power in direct and complete forms, it rejects the pessimistic reading that democratic politics is doomed to irrelevance or only sporadic, "fugitive" appearances.[19] As I suggest more fully below, the awareness and acceptance of democracy's uncertain and questionable status open the way both to recognizing the need for and to developing strategies that can make the difficulties of democratic politics more easily endured. With such strategies, I suggest, the thrust of radical democratic politics would shift from the attempt to achieve full autonomy and popular power to the work of negotiating democracy's dilemmas in the most sustainable and inclusive way possible.

The vision of the radical and uncertain nature of democratic politics elaborated in the chapters that follow also challenges another well-known school of radical democratic thought, that of the tradition of critical theory exemplified by Jürgen Habermas and others following in his wake. In the first chapter I address directly the work of Seyla Benhabib, whose "deliberative model of democratic legitimacy" explicitly relies on the work of Habermas's discourse theory of ethics. Although endorsing the fundamental value of equal and reciprocal deliberation to democratic politics, I argue nonetheless that the establishment of a democratic community, including the procedures of deliberation themselves, will at certain moments require nondeliberative, even forceful, means, the legitimacy of which can be confirmed only after the fact. Indeed, the conditions that make equal and reciprocal deliberation possible — including the willingness and ability of citizens to be invested in the outcomes of rational and general discussions — must themselves be laid at times by less than democratic, deliberative, or open and inclusive means. The silence of Benhabib's theory of deliberative democracy on such issues is, I argue, emblematic of a more general limitation of the mode of political theory her work involves. Although she, along with Habermas, accepts that the legitimacy of any particular set of political practices, institutions, or ideals, must always be open to question, her theory has no room to grapple with the practical effects of the deeper questionability that haunts all democratic action. The rationalist goal of producing a regulative ideal of democratic deliberation, argued as it must be from the perspective of perfected procedures of rational deliberation, against which actual practices are judged, has little to say about some of the most crucial questions raised by the necessity of acting in a political world in which one must frequently risk one democratic value in one's effort to respect another.

This is meant to suggest one advantage of a theory of democratic politics that highlights the nonsimultaneity of the people's self-foundation and the paradoxes and dilemmas that follow from it. Such an approach brings out more clearly both the difficult — because strategic, necessarily pragmatic and prudential — nature of democratic political practice and the corresponding necessity of strategies designed to make engagement in democratic action more easily endured. For the practice of democratic politics is particularly trying. It requires that one not only act on the basis of uncertain grounds and with questionable legitimacy — in the name of a people not yet, and never fully, in existence — but also that one frequently put at risk, perhaps even knowingly sacrifice, certain of its own ideals, yet without ever knowing in advance the full consequences of one's choices. The frustrations, doubts, and existential burdens that this entails — the more so the more seriously one takes one's democratic responsibilities — make democratic engagement anything but an easy endeavor (especially, as I argue in the final chapter, under contemporary conditions). Thus, although no theory of democracy can simply answer its fundamental questions, a democratic theory attuned to the ineradicable nature of its difficulties and dilemmas, unlike a more rationalist and perfectionist approach like Benhabib's, can suggest, as more than an afterthought, the need to develop strategies that help sustain, rather than discourage, democratic energies.

Central to the book's argument, in short, is the claim that for a more robust, egalitarian, and participatory form of democratic politics to be made sustainable, one need not only foster democratic identifications and the people's social spirit but also develop ways of respecting the constitutive incompletion and uncertainty of the democratic "we." For the condition of democratic incompletion and noncoherence of its basic principles — which I have been referring to as the third form of democratic openness — threatens to undermine democratic attachments and energies unless it is responded to in effective ways. These responses, I argue, constitute a fourth form of openness essential to a sustainable experience of the radical nature of democracy. Such responses would, among other things, take the form of resisting the more forceful and pseudo-democratic productions of the democratic "we," ones that Rousseau's story of the legislator can also be read as alerting us to. Affirming rather than denying democracy's constitutive incompletion, such a mode of democratic politics would require attitudes of forbearance, self-limitation, and openness to collective self-questioning. These would complement more classical modes of liberal dissent and contestation by working to limit the force involved in forming a democratic community, in part by actively contesting claims to be able to achieve, or to have actually achieved, democratic openness or generality.

An effectively egalitarian and participatory project of democratic politics would, then, have to abandon any hope of solving the problem of uncertain democratic legitimacy and the difficulties involved in the people's perpetual "state of transition." It would need, instead, to turn to developing means of better negotiating the difficulties and dilemmas posed for democratic citizens by such a political condition. At the heart of the book's final chapter is my argument for the need to develop a distinct democratic ethos, rooted in and supported by a different language of democratic responsibility, that could better enable citizens to remain within the difficult space of democratic politics. Such an ethos would require cultivating specific forms of "civic virtue" appropriate to democracy's questions and dilemmas. These would take the form of ethical, psychological, and rhetorical strategies designed to foster a more widespread willingness to engage in democratic action, despite the inevitable frustrations and disappointments that come with the impossibility of ever fully achieving democratic openness or commonality.

Plurality and the Radical Openness of Collective Self-Construction

To give the reader a richer sense of the nature of the openness at the heart of democratic politics, I analyze, in Chapters 2 and 3, two separate attempts to build a theory and practice of democratic politics out of the experience of political freedom itself and the constitutive uncertainty and plurality that characterize the democratic "we." Both Hannah Arendt's writings on the nature of political freedom, which I consider in Chapter 2, and the more directly deconstructive, or post-structuralist, work of Ernesto Laclau and Chantal Mouffe, which is the focus of Chapter 3, offer important insights into the value and complexity of democratic openness, particularly in the emphasis they give to plurality — of perspectives, of political visions, of identities — as a constitutive element of democratic freedom. Yet although both their theories have deeply informed the overall perspective of the book, especially with respect to the role of plurality in the experience of democratic politics, I argue that each in its different way downplays the kinds and degree of closure necessary to democratic openness. Painting too simple and optimistic pictures of democratic openness, neither Arendt nor Laclau and Mouffe ultimately take the full measure of the difficulty of respecting the radical and questionable nature of democracy in ways that move beyond *theories* of openness to a more sustainable *practice* of democratic politics.

For Arendt, *freedom* is the central experience, and value, of politics. In her egalitarian and radical, although rarely explicitly democratic, theory of politics, freedom is a matter of *action*, which means that it involves an experience of contingency, plurality, and the possibility of unpredictable, radically new beginnings. In her brilliant descriptions and analysis of political freedom as action — including a powerful critique of Rousseau's theory of sovereignty and the general will — I argue that Arendt illuminates in profound ways the constitutive openness of democratic politics. Such openness would, from this Arendtian perspective, be understood as the difficult but invigorating process of being together as equals who have the task of constructing together what it is each shares as members of the same community, including the need to respect their fundamental diversity, or nonidentity.

For both Arendt and her readers, the central question that hangs over her account of political freedom is how to preserve its own conditions, given how its fundamentally fragile, contingent, and open-ended character resists both settled institutions and simple collective identifications. At the center of Chapter 2, then, is a consideration of Arendt's argument for the capacity of the act of political *promising* to reconcile freedom, characterized by openness and contingency, with freedom's own need for stable, lasting foundations. By closely tracking through a number of Arendt's texts the figure of the promise — as seen in her discussion of the Mayflower Compact, the Declaration of Independence, and the U.S. Constitution — I argue that the promised reconciliation of freedom and foundation can never take place. In its stead, a different relation between them turns out to be at work, one in which the openness and plurality of freedom, and the political realm it makes possible, are themselves necessarily dependent on the closure of a variety of phenomena that Arendt labels nonpolitical, chief among them sovereignty, rule, and violence. In her attractive vision of a purified form of political action, in which political openness could be experienced without contamination by nonpolitical closures, Arendt ultimately minimizes the costs and risks necessary to the experience of freedom — the acceptance of which, I argue, must be at the heart of any fully democratic politics. Nonetheless, I argue, the very collapse of her sharp distinction between political freedom as openness and the nonpolitical experiences of rule and forceful closure itself reveals important aspects of the always "promised" and questionable nature of democracy. In its very attempt to escape what she considers democracy's (and Rousseau's) "vicious circles" of foundation, Arendt's text offers further evidence of the nature, and severity, of the paradoxes that afflict both political theory and practice once absolute, unquestionable foundations have disappeared, and the people are left continually to call, or promise, themselves into existence.

As with the work of Arendt, the writings of Ernesto Laclau and Chantal Mouffe articulate a pluralist and pluralized understanding of democratic politics and openness. Indeed, they explicitly argue for a theory and practice of "radical and plural democracy." Theirs is a radical conception of democracy: radical in its advocacy of the expansion of the democratic logics of equality and contestation into as many social spaces as possible; and radical in its sustained critique of essentialist views of identity, seeing identities instead as radically contingent, born of a process of constant articulation and re-articulation in relation to other identities and to the experience of "otherness" itself. It is a plural understanding of democracy in that they celebrate both the diversity of identities that constitute any "individual" and the plurality of political struggles, many of them over issues of identity, that today make up democratic politics. Indeed, Laclau and Mouffe hold that the recent proliferation of new social struggles and politicized identities and the generalized increase in sites of political conflict offer possibilities for the overall expansion and radicalization of democracy. In the central role they give to contingency in democratic politics, Laclau and Mouffe follow in the tradition of democratic thought we first saw in Tocqueville and Lefort: in the collapse of natural roles and hierarchies, a democratic logic of egalitarianism and freedom is born, as more and more of society is seen as open to free choice and collective reconstruction.

To seize the opportunities that such developments provide for the construction of a new democratic community, Laclau and Mouffe argue, we must recognize and affirm plurality, conflict, and uncertainty as constitutive aspects of democratic politics rather than lament them as obstacles to finding the true will of "the people." Indeed, if we follow the logic of the third form of democratic openness mentioned above — the openness of incompletion — democratic politics for Laclau and Mouffe is constituted around two "permanent tensions": the tension between the democratic principles of equality and of liberty, and the tension between the plurality of different struggles fought in the name of democratic freedom, on the one hand, and the necessity of articulating them together as part of a larger democratic struggle, on the other. Democracy's animating principles, that is, have no necessary coherence, especially to the extent that one pushes for their fullest practical application and works to respect not only the logic of equivalence and generality but also the plurality and diversity of democratic freedom's constituent elements. Much of the specificity of what they call radical and plural democracy, according to Laclau and Mouffe, thus lies in the recognition and even enhancement of such tensions. The openness of their "radical and plural democracy" would consist not only in the increasing sites of egalitarian struggle, in challenging all naturalized categories of identity, and in the active valuing of the openness of individual and collective identities as important spaces of freedom. It also consists in the refusal to claim full universality for one's particular interpretation of democratic principles, given what they argue are the "constitutive exclusions" necessary to any particular negotiation of democracy's plurality and conflict. Affirming the way in which democracy is constituted around tensions that are impossible to reconcile fully or finally, radical and plural democracy would be the name for a politics of openness, questioning and contestation, struggling against all forms of political closure.

There is much of real value in Laclau and Mouffe's conception of radical and plural democracy, and the parallels with the vision of the radical nature of democratic openness advanced in this book are often very close. Indeed, it is the great merit of the writings of Laclau and Mouffe, as well as those of Arendt, to illuminate more clearly the form of openness that in some ways lies behind all the other forms of democratic openness we have just seen elaborated. That is, both theoretical approaches, in their distinct ways, bring out the constitutive, even ontological, openness and fluidity of democratic and political freedom. Both allow us to better understand the central democratic experience of being together as diverse equals who must continually construct both what we share as equals and how we are distinct, as well as how the complex lines between and within equality and plurality are to be drawn. As we have seen indirectly in this introduction, the different forms of openness discussed so far all emerge out of this most fundamental kind of democratic openness and uncertainty — the fact that democratic equality and identity must remain forever open to question because they can be provisionally determined only through the collective and never-ending efforts of the diversity of individuals who make up the always "promised" people. Such openness, that is, lies behind both the "positive" openness of generality and revisability that characterizes the ideal of democratic autonomy and the more difficult, "negative," openness of democratic conflict, tension, and incompletion. What both Arendt and Laclau and Mouffe highlight is the importance to democratic politics of recognizing and in some way affirming this collective uncertainty as the basic condition of democratic freedom.

Yet, as I argue with respect to the other theorists discussed earlier, even the forms of democratic openness affirmed by Laclau and Mouffe will themselves always be limited, given that they, too, are possible only on the basis of certain closures of their own. Any form of openness requires some degree of closure, that is, and, as I try to demonstrate in the chapters on Arendt and Laclau and Mouffe, neither democracy nor the affirmation of the condition of contingency can furnish a rule to judge the proper weight to be given to their competing demands. As a result, a politics of questioning and openness is burdened by the necessity of making contingent, often risky, political decisions about its specific forms of openness and closure. Not only will the democratic paradoxes and dilemmas that we follow throughout the book always require particular forms of negotiation, but the specific kind of political practice advocated by Laclau and Mouffe, one that aims to affirm the constitutive tensions and incompletion of democracy, is particularly challenging and will require specific strategies and "habits of the heart" to be made sustainable. Indeed, as I argue in the final chapter, the general increase in the politicization of social relations, especially given today's democratic deficits and closures, actually threatens to make the experience of democratic ambiguity and difficulty quite dangerous, even self-defeating. It is as likely to breed citizens' anger, resentment, and cynicism—and even, paradoxically, further depoliticization—as it is to foster a greater openness to plurality and otherness, or to competing conceptions of what Mouffe calls the democratic "common bond." Laclau and Mouffe, unfortunately, give little consideration to the limits such conditions pose, or the difficulties they cause, for a politics of radical and plural democracy. Instead, by their general failure to address these questions, Laclau and Mouffe imply that the simple knowledge and theoretical affirmation of democracy's constitutive conditions can by themselves lead to a new form of democratic practice.

The Virtues of Another Democratic "We"

One of the aims of the fourth and concluding chapter is to begin to push beyond the overly formal and theoretical "affirmation" of democratic openness that characterizes not only Laclau and Mouffe's writing but also much other deconstructive and post-structuralist approaches to politics.[20] It is, I argue, only through developing ways of better negotiating the constitutive uncertainty of collective self-construction that the risks and burdens of democratic politics can be taken up in the wider and more energetic ways that Laclau and Mouffe and other radical democrats call for. Such a task is especially daunting under present conditions, particularly in the United States, where the democratic deficits and political closures are such that it is increasingly hard to see how the people can be said to rule, even in the most minimal, liberal, or "realist" interpretation of that principle. Democratic citizens and actors are faced instead with an acute contemporary version of Rousseau's paradox of effect and cause. With hyper-individualist and market logic undermining the psychic and financial investments necessary to vibrant democratic public institutions and spaces, the American political landscape, I argue, is composed increasingly of overlapping and mutually reinforcing forms of political alienation and disenchantment, affecting both the politically committed and the politically disconnected. What are urgently needed, then, are ways to reverse what I call the vicious circle of public disinvestment and to restart the positive cycle of democratic identification, through which citizens can see themselves as equal and active participants in a democratic community, sharing a larger fate and willing to act in concert with others to improve and sustain its democratic character.

In the final chapter, I turn to a recent theoretical analysis of the democratic deficits of American politics offered by Michael Sandel. Proposing a "civic republican" critique of what he terms "procedural liberalism," Sandel calls for a retrieval and updating of republican conceptions of political freedom and civic virtue, ones able to supply the sense of active democratic control and strong community life that are undermined by procedural liberalism's overreliance on individual rights and its misguided quest for moral and political neutrality. Although there is much to be learned from Sandel's critique of contemporary American liberalism and its inability to sustain the kind of political identifications that democratic politics requires, I argue that the kinds of civic republican calls to political virtue and responsibility that Sandel advocates are themselves more likely to further exacerbate "democracy's discontent." By generally ignoring democracy's constitutive paradoxes and dilemmas, and holding instead to the ideal of strong and clear collective identifications, Sandel's and related demands for a more virtuous form of political and community life take on a moralistic cast that works to undermine the very democratic energies the demands aim to produce.

The threat of moralism, and the depoliticizing effects it can produce, I argue, attaches not only to the community-oriented moralism of Sandel and other virtue theorists but also to left-liberal and radical democratic calls to civic virtue and political engagement. As the earlier chapters show, the tensions that exist between democracy's basic principles — of openness and closure, of liberty and equality — mean that all democratic action runs the risk of violating, or compromising, certain of its principles in the very attempt to respect them. The lack of any pure, or fully self-consistent, form of democratic politics, I argue, particularly in today's simultaneously depoliticized and hyperpoliticized context, makes all democratic action and calls to political responsibility easy targets for cynical demystification, just as the failure to fully respect democratic principles can be used as evidence for the pointlessness of any democratic action at all. In a similar way, given the fundamental uncertainty and ambiguity of the democratic "we," the necessity of speaking in the name of a democratic community that one's rhetoric and actions are themselves designed to bring into being can, from the perspective of those who hold a competing vision of the democratic "we," be challenged as evidence of dishonesty or hypocrisy.

More generally, I argue that left-liberal and radical calls to challenge entrenched power and injustice can all too easily provoke resentment and anger — and once again, cynical demystification — when they come to appear as moralistic and self-righteous calls for others to cleanse themselves of their implication in injustice and its suffering. Indeed, the tendency of democratic activism and calls to political responsibility to provoke such counterproductive reactions is particularly strong today, given how little space is free from power and injustice under modern conditions and how strongly the vicious circle of public disinvestment can push people toward political withdrawal and cynical self-justification.[21]

For calls to political responsibility and civic virtue to have any chance of success today, they must explicitly acknowledge, in the very language of their appeals, the impossibility of any pure form of democratic politics. More specifically, a democratic language of responsibility needs to incorporate within its calls to engagement a compassionate understanding of the inevitable trespass, failure, frustration, disappointments, and incompletion that characterize all democratic action and all democratic (and nondemocratic) actors. Caught inevitably in the very systems of power, inequality, and injustice that they are working to challenge, democrats, radical and otherwise, need languages that can open up such systems to critique in non-alienating and non-guilt-laden ways. Future-oriented languages of responsibility, I suggest, might better avoid moralism, and thus defuse cynicism, anger, and resentment by concentrating not so much on our implication in, and responsibility for, the injustices and suffering of the past as on the different potential each of us has, through our very implication in different forms of power, to help bring into being a more democratic and just future. Such forms of democratic rhetoric would at the same time work to make it easier to accept the frustration and limitations of democratic action, and the impossibility of ever once and for all discovering and securing a clear sense of the democratic "we." Such languages of democratic responsibility would aim to encourage the development of "second-order" civic virtues — those of compassion, forgiveness, self-critique, and self-limitation — better able to respond to the uncertainties and difficulties involved in (never quite fully) achieving the first-order democratic virtues and identifications. They would thus hope to resist both the inclination to avoid political activity altogether and the drive to achieve democratic identifications through force — whether by physical violence or simply the coercion of moralistic condemnation, ostracism, or the force of unchallenged political consensus.

Such civic virtues, as expressed in and supported by a nonmoralistic language of responsibility, would thus be distinct from those celebrated in the communitarian and civic republican traditions. They would not be grounded in a clear sense of the community and the moral obligations that are owed to it but would instead be designed as responses to the lack of a clear communal identity and to the inadequacy of simple moral codes. They would also aim to assist in the difficult work of negotiating the dilemmas that emerge from democracy's plurality — both the plurality of its (often competing) principles and the difference and otherness that constitute relations between political equals. Yet the virtues aren't precisely liberal ones either. For their aim would be to support a much more robust and participatory form of democratic politics, with a greater sense of indebtedness and dependence on those with whom one shares "community," than liberal emphases on individual freedom and rights generally allow. They would in this sense grow out of a critique of liberal individualism, but not one grounded in a strong sense of community and collective identity so much as in a critique of self-identity as such, whether of the "individual" or of the community. Yet at the same time, such "virtuous" political practices, embodied in and sustained by a compassionate language of democratic engagement, are precisely suggestions for going beyond the formal ethical injunctions of "classical" deconstruction, for they would be rooted in, and responses to, the actual lived experience of democratic politics and the suffering it entails.

Such new forms of civic virtue would, in short, emerge from a different, in some ways even more radical, understanding of the democratic "we." Without abandoning the classic democratic orientation toward the common good and a strong conception of equality, I argue in the final chapter that respecting the radical nature of democratic openness requires forms of mutual address that are provoked by a different kind of democratic identification. A more compassionate language of democratic responsibility would be fostered in part by a conscious identification with others understood not so much as those who share with us a common essence of a single community but rather as *fellow sufferers from identity* and its rage-filled demand for security, with all the greed, resentment, and dogmatism such an impossible desire brings in its wake. Approaching one's fellow citizens with an understanding of the ease with which we are *all* (including democratic critics of the status quo) trapped in limited identities and identifications might allow such political critique to be heard less defensively, or with greater "openness," and thus to assist the work of collectively dislodging and reworking those identifications in more democratic ways. The virtue of political compassion would also be grounded in a democratic recognition of our radical indebtedness to and dependence on one another, and of the space of mutual appearance and need that we therefore share. Yet the precise nature of what we "have" in common, or the exact way in which we are in debt to each other and the responsibilities we owe each other, would, as democratic questions, necessarily remain uncertain. Although we may together form a *public*, perhaps even a people, it is never in the sense of a community that *is* us, or that exhausts our being. Those equals who are before and within us, in their very familiarity *and* otherness, constantly call us, and our "we," into question: What exactly do we share, we constantly ask ourselves, other than the burdens of identity and the experience of this space and the encounter that it allows? To ask and try to answer these questions is to respect the democratic condition. And to affirm, in the very language of responsibility with which one addresses one's fellow citizens, this radical condition of being-together offers at least the chance of more easily negotiating the irresolvable democratic tension between the "we" understood as a set of common needs, rights, and duties and the "we" understood as perpetually uncertain and open to reformulation.

CHAPTER ONE

The Rule of the People?

Collective Autonomy and the Wagers of Democratic Openness

What Rousseau said of the state of nature applies very well also to democracy: it no longer exists, it perhaps never did exist, and probably never will. And yet as with the state of nature, we need the concept of democracy with its strange temporality for the critical function it performs.

— Robert Bernasconi, "Rousseau and the Supplement to *The Social Contract*: Deconstruction and the Possibility of Democracy," *Cardozo Law Review*

Philosophy and democracy were born at the same time and in the same place. Their solidarity comes from the fact that both express the refusal of heteronomy — the rejection of the claims to validity and legitimacy of rules and representations just because they happen to be there, the refusal of any external authority (even, and especially, "divine"), of any extrasocial source of truth and justice, in brief, the putting into question of existing institutions and the assertion of the capacity of the collectivity and of thought to institute themselves explicitly and reflexively. To put it another way: the struggle for democracy is the struggle for true self-government. As the aim of self-government does not accept any *external* limits, true self-government entails explicit self-institution, which presupposes of course the putting into question of the existing institution — and this, in principle, at any time. The project of collective autonomy means that the collectivity, which can only exist as instituted, recognizes and recovers its instituting character explicitly, and questions itself and its own activities. In other words, democracy is the regime of (political) self-reflexivity.

— Cornelius Castoriadis, "The 'End of Philosophy'?" *Salmagundi*

In a democracy, "the people" rule themselves. They are free because there are no grounds for authority and collective decisions other than those that they give themselves. In this chapter I explore this logic of autonomy and the openness it lodges at the heart of democracy, beginning with the work that the philosopher Cornelius Castoriadis has devoted to the topic. As Castoriadis argues in his account of the Greek polis and the "invention" of democracy, the disappearance of natural and divine foundations that is the source of the community's freedom also means that nothing can simply be assumed as naturally true or authoritative. Everything having to do with the life of the polis becomes open to question and debate. Indeed, according to Castoriadis's especially acute formulation of the classic argument for democratic autonomy, democracy is the very regime of openness — an ideal that extends beyond the simple fact of debate and questioning to include the form of self-rule itself. For it to be the people ruling themselves, rather than some part of the community ruling another part, the space of debate and decision must, first of all, be open to all equally, with, second, the debate directed toward the common good that all share in rather than any individual or special interest. Third, the principle of democratic autonomy requires that the people rule themselves directly, without mediation; it must be the people themselves who rule rather than representatives or officials, and their laws and decisions must always remain open to revision or reversal.

In the attractive picture of radical democracy and democratic openness that Castoriadis paints, the rejection of all grounds other than those that the people themselves declare renders everything, including the people's own decisions, questionable. But what about the people themselves? Who exactly are the people, and how do they come into being? What too few analyses of democratic autonomy grapple with, and in this, too, Castoriadis is exemplary, is the way in which the people themselves — understood as a self-directing political community of equals guided in its most important political decisions by something like the common good — are rendered questionable by their own logic of self-rule. Although he argues that democracy is a collective response to what he calls "the paradox of creation," Castoriadis nonetheless avoids the most difficult paradoxes of democratic foundation and the dilemmas it bequeaths democratic politics. For the openness that autonomy brings with it is both more profound and more limited than Castoriadis and others maintain. In what is the central paradox within the ideal of collective autonomy, the very fact that the people have no ground prior to themselves means that they can come into existence only through some degree of *heteronomous* closure. It is that closure which makes possible the openness and questioning of democratic freedom. Yet that closure also undermines the autonomy, and with it, the clear identity, of the people.

It turns out, that is, that for the people to be free and in charge of themselves, their identity must remain uncertain. I argue that by taking as its central problem the necessity of founding, or *forming*, rather than discovering, an autonomous "people," the text of Jean-Jacques Rousseau's *On the Social Contract*, despite, at times, Rousseau's own intentions, allows one to see more clearly both the dilemmas of democratic autonomy and the dangers involved in denying them. According to Rousseau's account, "the people" must call themselves into being, through the mutual promise of the social contract, in such a way that all are equal members of the "body politic" formed by the intersection of their different wills. This ideal point of commonality, which Rousseau designates as the general will, transforms a multitude of individuals into a people, guaranteeing both individual and collective freedom, and with it, legitimate authority. But as we see through a close analysis of the role of "the legislator" in Rousseau's account of the founding of the people, his text also tells a very different, even paradoxical, story, one in which "the people" never simply, once and for all, come into existence but must instead be continually founded and refounded, called into being from a position other than that of the people themselves, and on the basis of conditions that are themselves never simply, or fully, democratic. The very freedom and autonomy that are the conditions of possibility for the people's democratic existence end up posing a threat to the *completed* existence of the people, rendering their identity forever uncertain and the legitimacy of their rule forever questionable. Contestation of the established sense of the people, and of the force necessary to achieve it, thus becomes central to democratic politics, yet in a distinct way. Grounded in the public recognition that no form of the people can *ever* be fully open or universal, democratic contestation would in this form work to block the temptation to *achieve* the ideal of democratic autonomy through the violent exclusion of those social or political elements that seem to resist its required commonality.

To give the reader a better sense of what is at stake for democratic theory and practice in my reading of Rousseau, I then consider the very different reading of Rousseau's paradoxes of the people's self-foundation as offered in Seyla Benhabib's writing on "deliberative democracy." Although Benhabib's deliberative theory of democratic legitimacy also places contestation at the center of democratic politics, her understanding of democratic openness is grounded not so much in the logic of collective autonomy as in the potential for rationality found in discourse and collective deliberation. Indeed, it explicitly relinquishes the goal of securing a substantive sense of the common good and turns to the procedures of public deliberation in a conscious attempt to escape from Rousseau's paradoxes of democratic foundation. For Benhabib, deliberation that follows the guidelines of Habermasian discourse ethics provides a means of securing a foundation for democratic equality and universality while simultaneously respecting the requirements of democratic freedom as openness.

Exploring the implications of what Benhabib herself calls the "wager" of deliberative democracy, however, I argue that her procedural ideal of democratic legitimacy can avoid Rousseau's paradoxes only by *presuming* the existence either of perfectly open and perfectly rational deliberation or of large degrees of equality and democratic social spirit. In the absence of such an ideal situation, the legitimacy of a deliberative *process* will necessarily be judged at least in part relative to the legitimacy of the *outcomes* that it generates and the substantive values it allows to be established in the political community. Under conditions of less than ideal deliberation and collective rationality, there is no guarantee that deliberation will offer the most effective means to democratic ends. Indeed, I argue that the establishment of a democratic community, including procedures of deliberation — an establishment that Rousseau's analysis has shown is a perpetual process, constitutive of everyday democratic politics — will at certain moments require nondeliberative, even forceful, means, whose legitimacy can be confirmed, if at all, only after the fact. Democratic politics is thus never free from the logic of foundation and the state of transition whose paradoxes and dilemmas Rousseau so brilliantly theorizes.

Despite Benhabib's best efforts to reconcile its antinomies, then, democracy remains forever torn by the fundamental tension that exists within democratic freedom itself between the value of openness — whether that of deliberation and contestation, or that of generality and inclusion — and the need for closure — in the form of decisions and established institutions, which, often through less than general or autonomous means, place limits on future contestation and political openings. Given this essential division within the very meaning of democratic freedom, I argue, no theory of democracy can ever lead us out of its fundamental paradoxes and dilemmas, as Benhabib and many political theorists before her (including, at times, Rousseau himself) seem to promise. Indeed, as I try to show throughout the book, no theory can ever be adequate to the experience of democratic politics. Rather than providing answers, democracy leaves us with a permanent set of questions, with no sure guide to the most democratic judgment or action in any given situation.

Nonetheless, despite its inability to solve or to avoid democracy's constitutive paradoxes and dilemmas, democratic theory does have the power to reveal their existence. Thus my readings of Castoriadis, Rousseau, and Benhabib aim to bring to light a set of risks and burdens inherent in any political action and judgment oriented toward the democratic ideals of equality and freedom. As I argue in this chapter's concluding section, such analysis can alert us to the need for new forms of civic virtue grounded in "ethical" strategies — of compassion, forgiveness, and self-critique — which, by making more bearable the burdens and risks of acting in the absence of clearly articulable universal norms, have the power to strengthen deliberative practices and identifications with democracy's always uncertain "we," and thus to reduce the likelihood of more forceful resolutions of democracy's dilemmas. Far from abandoning the universalist grounds of democratic politics, as Benhabib is given to worry, such new forms of civic virtue would amount to the cultivation of a different relation to democratic universality, one that is better suited to negotiate the difficult freedom its constitutive openness brings with it.

1

Autonomy as Collective Self-Institution:
From the Demos Questioning to Questioning the Demos

For Castoriadis, the logic of democratic autonomy first emerges in the Greek polis, when "the community of citizens — the *demos* — proclaims that it is absolutely sovereign (*autonomos, autodikos, autoteles*, self-legislating, self-judging, self-governing, in Thucydides' words) [and] affirms the political equality (equal sharing of activity and power) of all free men."[1] Democracy, or the rule of the people, involves the self-conscious institution, and definition, of the community, by itself. For Castoriadis, the Greeks' invention of democracy was simultaneous with (and ultimately indistinguishable from) their invention of politics and philosophy. With the creation of politics, laws (and community norms in general) cease being inherited unquestioningly from one's ancestors or received from God or the gods. They are, instead, understood to be "created by men after a collective confrontation and discussion about right and wrong law" (94). Politics thus arrives in the world along with philosophy, defined by Castoriadis as "the explicit questioning of the instituted collective representation of the world" (95).

The Greek invention of democracy involves the direct engagement

with the "law" of freedom and self-creation that, according to Castoriadis, in fact governs all societies, however effectively "heteronomous" they
are in practice. Democracy is the regime that takes upon itself the burden — but also the possibility — of history and of creation, of the fact that
"there is not and cannot be a rigorous and ultimate foundation of anything — not of knowledge itself, not even of mathematics" (83). The fact
that, within "the Greek vision of the world and human life, the nucleus
of the Greek imaginary," there is no order in the world prior to that
which we give it, opens up the space for judging and choosing as well as
for responsibility and autonomy. It opens up the space of the law as something that must be created or declared rather than simply received.

Democracy is thus constituted around a fundamental openness: the
primitive closure of tradition, with its repetition of past practices and
norms, is broken. Democracy is born the moment that the existing form of
society becomes questionable and the community becomes conscious of
itself as its own creator, no longer bound to what has come before.
Democracy, then, is also the regime of freedom and questioning. Such
openness and questioning, however, must extend to the community itself
and its collective identity. As the community recognizes and declares itself
to be autonomous, to have no other ground than the one it gives itself, it
paradoxically renders itself questionable (and its "grounds" less than
secure). The polis can no longer take for granted who "it" is but instead is
engaged in an interminable process of creating, questioning, and re-creat-
ing its identity. It might, in fact, be said to *be* that very process of self-institution through self-questioning. Castoriadis suggests something of this
when he writes that "what is important in ancient Greek political life . . .
is the *historical instituting process*: the activity and struggle around the
change of the institutions, the explicit (even if partial) self-institution of the
polis as a permanent process" (97, emphasis in original).[2]

The practice of autonomy, whereby the people give themselves their
own law, can thus be seen to require a radical openness and flexibility in
its political arrangements. Since the community itself is sovereign, nothing must be allowed to get in the way of the community interrogating and
determining itself. True autonomy, Castoriadis argues, takes the form of
direct democracy. This means, most importantly, that the rule of the people is fundamentally at odds with all forms of "representation." Nothing
must get in the way of the people themselves deliberating over and determining their own affairs; indeed, "for classical political philosophy, the
notion of 'representation' is unknown. . . . Democracy is the power of the
demos, unmitigated in matters of legislation" (99). The sovereign body is
simply "the totality of those concerned," and because "representation is
a principle alien to democracy," "whenever delegation is inevitable, dele-

gates are not just elected but subject to permanent recall" (99). For once "representatives" are made permanent, "political authority, activity, and initiative are expropriated from the body of citizens and transferred to the restricted body of 'representatives,' who use it to consolidate their position" (99). For the same reason, Castoriadis argues, there is a fundamental difference between the polis and anything like a state in its modern form. Indeed, "the very term 'State' does not exist in ancient Greek" (100). Although there was a role for "a technical-administrative mechanism," it was left to slaves, was strictly monitored, and had a minimal, nonpolitical function. "The idea of a 'State' as an institution distinct and separated from the body of citizens, would not have been understandable to a Greek" (101). In short, nothing must be allowed to block the transparency of the people's relation to itself.

The openness and transparency essential to democratic politics entail not only the community's resistance to its own sedimentation into an institution separate from itself but also the creation of a fundamentally transparent, *public* space for their continual self-institution. According to Castoriadis's reading of the Greek polis, the autonomy of the people requires that whatever is of importance to their common, political, affairs appear publicly. Thus, for example, the presentation of the laws involves their engraving and public exposure for all to see and discuss. More broadly, "law materializes in the discourse of the people, freely talking to each other in the *agora* about politics and about everything they care about before deliberating in the *ecclesia*" (103). The creation of the public space, then, is "equivalent to the creation of the possibility — and actuality — of free speech, free thinking, free examination and questioning without restraint" (103). The community must be able to see, engage, and discuss with itself for it truly to be sovereign. This requirement of public exposure and openness is the corollary, then, of the requirement that the people themselves, rather than some other entity, determine the rules by which they live. Decisions on common affairs must be discussed and decided by the community itself, free to question, know, and revise itself at will.[3]

When one pushes on Castoriadis's own account of political autonomy, however, things begin to get more complicated than the terms of his analysis generally allow. As Castoriadis makes clear, the autonomy of the polis depends not only on the direct, or immediate, nature of its relation to itself — its resistance to all forms of representation — but also on the preservation of what Castoriadis calls "the unity of the body politic." Such "unity" requires that political decisions "be made on general grounds only" (102). It is only when this condition is met, only when political decisions are not only made *by* the community as a whole but made about, and on the basis of, genuinely *common* concerns, that it can be said that the community is ruling itself. If "particular" interests are allowed to be the source of a collective decision, the decision ceases to be the community's autonomous action and becomes instead the victory of one portion of the community and its interests over another. The community, that is, can truly be said to be *self*-determining only when it considers what is common to all its members, what gives the community its *identity*, what they share in such a way as to make them into a single community. Autonomy, then, would only be possible on the condition that there existed a high level of actual commonality among the members of the community, some significant sense of shared identity. Only when there is a large degree of similarity of beliefs, values, and actual practices — and thus some fairly clear sense of what is common to all members of the community — can there be said to *be* a community, in Castoriadis's sense of a collective "self" that can "rule" itself.

This notion immediately raises the question, however, of where this commonality comes from. Even while Castoriadis writes that "the unity and very existence of the political body is 'pre-political,' at least insofar as explicit self-institution is concerned" (he writes that "the community 'receives itself,' as it were, from its own past" [101]), Castoriadis nonetheless makes clear that this "raw material" must itself be transformed into a fully *political* form. For the community to be autonomous, its past self must not be accepted unquestioningly but rather self-consciously re-created into a form the community itself chooses. In particular, the prepolitical existence of the community must be restructured so as to meet the demands of generality. Castoriadis mentions as an example of this process the way in which the traditional tribal divisions of Athenian society had to be "reformed" into a "balanced composition" that would be "neutral as to territorial or professional particularities" (102). Indeed, if there are no necessary laws of political development and no natural order to the world — assumptions that are central, in Castoriadis's account, to both the Greek "vision of the world" and to democracy — then the "unity" of, or the commonality within, the polis can only be a political achievement. There is not, and should not be, any preexisting, prepolitical standard for what is common to all members of the community, or what their general, as opposed to particular, concerns are. For the community to be truly free and self-instituting, its members' commonness must itself be produced through their own action, rather than something necessary or natural.

But this conclusion returns us, although in a way that Castoriadis never addresses, to his own "paradox of creation." As Castoriadis describes it, the lack of absolute laws or norms on the basis of which a society can either be chosen or judged necessarily involves one in a paradox of "creation presupposing itself." "Judging and choosing always take place within and by means of an already existing socio-historical institution" that is itself in need of justification or ground, "or else spring out of a new creation in the face of which no criteria are available except the ones this new creation establishes for the first time" (94). What is at stake now, however, is not merely a norm for judging and choosing on a particular issue but rather a norm for judging what the community itself is. According to what standard should "the community" judge what makes it a community? How can this standard not be either circular (relying on a prior standard that is itself in need of support) or arbitrary? In other words, how can a democratic, autonomous community be produced democratically, or autonomously?[4]

The simple answer, which Castoriadis consistently avoids facing, is that it cannot be. What Castoriadis himself calls the necessary "element of arbitrariness" in "the self-definition of the political body" — the way in which "*who* posits the *Grundnorm* . . . the norm ruling the positing of norms . . . is a *fact*" (98) — rules out the kind of autonomy he argues for in the rest of the essay. Whatever sense of common identity and generality there is, if it is not the residue of a past, prepolitical (unconscious) community, can only be the effect of a political intervention that by definition cannot be an autonomous act — in the sense of a general act of the whole community — given that it is the act that creates the community *as* a community. This is, indeed, the central paradox of democratic political foundations (the effects of which, as we see in the pages that follow, radiate out into democratic politics more generally): the very conditions of freedom and autonomy — the lack of natural, unquestionable grounds for judgment and action — rule out the possibility of full political autonomy. Instead, what one might call the political community's "relative autonomy" can only be achieved through non-autonomous acts of outside intervention.[5]

The process, for instance, whereby the particularities of the Athenian tribes were "neutralized," and a new, more unified people brought into being, was not itself a neutral, or general, act. It was the decision of a particular body of people to transform the political "body" of the Athenians according to a particular, necessarily exclusive, vision of the community — of what it values, who it includes, and on what terms. As Castoriadis's example suggests, the act of instituting the people cannot but be exclusive: for the Greeks, he reminds us, "this 'who' [the point of commonality from which the *Grundnorm* is posited] is the body of adult, male, free citizens" (98), not the entirety of those affected by that group's decisions. The common identity of "the Athenians," like all collective identities, must be posited from a point that is not (yet) a general one. And it is, in part, through the more or less forceful exclusion of certain other identities (in this regrettable case, women, foreigners, and slaves), as well as other ways of organizing the community, that a sense of what is common to "we the Athenians" is constituted. Although democratic principles demand that such exclusions be open to challenge and the boundaries of the demos expanded as widely as possible so as to respect the basic equation of the rulers and the ruled, some such exclusivity is constitutive of collective identity as such.[6]

That identity must, in turn, because of its fragile, non-autonomous grounding, be constantly reinforced and reproduced. This explains the importance of "the education (*paideia*) of the citizens as citizens," the practice whereby one is trained to become "conscious that the *polis* is also oneself" (104). The successful "education" of a citizen to identify with the polis "as himself," so as to learn how to act with the general interest of the community at heart, requires that the citizen be educated into a particular form of community. Only after this training, and the achievement of a significant degree of overlap between his particular beliefs, values, or interests, and those of other members of the community, will he be able to recognize "general" concerns (the proper topic for political discussion), as distinct from "particular" interests.[7] In other words, the "how" — how to recognize generality and act on its behalf — can only be taught through the "what" or the "who" — on the basis of examples of the more or less successful, but always particular, forms of generality characteristic of the Athenian people. The initial determination of the particular vision, or form, of community, on the basis of which certain concerns are seen as general, cannot itself be a general, autonomous act. The relative degree of autonomy of the Athenians that Castoriadis describes in his essay, then, is possible only because a lot of work has been done to achieve it through the more or less forceful production of commonality. Although Castoriadis mentions the means of such production in passing, his analysis has no room for the constitutive necessity of such procedures and the effect that their non-autonomous character has on the possibility of collective autonomy.

The Closures of Democratic Openness

The fact that "the people" come into existence only through the intervention of an outside force, and thus not from "the people" themselves, means, then, that the people can never *fully* come into being. They are, instead, in need of perpetual re-institution, a process that can never be complete and that, because it must be performed from a point that is never itself fully general, will always remain deeply contestable. In other words, the identity of the people is more deeply questionable — in the sense of being both *uncertain* and *open to challenge* — than Castoriadis's discussion of autonomy can account for, predicated as it is on the possibility of the community being fully present and present to itself. The further twist, however, is that for the very same reasons that the identity of the people is more deeply questionable than Castoriadis assumes, it is also *less open*. The ability of the polis to remain fully present to itself and fully open to revision — the two points are inextricably linked — is in fact compromised from the very beginning, from its origin in Castoriadis's own "paradox of creation."

For example, as part of his claim that the polis is fundamentally distinct from the modern notion of the state, Castoriadis argues that Aristotle's *Athenaion Politeia* is consistently mistranslated as "The Constitution of Athens." Its correct translation, he argues, is "The Constitution of *the Athenians*" — not merely for grammatical reasons but also because it more accurately captures the sense that, for the Greeks, the polis *was* simply those members present for its discussions and decisions. It had no separate identity apart from such assemblies. As attractive as this account of the temporality of collective identity may be, however, it is, in the end, too simple. As Castoriadis himself acknowledges, "the political community exists at a level which is not identical with the concrete, 'empirical' reality of so many thousands of people assembled in a given place at a given time. The political community of the Athenians, the polis, has an existence of its own: e.g., treaties are honored irrespective of their age, responsibility for past acts is accepted, etc." Although he is no doubt right to argue that such a distinction is not the modern one between a "state" and a "population," it is too simple to claim instead, as Castoriadis does, that it is merely a distinction "between the continuous corporate body of perennial and impersonal Athenians and the living and breathing ones" (101). For the present assembly can *be* the assembly of "the Athenians," rather than a random collection of individuals, only by acting *in the name of*, "identifying" with, and thus feeling itself bound to, the decisions and engagements of a past group of different individuals acting under the same name. Indeed, the freedom and questioning that are fundamental to the autonomy of the assembled Athenians are only possible within the constraints of the Athenians past decisions and established practices (even when these constraints do not take the form of state institutions in the modern sense).

In one sense, then, it is fair to say that the Athenians inherit their political existence from their past selves. The community's self-questioning must begin from a point that cannot itself be fully questioned since it provides the terms and assumptions of who the community is (as well as why, and what, it should question). Even the most "free" and "unrestrained" questioning and discussion are always in part governed by a sense of belonging to a project begun in the past and worthy of continuing into the future; they are thus directed by and toward some notion of "who" the community "is" — that is, how it has acted and been organized in the past and how it should continue to be.

In a related form of "closure," of course, all debate and contestation must be structured by rules about who can speak, when they can speak, in what ways, on what topics, and so forth. These apparently merely "procedural" rules in fact inevitably allow some members of the community and some issues to be heard more easily or loudly than others. The community can never, therefore, be directly present to itself, as Castoriadis's model of autonomy assumes. Instead, even in the most "free" and "open" systems of self-rule, the people will always suffer from these two forms of de facto institutionalization or closure whereby the community is "present" to itself, is a community, only on the basis of, in the name of, or through the mediation of a particular interpretation of its past self, and through particular, necessarily substantive rules of procedure and debate. Both these forms of closure, in turn, obviously become more pronounced the more ideologically and materially divided, or simply diverse, the community becomes. As I later suggest at greater length, Castoriadis can ignore these phenomena only by assuming the prior existence of what can only be a political achievement: the existence of a "unified" "people" with a strong sense of commonality.

The transparency and openness central to Castoriadis's notion of autonomy can at best be partial, then, because the freedom of the polis to question, revise, and re-create itself depends, paradoxically, on the establishment of some previous version of itself.[8] The divided nature of the people's "presence," and the paradoxical relation between the openness of questioning and the closure of collective identity, is shown in a particularly interesting way in Castoriadis's treatment of the Athenian practice known as *graphe paranomon* (accusation of unlawfulness). According to this procedure, one citizen could accuse another of having induced the *ecclesia* to approve an "unlawful law." Given that there was no "constitution," or separate "fundamental law," to which one could appeal, the case was tried before a popular court made up of a large random sample of the citizenry, who decided whether the law should stand. That is, the people themselves had to decide; the demos had to appeal "against itself in front of itself" (107): one version of "the people" judged whether the decision of another version of the people was in fact consistent with the (spirit of the) people's law.

Such a decision amounts, in the end, to a determination of who the people "really" "are": Are "we" the sort of people who would approve of such a law? Is it consistent with the kind of community we are and want to be? Yet in the very effort to determine what the people's law "is" and whether it is "true" to who the people are, the "identity" of the people is rendered deeply uncertain. In what form(s) does the people exist during the course of this procedure? Where exactly *is* the people? In one sense, they exist only as they are staggered across the different stages of their conflicting determinations. Yet in another sense, their "true" identity emerges only as an *aftereffect* of the deliberations designed to determine what they are supposed *already* to be. Even as the procedure reveals the identity of the people to be constitutively uncertain, never fully or finally coming into presence, it also confirms how even the most radical, open-ended form of popular self-questioning is nevertheless severely constrained. Not only does it take place within certain assumptions about who the community "is," but it must also at some level be directed toward "discovering," or remaining true to, the "real" identity of the community that is presumed already to exist.

The ideal of autonomy is thus at odds with itself. On the one hand, it demands a radical openness: to ensure that the community be immediately in touch with and in control of itself, the political body and its institutions must remain fully open to questioning and transformation. They must, in a sense, *not* know who they are. And yet, on the other hand, the same demand that the community be in direct control of itself requires the establishment and careful preservation of a particular, common identity. The people, in this sense, *must* know who they are — political action is directed toward making this identity known and acting to protect it. It is clear that, at the very least, these imperatives push in opposite directions. If a strong enough commonality has been achieved to ensure anything like the latter sort of autonomy, questioning will risk no longer being meaningfully radical, operating within quite strict constraints of shared assumptions and common values. If, however, the openness and questioning are to be radical, they will inevitably render questionable the unity and generality of the community itself. In the face of any kind of disagreement, or internal heterogeneity (which, given the non-autonomous nature of political foundation, is virtually assured), it will be impossible for both demands of autonomy to be satisfied.

This problem is not merely a conceptual one, nor an issue that applies only to the moment (real or hypothetical) of the community's foundation and the production of citizens oriented toward the general good. It is relevant any time the community is divided over an issue that touches on its identity as a community — which is to say, it is relevant for any important political issue in a democracy. Returning to Castoriadis's example of *graphe paranomon*, there may not, in any particular debate, be a "real" or "true" Athens that can be found to resolve the dispute about what constitutes a proper law, nor even any likelihood of producing consensus about it in the near future. Without any way of knowing for sure — or autonomously — what being faithful to the collective endeavor requires of us, or even what is an appropriately "general" concern, any decision in a situation of conflict necessarily amounts to the forceful imposition of one version of the "community" onto those who don't share it.

In short, Castoriadis ignores a basic tension between autonomy-as-openness and autonomy-as-commonality, and with it the exclusive, ultimately forceful, nature of the production of commonality. He can do so logically only on the assumption that there is some natural commonality, or shared identity, that makes the people into a people prior to, or separate from, politics (perhaps as their ultimate telos, given some natural tendency toward agreement through discussion).[9] Only on the basis of some such assumption — that is, only if "the people" are understood to exist as an *identity*, prior to their own construction of themselves through political and rhetorical acts of *identification* — could "the people" possibly be fully present to themselves in the way necessary to satisfy both demands of autonomy. Without such an assumption — which Castoriadis's opening description of the Greek worldview would seem categorically to rule out — the people's "identity" must be seen as both more deeply questionable *and* more constrained and constraining than it appears in Castoriadis's account. It is because the people have no ultimate foundations, but instead must repeatedly posit or perform themselves into existence, that their identity must be a product of constraint and closure. And it is, among other reasons, because collective identity can be produced only through such (always incomplete) closure that it must, in order to be democratic, be radically questionable and contestable.

A Permanent State of Transition: Toward a Different Understanding of Democratic Openness

By neglecting the paradoxical nature of the people's self-institution, and in particular how it rules out the people ever coming into full self-presence, analyses like that of Castoriadis actually threaten to strengthen a closure at odds with his ideal of openness and free questioning. For assuming the possibility of the community being fully present to itself can help fuel a desire for a clear, unified, homogenous collective identity, one of the built-in risks of the logic of autonomy. The demand that "the people" rule themselves, without mediation, or disruptions by elements of "particularity," produces a pressure to repress or expel those elements of the community that do not "fit" the reigning definition of the people. (This is, in fact, part of the source of the ideal of a static, collective identity separate from the actual members themselves — for "Athens" rather than "the Athenians" — whose closure Castoriadis argues is incompatible with democratic politics.) At the very least, an emphasis on preserving the unity and generality of the political community, without an awareness of the non-autonomous, contestable way in which collective identity is produced, makes its inevitable closures harder to question and contest and loosen. It makes it that much more likely that the ideal of unity and generality will be appropriated by those intent on enforcing more restrictive, less questioning modes of political community. In short, the inclusion and commonality that are both so central to the ideal of democratic autonomy simultaneously fit together and challenge each other. As a result, to preserve the openness of democratic autonomy — the freedom and questioning that are essential to resisting tradition and "natural" laws — it is necessary to recognize the limits to such openness and questioning.[10]

Indeed, the dangers and dilemmas that Castoriadis's analysis faces suggest the need for a different approach to democratic theorization — especially for those who wish to respect the *radical* nature of its basic principles. Such an approach would begin from the acceptance of the constitutive impurity of the people and the necessarily incomplete nature of their autonomy. It would appreciate the value of democracy-as-collective-autonomy, but it would also accept that "the people" is an entity that needs to be constantly formed from points that are not yet "the people." That is, although the logic of democratic autonomy cannot simply be dispensed with, neither can it be the only logic of democratic politics and theory. Indeed, all of the pitfalls that ensnare the logic of the people's self-rule are exacerbated and made potentially more violent the further one moves from the simple and culturally homogenous model of society that Castoriadis takes for granted in the Greek polis. An approach that rejects the adequacy of such a model of democratic community would, I am arguing, better protect democratic openness-as-questioning by more easily identifying otherwise hidden forms of closure, and by making less likely the demand for, and perhaps the attraction of, violent, "purifying" exclusions.

Rather than beginning from the assumption that a unified — or ideally unifiable — version of the people exists to be adhered to, a preferable mode of democratic theory and practice would accept that democratic politics is stuck permanently in a state of transition, or formation. From such a perspective, the central democratic task would no longer be that of "discovering" the common good or the people's true interest but would rather lie in the *formation*, out of otherwise conflicting interests and identifications, of a large degree of equality, together with the shared creation of spaces and practices through which our common fate and always uncertain community can be continually defined, negotiated, and contested. From this angle, of course, democratic politics becomes a lot more obviously difficult, both as a practical and theoretical matter. The necessary, but always insufficient, balancing of the demands of openness and closure, and of commonality and diversity, becomes a never-ending challenge. Creating a sustainable practice of democracy, then, one in which more than a small minority of citizens would take active roles, would require learning to maintain and respect not just the openness of democratic commonality and democratic contestation but also the radical openness and uncertainty of democratic identity — both individual and collective — that result from the members of the community having continually to construct the terms of their own commonality, without preexisting guidelines. The more seriously the principles of democratic autonomy are taken, then, the more difficult the experience of democratic politics becomes — and, with it, the more necessary such new forms of civic virtue.

Thus, despite the admirable clarity and insight of the connections Castoriadis draws between democratic autonomy, the disappearance of all nonpolitical grounds, and the openness and questioning that the disappearance makes central to democracy, his analysis nevertheless falls away from its own best insights. Although he correctly speaks of democracy as the regime of risk and of its need for strategies of self-limitation, his attachment to an uncomplicated vision of collective autonomy prevents him from addressing the risk that comes from that same ideal — and the greater risk that comes from maintaining the ideal while forgetting its own paradoxes. Rousseau's *On the Social Contract*, by contrast, rather than assuming the existence of the political community, is centered on the question of how the community comes into existence in the first place. As a consequence, it is, in its unique way, attuned from the start to the paradoxes and dilemmas that Castoriadis avoids. As I argue in what follows, by suggesting the simultaneous necessity and danger of the logic of autonomy and the common good, and by making clear the rhetorical, always uncertain, character of "the people," Rousseau's text offers more resources for resisting attempts to naturalize, and thus close off, the identity of the people (including his own famous attempts at various points in the *Social Contract* and elsewhere). At the same time, however, in identifying so incisively the paradoxes of openness at the center of democratic autonomy, Rousseau also makes visible the questionable nature of "democracy" itself and the difficulties involved in both its practice and its theorization. Indeed, despite Seyla Benhabib's best efforts to solve Rousseau's paradoxes with her deliberative conception of democratic legitimacy, I argue that their existence directs our attention to certain constitutive burdens and dilemmas involved in the experience of democratic politics, ones that any theory of democracy needs to recognize and any practice of democracy needs — through new forms of civic virtue — to address.

2

> A true democracy has never existed and never will exist.
> — Rousseau, *On the Social Contract*, II/iv/85

> All of my ideas fit together, but I can hardly present them simultaneously.
> — Rousseau, *On the Social Contract*, II/vi/65

Rousseau's Legislator and the Democratic Paradox of Effect Becoming Cause

One particular moment to turn to for a better sense of the problems involved in forming a democratic people, and for a more articulated sense of how the people only come into existence through outside, non-autonomous, rhetorico-political intervention, is Rousseau's discussion of the legislator in book 2, chapter 7, of *On the Social Contract*.[11] Rousseau's primary concern in *On the Social Contract* is, of course, to work out the arrangements necessary to making political authority legitimate. Rousseau establishes early on that those grounds must be the people themselves; the only legitimate form of government is one in which the people rule themselves. Given what Rousseau posits as the natural freedom and independence of individuals, however, legitimate authority requires not just collective autonomy but individual autonomy. The people themselves must be grounded in a unanimous agreement. "Since no man has any natural authority over his fellow man," Rousseau writes, "and since force produces no right, there remain only conventions as the basis of all legitimate authority among men" (I/iii/49). For authority to be authority, and not force, it must at some point be accepted, or willed, by all those it constrains. In other words, it is not enough simply to locate legitimacy in the requirement that the people rule themselves. What must first be understood is

the act by which a people becomes a people. For this act . . . is the true basis of society. Indeed, if there were no prior convention, what would become of the obligation for the minority to submit to the choice of the majority . . . ? The law of majority rule is itself an established convention, and presupposes unanimity at least once. (I/v/52)

The task Rousseau faces is to discover how to transform a mass of heterogeneous individuals into a single entity such that their common existence is regulated by an authority that comes from and applies to each individual equally. Only on those conditions — only when each individual's equal natural freedom is preserved by the transformation it undergoes in the new, conventional authority — can the people themselves be said to rule, rather than some part of the people ruling another part. "The fundamental problem" then becomes to "find a form of association that defends and protects the person and goods of each associate with all the common force, and by means of which each one, uniting with all, nevertheless obeys only himself and remains as free as before" (I/vi/53).

The problem is "solved," Rousseau initially claims, in the form of the social contract, according to which "each of us puts his person and all his power in common under the supreme direction of the general will; and in a body we receive each member as an indivisible part of the whole" (ibid.). Through the simultaneous and "total alienation of each associate, with all his rights, to the whole community," the community to which one supposedly "gives" oneself is actually *born*. "Instantly," Rousseau writes, "in place of the private person of each contracting party, this act of association produces a moral and collective body, composed of as many members as there are voices in the assembly, which receives from this same act its unity, its common self, its life, *and its will*" (ibid., emphasis added). Because each individual is destroyed and then remade as an equal part of the new collective body, the community's law *is* now the "individual"'s law. And because "obedience to the law one has prescribed for oneself is freedom" (I/viii/56), the individual thus remains as free as before. Each individual is now ruled by the general will, the point of commonality that exists between them all and that forms the core of "the people"'s identity. Being common to all members of the community, the general will is the point from which all may both collectively and individually rule themselves. Rousseau explains this a few pages further on, at the start of book 2:

The general will alone can guide the forces of the State according to the end for which it was instituted, which is the common good. For if the opposition of private interests made the establishment of societies necessary, it is the agreement of these same interests that made it possible. It is *what these different interests have in common* that *forms the social bond*, and if there were not some *point at which all the interests are in agreement*, no society could exist. Now it is uniquely on the basis of this common interest that society ought to be governed. (II/i/59, emphasis added)

What forms this general will is the mutual promise that is the social contract. Everyone agrees to place all of their resources at the disposal of the community they together will form, and promises to abide by the decisions that the majority of the community takes in the name of its common life and interest. The promise is one that each makes to every other prospective member of the community, rather than to anyone or anything that exists prior to the promise. In Rousseau's words, "as each gives himself to all, he gives himself *to no one*" (I/vi/53, emphasis added). Any other arrangement would destroy the autonomy that is the essence of the contract's legitimacy, for it would place the community and its members under the power or authority of something external to it. The only guarantor of the promise that calls the community into being, then, and thus the only guarantor of the *generality* of the communal will, is the community itself.

Although everyone is equal, then, in a formal, and negative, sense — each contractor is equally bereft of her previous freedom and powers — there can be no common standard, at the moment of contracting, for judging the equality of their treatment, nor any guarantee that one will be found. This raises an immediate problem, however. Because the act of association has no common grounds to support it but must itself produce those grounds — because each "gives himself to no one" — the people's collective *identity* is "grounded" over an abyss. Without any common standards to judge the generality of the people's will, there remains an essential uncertainty about whether "the people" in fact exist, since they are nothing more than the point of commonality between all the different contractors. If the people do exist, it is at this point *in name only*, their mutual promise a collective self-naming.[12] In many ways, I want to argue, the remainder of Rousseau's text can be read as the simultaneous resistance to and description of the effects on the people's autonomy, and on democratic politics more generally, of the abyss out of which the people have to promise themselves into "existence." Indeed, the rest of book 1 and much of book 2 of *On the Social Contract* consists of different, but always unsuccessful, attempts by Rousseau to reformulate the social contract in such a way that it can overcome its initial dilemmas.

In an initial attempt to shore up the people's foundation so as to give them bodily existence, Rousseau immediately redescribes the social contract in the following chapter in a way that attempts to cover up the abyss over which the people must call themselves into being. "This formula," he writes of the social contract,

shows that the act of association includes a reciprocal engagement between the public and private individuals [*un engagement reciproque du public avec les particuliers*], and that each individual, *contracting with himself so to speak*, finds that he is doubly engaged, namely toward private individuals as a member of the sovereign and toward the sovereign as a member of the State. (I/vii/54)

Referring to the way in which each member of the political community has a dual role — as a citizen, or member of the sovereign, and as one subject to the decisions of the sovereign — Rousseau describes "the act of association" as taking place *within* each individual. The individual as a member of the sovereign contracts with the individual as a member of the state (or as a subject). The individual as author of the law contracts with the individual as recipient of the law, thus guaranteeing her freedom and autonomy by giving herself her own law. This figure of the contract internal to the individual contractor can be seen as a further paraphrase of the description that immediately precedes it, that of the contract as including "a reciprocal engagement of the public [person] with [the] individuals [who make it up]" (my translation). Yet neither formulation accurately describes the social contract. By covering over the abyss that forms its ground, they merely displace the fundamental question: where does "the public," or the public/sovereign "side" of the individual, come from? Since this is what the contract is designed to bring into being, the contract itself can hardly take place *between* the public individual and the private individual. One can only conclude that, at least at this point in Rousseau's text, the people have yet to give birth to themselves as a political body.

A few chapters further on, in the beginning of book 2, Rousseau proposes another such formulation, this time concerning not the social contract itself but the general will it is supposed to bring into being. He writes,

The engagements that bind us to the social body are obligatory only because they are mutual, and their nature is such that in fulfilling them one cannot work for someone else without also working for oneself. Why is the general will always right and why do all constantly want the happiness of each, if not because there is no one who does not apply this words *each* to himself, and does not think of himself as he votes for all? (II/iv/62)

Rousseau here correctly describes both the formal conditions for the legitimacy of the general will — according to which "everyone necessarily subjects himself to the conditions he imposes on others" (II/iv/63) — and the way decisions might be taken when a properly functioning general will is in place. But such a decision-making procedure would be effective at *producing* a truly general will (one that is "always right") only if there were in fact some reason (material or psychological) for taking oneself as a model for everyone else in the community, and, more important, only if there were some reason for others to *accept* one's version of the model citizen. Absent such a basis, the practice of everyone thinking of themselves when voting for all would just as likely lead to chaos, and would certainly guarantee nothing about the mutuality of the collective engagements, and thus nothing about their obligatory quality.

As Rousseau himself writes two paragraphs later, "what generalizes the will is not so much the number of votes as the common interest that unites them" (II/iv/63). The social contract can be said to succeed at bringing the general will, and thus the people, into being only to the extent that such an interest exists and there is a general, or agreed, sense of what counts as general, common, and equal.[13] That common standard is, however, precisely what the contract itself was supposed to supply. In its absence, how are we to find the common judge for deciding who or what the common standard is or should be? The social contract cannot itself provide such a standard.[14] Until the conditions on the basis of which this performative act is to take place are themselves equal, or a common interest already exists and is commonly acknowledged, one cannot say with any certainty whether the social contract has in fact achieved what it was intended to achieve.[15]

There is thus much reason to doubt Rousseau's frequent suggestions that the mutual promise of the social contract, simply by being performed, is enough to form a new political "body," of which all the individual "members" are fully and indivisibly a part. Although it may be true that "as soon as this multitude is thus united in a body, one cannot harm one of the members without attacking the body, and it is even less possible to harm the body without the members feeling the effects" (I/vii/55), it is by no means certain when, if ever, this collective embodiment takes place, or how one would even recognize it if it did. Although Rousseau writes that "through the social compact we have given the body politic existence and life; the issue is now to give it movement and will through legislation" (II/vi/65), it is nonetheless clear that Rousseau realizes, at some level, that the creation of the general will as the "point" that holds the body politic together remains in danger — despite the apparently airtight form of the social contract, despite its refiguring as a contract within the individual, and despite the subtlety of the word "each."

This is particularly evident if one turns to the first version of *On the Social Contract*, known as the Geneva Manuscript.[16] There the issue of laws and legislation seems to arise less as something added to a preexisting political body than as something essential to its very constitution. In particular, the law emerges as the solution to the problem of how the general will, or the common good, can be *known* to otherwise particular individuals.

In order for each person to want to do what he ought to do according to the engagement of the social contract, each must know what it is that he ought to want. . . . But since *the State has only an ideal and conventional existence*, its members have *no natural and common sensibility*, by means of which they are promptly alerted to receive a pleasant impression from what is useful to it and a painful impression as soon as it is harmed. (I/vii/177, emphases added)

If the general will lacks the *natural* connection between members that Rousseau elsewhere imputes to the "body politic," how can the general will — even assuming it exists — "manifest itself on all occasions?" "Will it always be evident?" Rousseau asks. "Will the illusions of private interest never obscure it?" The answer lies, Rousseau claims, in "the most sublime of all human institutions, or rather by a celestial inspiration that taught people to imitate here on earth the immutable decrees of the divinity." The answer lies, that is, in the law. Law is

this healthy instrument of the will of all that reestablishes, as a right, the natural equality among men. It is this celestial voice that tells each citizen the precepts of public reason, and teaches him to behave according to the maxims of his own judgment and not to be constantly in contradiction with himself. (I/vii/178)

Without the law, each individual is inevitably at odds with himself, unable to recognize and communicate with that part of himself that is general. Both singly and as a whole, the people will be torn apart without the general voice of the law keeping them in harmony.

It should be clear by this point, however, that the attempt to use the generality of the law to shore up the endangered generality (and existence) of "the people" as a sovereign will runs into the same dilemma as did Rousseau's previous such efforts. It falls into the trap once more of presupposing the object that is in need of its support: the law's generality cannot be used to secure and orient the people's vision toward the general will, given that the law requires as one of its defining characteristics precisely the absolute generality of the people's will. The people must already exist as fully general in order to serve as the source of the law's generality. The generality of the law can be assured, and effective in securing the people's generality, only if the people are already general. That is, without some commonly accepted basis for distinguishing the general from the particular, how can one be sure that what one is hearing is the voice of the law, or one's own "true" voice, and not that of an imposter?

Even following the "narrative" of the final version of *On the Social Contract*, according to which the law is explicitly figured as merely an addition to an already formed body politic, Rousseau eventually runs into the same problem. At the conclusion of the chapter titled "On Law," Rousseau himself finally makes explicit the issue that his project inevitably confronts. There he reminds us that the people themselves should regulate the conditions of their own association — they must be the authors of their own laws. And yet by themselves they do not yet have the means to uncover the generality that must be the ground of their laws. How will they be able to develop appropriately general laws? Rousseau asks.

Will it be in common accord, by sudden inspiration? Does the body politic have an organ to enunciate its will? Who will give it the necessary foresight to formulate acts and publish them in advance, or how will it pronounce them in time of need? . . . How will a blind multitude, which often does not know what it wants because it rarely knows what is good for it, carry out by itself an undertaking as vast and as difficult as a system of legislation? By itself, the people always wants the good, but by itself it does not always see it. (II/vi/67)

The people cannot give themselves their own law because they are too blind to see the generality of their will. Although Rousseau continues to write as if the people does exist as a political body, they are at best paralyzed by their lack of an "organ" able to express their will and give them movement. Indeed, their blindness and incapacity render them a "multitude," in need of outside intervention to mold them into a real people, to put them in touch with themselves, with the general will that is supposed already to be theirs.[17]

In a passage worth quoting at length, Rousseau elaborates on the required work of construction:

The general will is always right, but the judgment that guides it is not always enlightened. It must be made to see objects as they are, or sometimes as they should appear to be; shown the good path it seeks; safeguarded against the seduction of private wills; shown how to assimilate considerations of time and place; taught to weigh the attraction of present, tangible advantages against the danger of remote hidden ills. Private individuals see the good they reject; the public wants the good it does not see. All are equally in need of guides. The former must be obligated to make their wills conform to their reason. The latter must be taught to know what it wants. (II/vi/67)

The people must be "taught" to judge in a properly general manner, trained to see the general will that is theirs, made to "recognize" their own generality. In other words, despite the initial promise, the social contract — whether by itself or with the help of the laws — has failed to remake the individual person into an indivisible "member" of a larger "body." Both the individual and the body of which it is supposedly a member continue to be at odds with themselves, unable to see, act, or move *as a people.*

In order, finally, to grant the people the "public enlightenment [that] results in the union of understanding and will in the social body," to provide them their long-promised embodiment (and with it their autonomy), Rousseau turns to the figure of the legislator. His task, as should by now be clear, is not an easy one. In Rousseau's words, he must be

capable of changing human nature, so to speak; of transforming each individual, who by himself is a perfect and solitary whole, into a part of a larger whole from which this individual receives, in a sense, his life and his being. . . . He must, in short, take away man's own forces in order to give him forces that are foreign to him and that he cannot make use of without the help of others. (II/vii/68)

The legislator is the outside, heteronomous force whose task it is finally to reconfigure the mass of individuals into a people, into a unified, autonomous body capable of knowing and ruling itself. To perform this task, he must be both of the people and apart from them, both inside and outside. His job requires, according to Rousseau, "a superior intelligence, who saw all of men's passions yet experienced none of them; who had no relationship at all to our nature yet knew it thoroughly; whose happiness was independent of us, yet who was nevertheless willing to attend to ours" (II/vii/67). In short, "Gods would be needed to give laws to men" (II/vii/68). What's more, the legislator's "function, which constitutes the republic, does not enter into its constitution" — that is, he can have no authority or power over those to whom he gives laws. The people, unable to divest themselves of their ultimate right to give themselves their own laws, are required to ratify whatever system of legislation the legislator proposes. Once they vote on his proposals, the legislator's job is done. He must be able, then, to "work in one century and enjoy the reward in another" (ibid.). Which is to say, finally, that "one finds combined in the work of legislation two things that seem incompatible: an undertaking beyond human force and, to execute it, an authority that amounts to nothing" (II/vii/69).

Yet the legislator's (and Rousseau's, and the people's) troubles don't end here. Even if one were to find a being capable of such a task, he would still be confronted by precisely the paradox he is meant to solve, and which we have seen haunt the entirety of Rousseau's text up to this point. For the same reasons that the people are not able to generate their own laws in a sufficiently general form, the people may not be able to understand and receive the proposals of the legislator. Given the very deficiencies in the people's constitution that it is the legislator's job to remedy, is there any greater likelihood that the people will be able to "recognize" *him* than they are to recognize themselves? Shifting his bodily metaphor from sight to hearing, Rousseau explains that the language of the legislator will necessarily contain much that cannot be "translate[d] into the language of the people," for whom "overly general views and overly remote objects" are beyond comprehension. "Each individual," Rousseau writes,

appreciating no other aspect of government than the one that relates to his private interest, has difficulty perceiving the advantages he should obtain from the continual deprivations imposed by good laws. In order for an emerging people to appreciate the healthy maxims of politics, and follow the fundamental rules of statecraft, *the effect would have to become the cause*; the social spirit, which should be the result of the institution, would have to preside over the founding of the institution itself; and men would have to be prior to the laws what they ought to become by means of laws. (II/vii/69, emphasis added)

Here Rousseau finally acknowledges as a paradox the dilemma that structures his whole text and the politics of democratic autonomy in general: to establish the commonality that is necessary to the people being a people, some such commonality must already be in place. The laws, as we have seen, are designed to maintain the people in their generality, establishing the common standards that make them into a community, keeping them true to themselves and away from the forces of fragmentation, particularity, corruption, and injustice. Yet for "an emerging people" to accept the laws as their own, they would already have to have a sense of themselves as a community with a common good, if not a general will — and thus as something more than a collection of individuals. They would, that is, already have to have the "social spirit" — a sense of who they are and what holds them together as a "we" — which it is the job of the laws to generate.

In other words, the commonality that is necessary to the general will, not having any natural source, must instead be established through the institution of, and common respect for, a set of laws. For it is only to the extent that such laws (or more generally speaking, political principles) are commonly understood to treat everyone as equals and are in practice (e.g., in functioning institutions) respected by the community as a whole that it becomes rational to see oneself as a member of that community and as implicated in a common fate. Yet without some willingness among the members of the people-to-be, prior to such a shared practice of community, to think of themselves as having obligations to the community as a whole, how will the laws necessary to that practice ever be decided on and accepted?

Rousseau's immediate "solution" to the paradox, it turns out, is for the legislator to trick the people into accepting his laws. In the face of the paradox of effect and cause, Rousseau explains, the founders of nations have historically had "recourse to the intervention of heaven and . . . attribute[d] their own wisdom to the Gods" (II/vii/69). By placing his proposals "in the mouth of the immortals in order to convince by divine authority those who cannot be moved by human prudence" (ibid.), the legislator might be able to persuade the people to accept his laws. If they can be convinced that they should be "subjected to the laws of the State as to those of nature" and taught to "recognize . . . the same power in the formation of man and of the City," they might be able to "obey with freedom and bear with docility the yoke of public felicity" (ibid.). The people's predicament is such that they not only require outside intervention to give them the laws that will make them whole but they can only accept the laws under false pretenses and in a way that denies their autonomy! They must feel themselves compelled to submit to them by the laws of nature and the force of the gods.

Autonomy and the Questionable Grounds of Democratic Legitimacy

Whether such a political foundation should count as an autonomous act of the people is clearly open to question. And as any kind of a practical solution to the paradox, especially in contemporary societies, it is obviously no help at all, at least for committed democrats. Yet however surprising, even far-fetched, one finds Rousseau's recourse to the legislator, and then to the legislator's ventriloquizing the Gods — especially in a text devoted to laying the foundations of popular autonomy — the legislator cannot for all that be dismissed as merely an embarrassing, or somehow inessential, component of Rousseau's text. On the contrary, the legislator plays a fundamental role in Rousseau's democratic project — the outlandishness of the figure, and of Rousseau's accompanying text, is, if anything, a sign of the seriousness of the dilemma Rousseau faces — and suggests important lessons for democratic theory in general.

More specifically, I argue the legislator is most profitably read as the figure for those elements and actions in democratic politics that prove *necessary to* the people's autonomy without being reducible to its logic. The crucial role given to the legislator can be read, then, as Rousseau's own implicit (perhaps only unconscious) "recognition" of the limits of his otherwise formal analysis, and of the logic of autonomy more generally. Unlike other theorists of autonomy, that is, Rousseau is forced, through the rigor of his own attempt at foundation, to "accept" that the people's generality and rationality are not simply there, and that "the people" themselves — in the sense of a legitimate political body guided in its most important political decisions by something like the common good — are unable to generate them alone. They must instead be produced and maintained through the political and rhetorical force of agents other than the people themselves (in their completed generality), and must be done in the face of a deep paradox. The necessity of the legislator makes explicit what can be read less directly in Rousseau's preceding chapters — that despite its design, the social contract cannot by itself bring the people into existence with any certainty. The people remain only promised, the initial gap at the center of their constitution continually in need of shoring up. The paradox of effect and cause that we have seen Rousseau eventually make explicit remains constantly in need of negotiation, because the people must repeatedly call themselves into being from a position other than themselves and through an appeal to the very generality that one is attempting to construct and instill in them.

The story of the legislator can thus be read as an allegory for the various non-autonomous political and rhetorical strategies that democratic actors themselves must engage in so as to construct the people's generality, to make and persuade them into an autonomous people. It is thus not surprising that immediately following Rousseau's treatment of the legislator there is a marked shift in the text, away from a concern with the *formal* conditions of the people's autonomous and legitimate existence and toward the *practical* question of discovering the particular strategies necessary for the people to come (more or less) into being.[18] Such strategies can be understood as Rousseau's own quite contestable suggestions for "jump-starting" the people's rationality (and thus closing what Seyla Benhabib characterizes as a gap between legitimacy and rationality) by making the people both more "general" and more oriented toward the general.

Chief among the interventionist strategies Rousseau's own text recommends for restructuring the people so as to assure their general, and thus autonomous, existence, are the following: (1) laws that establish and maintain a minimum level of equality among all the citizens; (2) the legislator's cultivation of the people's "mores, customs, and especially . . . opinion," which Rousseau sees as laws "engraved . . . in the hearts of the citizens" and which form "the true constitution of the State" by "preserv[ing] a people in the spirit of its institution, and imperceptibly substitut[ing] the force of habit for that of authority" (II/xii/77); (3) censorship, which has the task of maintaining healthy opinion; and (4) civil religion, whose "simple dogmas" — the existence of a benevolent God and of the afterlife, the happiness of the just and the punishment of the wicked, the sanctity of the social contract and the laws, and the unacceptability of religious intolerance — help preserve the social spirit, and thus hold the community together. A more detailed reading of *On the Social Contract* makes it very clear that for Rousseau, these and other very specific efforts are needed to make the people into a people and to keep them that way, whatever one makes of the merits of his particular suggestions. These can be understood as ways that make it easier for the people to be rational by making them more general (laws enforcing equality; common mores and customs) and by orienting them toward the general or the universal (civil religion's "sentiments of sociability").

Far from overcoming the paradox of effect and cause, however, the strategies designed to achieve and sustain the people's generality must themselves confront it. The practical question remains, that is, how the system of mutual supports Rousseau proposes — the laws that establish equality of material conditions, the "laws of the heart" that are necessary to the effectiveness of such regulations, and the censorship and civil religion that keep those "mores" in good form — can ever get off the ground, especially through democratic — that is, autonomous — means. How can individuals be made to attach themselves to and identify with the State and their duty to obey its universal norms — how can one generate Rousseau's "social spirit" — if they don't already see themselves as represented by it, or see their will in the will of the community as a whole? Yet in the absence of that social spirit, what resources are there to achieve a truly general, or representative, general will? (In Rousseau's formulation, it is the laws that have the job of producing the social spirit, even as that spirit must be in place for the people to be able to accept the laws.) To lay the conditions for the people to become a people, one must appeal to a sense of the people *as* a people; yet the success of that appeal depends on those conditions already being in place, or at the very least being imaginable. The paradoxical task of the legislator — or rather, of all democratic political actors — then, is to make an appeal that sets the conditions for its own proper reception: one must appeal to the political community in such a way that its members will accept the regulations that will make them into the kind of (general) people able to "hear" such an appeal.

The work of (re)founding the people is thus never ending. If "the people" ever come into existence, it can only be in the form of *claims* made about them, on their behalf, or *in their name*. The paradox at the heart of the people's identity is (temporarily) bridged, that is, only through the rhetorical or argumentative force of such claims. If the social contract is understood as creating the promise, or the "name" of the people, such efforts amount to attempts to produce the "body" that corresponds to that name. These include rhetorical efforts designed to foster *identifications* with practices of universality, fairness, and reciprocity, and with a particular version of the people — a particular sense of what they do have, and should have, in common and the norms that should govern their shared existence — together with efforts to *institutionalize* that vision in the form of a particular set of commonalities and normative standards and a particular mode of material and formal equality able to support and sustain those identifications. Hence the need not only for something like Rousseau's laws that establish a minimum level of equality, but also for institutions like civil religion — through which people are trained to identify with the community by learning and repeating certain dogmas of "sociability" — and the censor — who teaches by "reminding" the people who they are and what they believe.[19] Although the specific procedures and institutions that Rousseau recommends may be deeply problematic (in part, as Benhabib suggests, because they are insufficiently attuned to the pluralist requirements of modernity), all democratic politics must nevertheless consist to some important degree in making such claims, in trying to call the people into being by persuading "them" to see themselves in a particular claim of generality, to get them to act *as if* the commonality is there, and by so doing, produce it (or accept policies that will do so).

Yet the freedom and openness of the people's foundation, which means that "they" must call themselves into being before they exist and thus from a point that is not yet "the people" themselves, rule out the possibility of there being any politically neutral source of generality, or definition of who the people are. One must speak and act in the name of the people before receiving the people's own sanction. As a result, one can never be certain of their identity or of whether one has successfully "achieved" it. There is only the name, which members of the community struggle and deliberate over without an external standard for knowing whose "name" is "correct."[20] And because such efforts have the task of producing the very ground they need for validation — the point of commonality or the general will that everyone shares and that guarantees legitimacy — there can be no guarantee of their legitimacy, or "accuracy," in the moment of positing. Any legitimacy could only emerge retroactively, after the people that is called into being ratifies the act of their institution as justified. For this reason, whatever legitimacy is achieved always remains questionable.

Not even the decisions or beliefs of a clear majority, then, can be said without doubt to "be," or represent, the people, and not even the most rational deliberative process can escape the difficult practice of having to call the people into being through non-autonomous rhetorical and practical interventions.[21] One can, nonetheless, distinguish between more and less democratic, and more and less forceful, modes of constructing the political community. Certainly the more inclusive the process of collective discussion and decision-making, the more widely supported the outcome, and the more the decisions reached lay the groundwork for as great or greater levels of participation in the future, the stronger will be their claim to democratic legitimacy. Yet as we saw earlier with respect to Castoriadis's vision of the people's rule, the democratic nature of the community is sustainable only to the extent that the drive to closure contained within the ideal of collective autonomy can itself be resisted through the institutionalized *affirmation* of the impossibility of ever completing the democratic community or of achieving democratic legitimacy once and for all. A sustainable form of democratic politics, that is, needs to invent forms of civic virtue that combine more classical strategies for jump-starting democratic identifications and the people's social spirit with newer ways of respecting the constitutive openness and uncertainty of the democratic "we" — thus making it easier to avoid the more forceful and less (even pseudo-) democratic productions of the people's identity, which Rousseau's story of the legislator can also be interpreted as referring to.[22] An effectively egalitarian and participatory project of democratic politics, in other words, must abandon any hope of solving the problem of uncertain democratic legitimacy and the difficulties involved in the people's perpetual "state of transition," and turn instead to developing forms of civic virtue better able to negotiate the difficulties posed for democratic citizens by such a political condition — captured in the Rousseauian dilemma of having to call the people into being from a not yet democratically sanctioned space.

3

Deliberative Democracy:
Bridging the Gap Between Legitimacy and Rationality?

On Seyla Benhabib's reading, Rousseau's recourse to the legislator amounts to an acceptance of a "trade-off between legitimacy and rationality" that the preceding chapters of the *Social Contract* had been implicitly articulating: "if the will of the people is the source of all legitimacy, then it can also fail in rationality, for the judgment which guides the people is not always right, nor do the people always know what is in their own best interest."[23] For Benhabib then, the legislator amounts to an "instance of idealized rationality," armed with insight into the people's own best interest and common good that by themselves they fail to achieve, and able to "compel" them (through appeal to the gods) "to conform their wills to their reason."

Although Benhabib expresses her indebtedness to Rousseau for articulating the basic grounds of democratic legitimacy, she nonetheless refuses to accept that the paradox he struggles with is, in fact, insoluble. Indeed, for Benhabib, Rousseau ends up in the bind he does "partly because he did not allow institutional mechanisms to incorporate rigorous deliberation and debate in the determination of the general will," believing that such debate would only produce factions (DR 30). In Benhabib's view, the deliberative model of democracy she endorses is able to explain how this paradox, based on "the hiatus between rationality and legitimacy," can be overcome. Of course, with her Habermasian belief in the fallibilistic nature of deliberative outcomes and their merely "presumptive" rationality, Benhabib certainly accepts that the legitimacy of all democratic decisions must remain questionable — indeed, it *requires* institutionalized contestability.[24] The questionability, or uncertainty, that is essential to democratic legitimacy, however, is never for Benhabib so serious as to raise doubts about the adequacy of deliberation to democratic politics, much less to affect the ability to establish a rational basis for democratic action, or the meaning of democracy itself. In the end, Benhabib's rationalist faith in the powers of deliberation succeeds only in solving Rousseau's paradoxes in the abstract — while, in the process, leaving unexplored the kinds of dilemmas and tensions that we have begun to see are so distinctive about the actual experience of democratic politics.

As Benhabib describes it, the deliberative model of democratic legitimacy holds that collective decisions are obligatory only because of the presumption that they "represent an impartial standpoint said to be equally in the interests of all." "This presumption," it further holds, "can only be fulfilled if such decisions are in principle open to appropriate public processes of deliberation" (DR 31). More specifically, a society's processes of collective deliberations must be "conducted rationally and fairly among free and equal individuals" if the decisions said to be in the common interest of all are to be accorded the presumption of legitimacy and rationality. "The more collective decision-making processes approximate this model, the more the presumption of their legitimacy and rationality increases" (DR 30–31).

Deliberative democracy thus takes "the discourse model of ethics and politics" as the source of its "general principles and moral intuitions." This model then would act as a regulative ideal for the fashioning of particular institutions and specific deliberative procedures in any practical situation. Benhabib describes "discourse ethics" in the following terms:

The basic idea behind this model is that only those norms, i.e., general rules of action and institutional arrangements, can be said to be valid which would be agreed to by all those affected by their consequences, if such agreement were reached as a consequence of a process of deliberation which had the following features: a. participation in such deliberation is governed by the norms of equality and symmetry; all have the same chances to initiate speech acts, to question, to interrogate, and to open debate; b. all have the right to question the assigned topics of conversation; c. all have the right to initiate reflexive arguments about the very rules of the discourse procedure and the way in which they are applied or carried out. There are no *prima facie* rules limiting the agenda of the conversation, nor the identity of the participants, as long as each excluded person can justifiably show that they are relevantly affected by the proposed norm under question. (DR 31)

Only to the extent that these conditions are actually met in practice can collective decisions be said to be legitimate, because they are reflective of the "impartial standpoint" so essential to moral validity. Yet the achievement of legitimacy, on this model, is simultaneous with the achievement of rationality, for the outcomes of such deliberative processes would carry with them strong claims to "practical rationality." This is so for three reasons, according to Benhabib. First, collective deliberations impart information. No single person can know all the information relevant to a decision that affects the whole community, nor can one person know in advance the various moral and political perspectives that might be held by all those affected by the decision. Second, deliberation forces people to reflect on their preformed opinions and the likely consequences of their preferences, thus allowing them to clarify them and their relative weights, as well as facilitating the recognition and more coherent ordering of preferences and opinions when they are in conflict. Finally, "the very procedure of articulating a view in public imposes a certain reflexivity on individual preferences and opinions" (DR 32). Having to garner support for our views among other members of the community forces us not only to present what we consider good reasons but also to consider "what would count as a good reason for all others involved. . . . Nobody can convince others in public of her point of view without being able to state why, what appears good, plausible, just and expedient to her can also be considered so from the standpoint of all involved" (DR 32–33).

In addition to the claim to rationality and legitimacy that such deliberations would bring with them, the deliberative model of legitimacy has, on Benhabib's reading, two additional, practical advantages. First, it gives up on the Rousseauian "fiction of a general deliberative assembly in which the united people expressed their will." Such a fiction "belongs to the early history of democratic theory." Instead, the "guiding model" must today "be that of a medium of loosely associated, multiple foci of opinion-formation and dissemination which influence each other in free and spontaneous processes of communication" (DR 35). Thus deliberative rationality and legitimacy can be reconciled with the scale, the complexity, and the diversity of contemporary (post)modern societies. What's more, such a model of legitimacy respects a further fundamental aspect of modernity: the fact of ineliminable "disagreement about the highest goods of human existence and the proper conduct of a morally righteous life." Deliberative democracy works on the assumption that "agreements in societies living with value-pluralism are to be sought for not at the level of substantive beliefs but at the level of procedures, processes, and practices for attaining and revising beliefs. Proceduralism is a rational answer to persisting value conflicts at the substantive level" (DR 34). Thus

Benhabib's belief in the ability of a deliberative model of legitimacy to escape Rousseau's paradox of effect and cause: although the definition or identity of the people remains questionable, with the precise nature of *their* generality or commonality open for debate, the legitimacy of that debate and of its provisional outcomes is nonetheless guaranteed by the generality of the *procedures* of deliberation.

In an admission whose importance we return to later, however, Benhabib accepts that "procedural models of rationality are underdetermined." The deliberative model of democracy sketched out above "suggests a necessary but not sufficient condition of practical rationality, because, as with any procedure, it can be misinterpreted, misapplied, and abused. Procedures can neither dictate outcomes, nor can they define the quality of the reasons advanced in argumentation, nor can they control the quality of the reasoning and rules of logic and inference used by participants" (DR 33). Rationality is, then, the ideal, but not always the real, outcome of collective deliberations that take discourse ethics as their model. Nonetheless, the condition of reflexivity that is a requirement of Benhabib's model of discourse — whereby any participant has the right to challenge the rules that structure deliberations and the ways those rules have been applied — "allows abuses and misapplications at the first level to be challenged at a second, meta-level of discourse. Likewise, the equal chance of all affected to initiate such discourse of deliberation suggests that no outcome is *prima facie* fixed but can be revised and subjected to re-examination" (DR 33).

For Benhabib, it is precisely this possibility of reflexive challenge and ultimate revision that explains how majority rule as a decision procedure can be normatively justified. For

in many instances the majority rule is a fair and rational decision procedure, not because legitimacy resides in numbers, but because if a majority of people are convinced at one point in time on the basis of reasons formulated as closely as possible as a result of a process of discursive deliberation that conclusion "A" is the right thing to do, then this conclusion can remain valid until challenged by good reasons by some other group. . . . [Thus,] if a large number of people see certain matters a certain way as a result of following certain kinds of rational procedures of deliberation and decision-making, then such a conclusion has a presumptive claim to being rational until shown to be otherwise. (DR 33)

This interpretation of the link between legitimacy, rationality, and contestation thus helps explain the long-standing liberal-democratic practice of maintaining separate ruling and opposition parties, along with parliamentary procedures of opposition, debate, impeachment proceedings, and so forth, all of which "incorporate this rule of deliberative rationality that majoritarian decisions are temporarily agreed upon conclusions

the claim to rationality and validity of which can be publicly reexamined"
(DR 33–34). Thus, for Benhabib, the reflexivity and revisability condition in deliberative procedures helps preserve the link between legitimacy
and rationality: by holding out the possibility of increased rationality *at
a later date*, the process can preserve its legitimacy even among those who
have grave doubts about the rationality of its *present* outcomes.

Of course, such situations cannot happen too often without serious
problems, both in practice and for the coherence of Benhabib's theory of
deliberative democracy. For were the presumptively rational deliberative
process to frequently render decisions that did not seem rational (or just,
or in the common good) to some significant portion of the community, or
were it even just occasionally to produce outcomes that seemed *deeply
unjust* to a significant constituency, how could the legitimacy of the
process any longer be assumed? What this suggests is a larger point that
poses serious problems for the ideal of deliberative democracy: given
what Benhabib herself admits is the impossibility of ever achieving a perfectly open, inclusive, egalitarian, and reflexive process of deliberation —
or system of public spheres — the legitimacy of the process will necessarily be judged at least in part relative to the *outcomes* that it generates, relative to the kinds of rights it establishes, the duties it imposes, the justice
of its distributions. If this is true, it would seem that Benhabib's purely
procedural model of democratic legitimacy would in practice necessarily
amount to something else: for democratic politics, even on Benhabib's
model, would frequently require us to make choices between honoring
certain substantive values (rights, justice, equality) and honoring the value
of process (deliberation), relative to the risks that such a process — in
those forms one is realistically able to establish at a given moment —
might pose to the achievement of our substantive values. In this context,
then, even the choice of establishing, or abiding by the outcomes of, deliberative procedures would itself be a function of substantive, pragmatic
factors — it would, that is, be a "wager" on the likelihood that deliberative procedures, in their actual, non-ideal form, will allow us to achieve
democratically the best outcome. At this point we can wonder just how
far we have come from Rousseau's paradoxes.

Making the Democratic Wager: A Politics Without Deliberative Guarantees

Benhabib's analysis ends up encountering this problem most directly
(although not explicitly) in her engagement with liberal criticisms of
deliberative democracy, where the issue is the possible tension between
an (imperfectly rational) process of democratic deliberation and liberal-

ism's desire to protect individual liberties and minorities from majority tyranny.[25] Although Benhabib accepts that liberal worries about the effects of unbridled majoritarian politics on civil and political liberties are not without foundation, she argues that the deliberative model of democratic legitimacy "can offer certain conceptual as well as institutional solutions to soften, and perhaps to transcend, the old dichotomy between . . . individual rights and liberties . . . and collective deliberation and will-formation" (TDM 77).[26]

This is so, according to Benhabib, because the deliberative model of democracy presupposes a discourse theory of ethics able to supply it with the most general moral principles upon which a more concrete set of rights would be based. Discourse ethics "proceeds from a view of persons as being entitled to certain 'moral rights'" — which Benhabib names as the rights to "universal moral respect" and "egalitarian reciprocity" — "that accrue to individuals insofar as we view them as moral persons" (TDM 78). The crucial move from recognizing these two moral rights to formulating "a principle of basic rights and liberties" would, in good Kantian fashion, consist in a "hypothetical and counterfactual moral reasoning procedure" that asked: "which most general principles of basic rights and liberties would [those individuals who view one another as beings entitled to universal moral respect and egalitarian reciprocity] also be likely to accept as determining the conditions of their collective existence?" The distinctiveness of the approach of the deliberative model of democratic legitimacy, however, as compared with its close cousins in the work of Kant and Rawls, is that it "would privilege a discourse model of practical debate as being the appropriate forum for determining rights claims" (TDM 78).[27]

That is, "what is distinctive about the discourse model is that although it presupposes that participants must recognize one another's entitlement to moral respect and reciprocity *in some sense*, the determination of the *precise* content and extent of these principles would be a consequence of discourses themselves" (TDM 79, emphasis added). This would happen, according to Benhabib, through a process of "recursive validation," whereby the normative constraints upon discourse (grounded in the two universal norms of discourse ethics) could themselves be challenged within the deliberation itself.[28]

For Benhabib, such a process of recursive validation, whereby the precise meaning and entailment of the universal, but very abstract, norms of discourse ethics are determined (and constantly revised) through collective deliberation, is in fact an essential part of the practice of existing "complex constitutional democracies." On the one hand, then, it is a mistake to say that in such societies even the most basic rights are "off the table," for in fact we are constantly debating and revising them, even when they cannot be abrogated by simple majority decisions. In other words, political debate in such societies allows the basic rules of the game to be disputed in the very playing of the game. There are no umpires in the game of constitutional democracy. On the other hand, to play the game, one has to respect the rules (even though they never simply determine specific results), for "one cannot challenge the specific interpretation of basic rights and liberties in a democracy without taking these absolutely seriously." Indeed, "when basic rights and liberties are violated the game of democracy is suspended and becomes either martial rule, civil war, or dictatorship; when democratic politics is in full session, the debate about the meaning of these rights, what they do or do not entitle us to, their scope and enforcement, is what politics is all about" (TDM 80).

Thus Benhabib can argue that "the deliberative theory of democracy transcends the traditional opposition of majoritarian politics vs. liberal guarantees of basic rights and liberties to the extent that the normative conditions of discourses, like basic rights and liberties, are to be viewed as rules of the game that can be contested within the game but only insofar as one first accepts to abide by them and play the game at all" (TDM 80). With the particular combination of attitudes that might be called "respectful contestation," deliberative democracy would thus offer the best of both worlds: able both to guarantee/respect rights and to leave those rights open to deliberation and contestation. Benhabib can thus be understood to be proposing deliberative democracy as a means of reconciling not only democracy and liberalism but also the tension within democracy itself — between the required openness of debate and deliberation and its need for the closure afforded by established rights and institutionalized procedures.

When we begin to press on this happy reconciliation, however, uncertainties emerge that raise important questions about the meaning and ambitions of Benhabib's deliberative democracy. To some degree, Benhabib seems to offer her "reconciliation" of liberal rights and democratic deliberation merely as an improved *description* of democracy, one that would "correspond to the reality of democratic debate and public speech in real democracies much more accurately than the liberal model of deliberation upon constitutional essentials or the reasonings of the Supreme Court." This would explain the importance Benhabib places on the existence of a public sphere "of opinion-formation, debate, deliberation, and contestation among citizens, groups, movements, and organizations in a polity," which she characterizes as "the concrete embodiment of discursive democracy in practice" (TDM 80). Yet clearly — as any democratically inclined interpreter of American or European political institutions and practices, for instance, would have to admit — Benhabib's improved description of actual constitutional democratic practice is an idealized one, which would be designed in part to move the practice closer to the ideal.[29] Indeed, Benhabib's aim is clearly to argue not only that rights are *already* open to deliberative reconstruction but that they should be *more* open to deliberation. At times in her essay, this would seem to involve not only an increase in the amount, inclusiveness, and quality of public discussion but also a shift in the effective power to determine the precise meaning of rights from present institutions (i.e., courts) toward the process of deliberation itself.

But how exactly would this turn to deliberation work? And wouldn't it involve certain risks? Benhabib suggests otherwise, arguing that because deliberative democracy's norms of universal moral respect and egalitarian reciprocity "allow minorities and dissenters both the right to withhold their assent and the right to challenge the rules as well as the agenda of public debate" (TDM 79), the worries of liberals about deliberative democracy bringing with it undue pressure to conform or the threat of majority tyranny should be allayed. The promise of the deliberative model of democratic legitimacy, indeed, is that the openness of democratic deliberation would contain within its own conditions of possibility certain safeguards against its abuses. There emerges a central ambiguity at this point, however. Benhabib supports her claim with the following: "for what distinguishes discourses from compromises and other agreements reached under conditions of coercion is that only the *freely given assent of all concerned* can count as a condition of having reached agreement in the discourse situation" (TDM 79). Of course, this clearly refers to the ideal conditions of discourse, however, not to those under which deliberation is likely to happen anytime soon. How would liberal fears be alleviated, then, in the transitional state, before the achievement of fully rational deliberation? How would the risks of deliberation be avoided today, under present less-than-ideal conditions?

In the earlier of the two versions of her essay from which I have been working, Benhabib seems to acknowledge the risks involved in moving toward a more deliberative practice of democracy. In an endnote discussing a series of contentious issues of religious and cultural diversity in liberal-democratic constitutional states (and touching specifically on the role of Islam in French public institutions), she argues that such issues should be determined at least in part by "an anonymous public dialogue . . . carried out in religious, educational, cultural associations and the media . . . but first and foremost [in] the communities affected by these decisions." Benhabib then states that "the wager of the deliberative theorist of democracy is that a *decision* around these issues *reached as a result of concurrent processes of public dialogue and deliberation* would be both more rational and more legitimate. The reason why I define this as a wager has to do with the rational underdetermination of procedures discussed above" (DR 49, emphasis added). Of course, by "wager," Benhabib may simply mean "a good bet," as in "the educated guess" of the theorist. But even so, the statement would seem to imply her recognition that granting an increased role for deliberative processes in determining a society's basic rights runs the risk that the outcome of such deliberation would, at least from some perspectives, be seen as weakening rights essential to justice or legitimacy.

This reading is admittedly made more difficult by the following passage, which immediately precedes the sentences just cited, and which seems to give a merely advisory role to public deliberation:

Such a process of deliberation could not and should not replace the constitutional and legal procedures for settling the question whether or not Koran schools should enjoy the same constitutional rights as other religious schools. Nonetheless, the participation of the affected religious and cultural community in such deliberative processes should be encouraged as widely as possible and they should be given the widest possible public access to present their points of view.[30] (DR 49)

Yet here, too, even as this would seem to alleviate the most severe grounds for liberal worry, risks of various sorts would remain. For opening up rights to greater deliberation, even if in a merely advisory capacity, could conceivably have the effect of undermining the legitimacy of established constitutional rights procedures when deliberative outcomes and the decisions of established bodies conflict (especially if they do so frequently and for distinct constituencies of citizens). On the other hand, choosing to rely on an institutionally weak form of deliberation would run the opposite risk of perpetuating antidemocratic institutionalizations of liberal rights, or otherwise unjust or less than fully rational situations that are locked into place by present institutions and relations of power. Finally, the wager Benhabib mentions could also — on an admittedly un-Benhabibian reading — be read as referring to the risk one takes by relying on (imperfectly rational) deliberative procedures to effect change, as opposed not to liberal rights but rather to other, nondeliberative, perhaps even forceful means of pressure and change.[31] The question of which of these various approaches is most democratic, in other words, can only be a pragmatic question about which risks are most worth running, a question that calls for a contextual judgment about the best way to bring into being one's preferred vision of democratic rights and procedures.

In short, the abstract compatibility of liberal rights with those rights characteristic of deliberative democracy doesn't guarantee the compati-

bility between any *existing* rights and the outcome of any *given* deliberative procedures. Nor, more generally, is there any necessary compatibility
between a reliance on deliberation and achieving an increase in democracy, justice, or rationality. Whichever approach one takes, one runs a
risk — indeed, in one sense a risk to "democracy" itself, whether in the
form of preserving its existing rights, achieving equality, or respecting its
essential procedures of argument and deliberation.[32] Given limited time,
knowledge, and resources, democracy's multiple principles will in effect
be in competition, making it difficult to know, before the ideal conditions
of deliberative legitimacy and rationality have been established, when to
deliberate and when not to. Does one, for instance, push to open up a
particular issue for debate, if doing so might jeopardize the political support needed to achieve other democratic goals, or if doing so now, given
the particular conjunction of political forces, might lead to a political
defeat that would further entrench antidemocratic opinions and practices? Is it best to put one's limited political resources into democratizing
deliberative procedures more generally, or into achieving other democratic ends — for example, justice in some particular case, or expanding
equality in specific social domains, or strengthening the political alliances
needed to fight other democratic struggles? Even accepting deliberative
democracy and its vigorous public sphere as a critical ideal toward which
one would like to move present political practice, it isn't certain that in
the here and now, in any given situation, a reliance on deliberation is the
best way of getting us to democratic, or rational, outcomes — or even of
bringing into being the conditions for fully open and public deliberation.
Situated as we are in imperfectly democratic contexts and with imperfectly rational deliberative procedures at our disposal, a choice to rely on
deliberative procedures (or indeed any other mode of decision-making)
can indeed only be a wager.

4

The Dilemmas of Democratic Openness

In the absence of an already rational body of people, and in the absence
of procedures that can guarantee rational deliberation, we are back to (or
rather, we have always remained within) Rousseau's paradox: how are we
to make the people rational — in the sense of oriented toward and able to
discover their common good and the rights and procedures necessary to
its continued respect — while at the same time respecting their autonomy?
And how can we act most democratically before having achieved such a

goal? The promise of Benhabib's deliberative model of democratic legitimacy to reconcile rationality and legitimacy, or simply liberal rights and
deliberation, would seem able to be fulfilled only if there already existed
the equality and commonality that deliberation itself is meant, among
other things, to achieve.[33] Or to describe the problem more directly in
terms of Rousseau's paradox of effect and cause: both the effectiveness
and legitimacy of deliberative procedures would seem to presuppose a
democratic social spirit, in the form of a general commitment to, and
practice of following, egalitarian and reciprocal rules of deliberation. Yet
such a social spirit is something whose achievement would itself seem to
depend at least in part on the prior existence of fair decisions and egalitarian institutions — or else must somehow be built out of not-yet-demo-
cratic materials. To argue this is not to *disprove* Benhabib, nor to reject
the value of deliberative procedures, understood as effective strategies in
particular cases for reaching more deeply democratic and legitimate decisions. It is meant, instead, to suggest that such an approach will itself *in
practice* run up against a series of difficulties and tensions that are constitutive of democratic politics, for the negotiation of which deliberation
itself has no necessary advantage over other approaches, and about
which, in general, theories of deliberative democracy have little to say.[34]

These difficulties and tensions, as I have begun to suggest, go beyond
the age-old conflict between liberal rights and the decision-making powers of democratic majorities. As I have argued throughout this chapter,
they reside in the very nature of democratic freedom and its fundamental — but always incomplete — openness, and the limits of Benhabib's theory are thus instructive for an understanding of democratic theory and
practice more generally.[35] In her rationalist belief that Rousseau's paradox
of effect and cause can be avoided in the deliberative model of democratic
legitimacy, and more generally in her theorization of democratic politics
from the point of its ideal *completion*, Benhabib repeats the overconfidence of many democratic theorists before her, failing to recognize the
intractability of the paradoxes that structure democratic freedom and
openness — and thus having nothing to say about some of the most
important and characteristic aspects of the actual experience of democratic politics, in which democracy is always *still to be achieved*, the people still-to-come. For Benhabib, the deliberative ideal posits a form of
openness — according to which the conversation is open to all, the topics
and rules of the discussion are always open to question, and the force of
the better argument carries the day — that is also able to grant the political body both legitimacy and stability (in the form of established institutions and procedures for deliberation, debate, and collective revision). Yet
in the absence of a neutral conception of the people — an absence that is

the very source of democratic freedom — there can be no guarantee that either the closure *or* the openness necessary to democratic contestation will not itself become a threat to democratic freedom and the legitimacy of debate. As a result, the existence of any given procedures of deliberation and debate can never be a guarantee of the kind or degree of questionability or openness necessary to democratic legitimacy. The ultimate effect of this paradox is to make it difficult in many situations to know what the properly "democratic" attitude requires in practice. The uncertainty, conflict, and paradox so basic to democracy render the very meaning of democratic openness and action uncertain, the site of endless conflict.

Of course, as we have seen, Benhabib would accept that in practice such openness will always be incomplete. For the rights and practices that constitute the public space of debate will always create, or grant access to, a *particular* space or spaces, making it possible for some to say and do certain kinds of things in certain situations, but not for anyone to say anything, at any time, for any reason.[36] However equal the access to the public space might be in formal terms, then, some members of the community, or groups within it, will always be situated in such a way as to have a greater ability to influence the outcome of the debate than others have — often by controlling the means and the terms of the debate itself.[37] (Indeed, Benhabib goes so far as to concede at one point that "there may be no act of republican founding that does not carry its own violence and exclusion within it.")[38] The particular *form* of the debate thus inevitably affects the debate's *content*. As a result, there can in practice be no politically neutral definition of "equal" access. In its absence, of course, all such constraints on debate must themselves be fully debatable. Yet the obvious dilemma is that they can be challenged only under conditions that they themselves have in part set.[39]

Ultimately, then, whether because of the limited set of options that the institutions of debate themselves make available, or perhaps because of a high degree of consensus about certain fundamental issues among most, or just the most powerful, within the community, there is always the possibility that debate and deliberation will be structured in such a way that a given version of the people is protected from effective challenge within the terms of the system itself. The existence of the public space and democratic debate provides legitimacy, however, only if the reigning version of the people is truly questionable — that is, it must actually be possible to revise the community's decisions, laws, and rights in meaningful ways. Yet when judging the existence of democratic legitimacy and freedom, how is one to know whether the decisions debated in the public sphere are truly up for grabs and never more than provisional? The difficulty —

both for proceduralist theories and for democratic actors — is that there is no politically neutral way of knowing when this is the case. There is no rule independent of a particular conception of "the people" and their rights for what constitutes being "open," no rule for how much or what sort of questioning and change is enough to prove "real" revisability. Given that all deliberation and contestation have to end at some point, and that there is no *procedure* of debate that doesn't to some degree help determine the *substance* of what is debated and what is decided, the criteria for judging adequate "questionability," and the legitimacy that goes with it, are always relative to a particular, not fully open, conception of the people. One can, therefore, find oneself in a situation that meets all the formal requirements of a deliberative (or other) model of democratic legitimacy — a set of laws and equal rights and a public space that allows those laws and rights to be challenged and changed — without, for all that, finding that the range of political options it makes possible includes those necessary to the actual "rule of the people," or one's preferred vision of a community of political equals.

The definition of what, for the purposes of democratic legitimacy, constitutes an adequate public space cannot, in other words, be separated from a judgment of what rights one thinks people do or should have — *how questionable* one judges the people to be depends in part on *what* is questioned and what the *likely answers* are. This is what Benhabib's proceduralism and her reliance on the idea of "recursive validation" fail to take seriously: for legitimacy to be found in the process of debate, one must be able to identify with at least the basic content of the rights and political practice of the community, and not merely with the procedures of debate and deliberation themselves and the underlying principles that explain and justify them. Otherwise, whatever changes and revisions that are in fact made as a result of political contest and debate will be merely inessential revisions to a scheme of rights and political institutions that do not actually allow "the people" to rule. A judgment that there exists a properly functioning public space, then, cannot be limited to the question of equal access to that space (even if agreement could be reached about what that entailed). It also requires that the space allow one the possibility of influencing the outcome of the debate that takes place within it.[40] From the perspective of those who hold a conception of the people that is unable to affect the debate, the reigning version of "the people" will effectively be *unquestionable*. The existence of "debate" and "deliberation" by itself accords that people, and the decisions made in its name, no legitimacy, since the public space is compatible with both injustice and illegitimacy. Indeed, the very reliance on deliberation, when the conditions are not in place for a truly equal and open exchange and evaluation

of ideas and opinions, can have the effect of offering democratic legiti-
mation to unjust procedures and unfair outcomes.[41]

How best, then, democratically speaking, to open up an effectively
closed system of debate and questioning? One cannot simply offer more
deliberation as the answer to unfair or inadequate deliberation, for the
question remains how to transform the quality of deliberation in ways
that make it more possible for critical voices, alternate visions of freedom
and commonality, to be heard. Nor is it simply enough, through a process
of recursive validation, to appeal to the underlying principles of openness
and deliberation whose respect is necessary for the reigning version of the
public space and debate to be able to claim legitimacy. Given that deliberation and questioning take time and resources and thus involve opportunity costs — including those of other forms of freedom — opinions about
what counts as sufficient respect for deliberative procedures of legitima-
tion will depend in part on one's larger, more than just procedural, vision
of the good (and realistically possible) society. It follows that various
means of shutting down, or disrupting the functioning of, existing procedures of deliberation and forms of "openness" — from political pressure,
to disruption of meetings, to computer hacking, shaming, and classic
forms of civil disobedience — can be seen as properly democratic modes of
opening (if not yet being fully open themselves). They cannot simply be
ruled out as nondemocratic, in the name of democracy's essential openness and its dependence on the activity of debate and deliberation.
Indeed, from the perspective of a version of the people excluded, by whatever form of closure, from effectively influencing political debate, more or
less forceful resistance to such exclusion can itself be argued to be more
democratic — because necessary to the rule of a *different* "people" — than
is negotiation within its confines. As the democratic theorist Claude
Lefort argues, "resistance to oppression" is at the basis of political freedom and all other democratic rights.[42]

Such forcefulness, however, is just one, particularly clear, example of
the forcefulness that is always involved to some degree in the struggle to
establish and maintain a particular version of the people, or political community. For the people's generality — the various forms of equality and of
social spirit that hold them together as a political community, and which
then go on to help make possible their own questioning and deliberation — must be built in part through modes of political action that fail to
respect the democratic demands of openness or autonomy. In the most
general sense, this refers to the fact that any given vision of the political
community must be brought into being against political (and other modes
of) resistance, even as what one is attempting to establish are forms of
commonality, together with the habits and beliefs that incline members of

the community toward what they have in common.[43] More specifically, as Michael Walzer has argued, most of the forms of democratic speech and action needed to sustain democratic politics against the inevitable drift toward greater inequality and loss of social spirit would fail to meet the criteria of legitimacy laid down in deliberative democracy's model of the rational exchange of arguments among equals.[44] Thus the forms of collective identification that must be established and maintained will always be with particular traditions, histories, and ways of being together, and not simply with the universal principles of democratic equality and debate. What's more, the work of establishing such identifications will, like much, if not most, democratic politics, depend on large amounts of organizing and mobilization. These will require multiple techniques of nonrational, non-argumentative persuasion — using images, strong metaphors, and emotional stories. Effective democratic mobilization will also depend more on displays of strength — demonstrations, letters and phone calls, lobbying — that are intended to bring pressure to bear on decision-makers and on the political opposition, rather than on efforts to persuade them of the rational correctness of one's own policies or beliefs. And such organizing, finally, will itself require, at least under any foreseeable modern form of democracy, effective leadership and effective followership, in which the values of critical debate and questioning will necessarily be kept within limits.

In short, then, even though active questioning and debate are essential to democratic political practice, the best democratic efforts to question one's own political positions and to foster an attitude of collective openness and self-critique will nonetheless always be limited. This is not only because debate will always have practical constraints, nor is it just because questioning itself is possible only on the basis of a structure of debate that inevitably helps channel it in certain directions and not others. The limits to democratic openness also involve more than the many ways we have just been looking at in which the people's perpetual refoundation depends on practices that frequently limit the scope of questioning and open debate. Democratic openness and self-critique are also limited, finally, because for "the people" to be able to rule, certain political principles and institutions will, and *should*, always be effectively non-negotiable.[45] Even if one accepts the Habermasian ideal of discourse as promising a route to rational moral and political decisions, procedures of debate and questioning can serve the purposes of political legitimacy only within the limits set by those substantive principles and institutions one holds to be necessary to justice and legitimacy. Given the necessity of working within a less than perfectly rational public sphere with less than fully free and open deliberation, we will be open to negotiate over and question our own position only to the extent that the positions of our interlocutors (or opponents) do not endanger those values or practices indispensable to the legitimacy of our own notion of the people (or the common good, or justice, etc.).[46] Thus even as the good democrat recognizes the ultimate questionability of her highest values and principles, efforts to institutionalize them so as to make them more difficult to challenge[47] — and, in the face of disagreement, to defend or establish them by force if necessary — are in principle entirely appropriate to democratic politics.[48]

Given the freedom at the heart of democracy, then, no *theory* of democracy can prescribe when such a right is appropriately invoked, nor, more generally, can we ever be certain what democracy requires us to do — "democracy" and the people's rule can be invoked on either side of such a debate. But this is to say that conflict is not only an ever-present possibility *between* competing conceptions of the people but that it resides *within* the very ideal of freedom, and thus within any single conception of the people. Because democracy is the regime of autonomy and freedom, it is structured around two demands, which push in opposite directions. The imperative that the people rule requires that a particular version of the people, including the space of debate, be established, through imperfectly autonomous means, and defended, at times even forcefully; that same imperative also requires that the people be no more than provisional, fully open to challenge and revision. In practice, then, one cannot avoid having to risk freedom — either through too much closure *or* through too much openness — in order to preserve it.

The predicament in which this places democratic political actors is all the more difficult, the more seriously we take democracy's principles. To make possible a democratic form of politics, in which the community gives itself its own rules, we must act in the general interest and attempt to bring into being a regime of equality and equal participation. Yet in recognition that our own notion of the general interest or the common good is not a universal one but necessarily involves closure and exclusion, we must make it possible to contest and revise it. For the sake of the rule of the people, the constitutive openness of the people's identity must be affirmed rather than denied. Nonetheless, because the debate and contestation required to maintain such openness must itself always be limited — in part by the closure necessary to its own preservation — it is impossible to say with certainty what keeping the people "open" requires in practice. The point here is not only that such "openness" can always be challenged as inadequately democratic from a competing notion of who the people are, but, more fundamentally, that each side of democratic freedom challenges the other. There is always the imperative to enforce closure in order to protect freedom and openness, even as this limits and endangers it; so, too, we must foster openness so as to make possible the rule of the people, despite the fact that such openness may ultimately endanger the people's continued existence. Nothing can free us from the paradox of needing *and* resisting both openness and closure, without having access to any rule about when or how much of one or the other is needed.

In short, we never know for sure what democracy calls for. The questionability that is the foundation of democracy, as the regime of freedom, renders the meanings of "democracy" and "democratic" fundamentally questionable. Yet the uncertainty of democracy cannot simply become its own rule; *identifying* democracy with questioning or questionability threatens to downplay the true difficulty of democracy. Because "democracy" is a series of questions that nonetheless demand answers (however provisional), its own questionability cannot *be* an answer.[49] No theory of democratic legitimacy, then, can be adequate to the experience of democratic freedom — to the necessity of speaking in the name of the people so as to call them into being, of deciding and acting even as any choice one makes will always threaten the freedom one wants to preserve. Democracy, instead, remains torn by the *risk* of practicing freedom, of having to give answers without properly autonomous or legitimate grounds, of risking, even violating, its own laws of freedom, openness, and autonomy, precisely in order to follow those same laws.

In the Name of the Always Uncertain "We": Civic Virtue and the Burdens of Democratic Freedom

The paradoxes and uncertainty that are so essential to democracy thus place a fundamental limit on its theorization. The difficulties of democratic freedom and openness are not, however, merely theoretical. Indeed, the challenge democracy poses to theorization is born precisely from the necessity of democratic action and judgment in the absence of clear grounds and unambiguously applicable principles. Yet although political theory can provide no answers to democracy's questions, in the sense of specific recommendations for how best to negotiate its conflicting demands in any given situation, it nonetheless has something important to offer democratic practice. Indeed, it is a central contention of this chapter, and of the book as a whole, that an analysis of democratic politics that begins from a recognition of the nonsimultaneity of the political community's self-foundation — such as that worked out in this chapter's reading of Rousseau and in the following chapters on later theorists of political freedom — has the advantage of bringing to light the risks and burdens that confront all those who must judge and act from uncertain, democratically "impure," grounds. By doing so it also draws our attention to the need for, and general contours of, strategies that might make such difficulties more bearable by democratic citizens and actors. Such strategies — which can be understood as specific forms of "civic virtue" — would be particularly important for those citizens who wish to take the principles of democratic politics *more* seriously than the present system allows, for it is during such attempts that the dilemmas of democratic openness are felt most acutely. And given the forcefulness that shadows all democratic foundations and decisions, strategies are especially needed to allow democratic freedom and conflict to be experienced in nonviolent ways. The new forms of civic virtue designed to respond to these difficulties would thus address the central dilemma facing democratic actors today: how to create a vibrant sense of democratic community able to generate widespread and active identifications, while also recognizing and respecting the radical openness of any shared collective identity.

Perhaps the most obvious difficulty in need of response that the previous analyses draw our attention to is the awkwardness of having to speak and act in the name of a people not yet in existence and thus prior to the people's own sanction, all the while actively contested by other "voices of the people." This is not an easy or comfortable position to occupy, and it is less so the more seriously we take our democratic, universalist responsibilities. And to have to do so from within the imperfectly democratic and rational context of the present system, with its own demands of limited time and resources and inevitable considerations of strategy, requires not only that we often, if not always, *risk* some aspect of democracy's ideals but also that at times we actively, even forcefully, *sacrifice* certain of its values (full participation, "liberal" rights, deliberative procedures, and so forth), precisely so as to respect others. This is not only a difficult position for citizens to take up and maintain but also one likely to provoke reactions that can make it harder to generate a democratic social spirit. It is all too easy for others — whether one's political opponents or those disengaged from politics altogether — to point to the questionable nature of the democratic "we" in whose name one speaks, and thus the doubtful legitimacy of those who do so, which is only compounded to the extent that less than fully democratic means must be used to bring it more fully into being. Preventing the uncertainty of the democratic "we," around which democratic politics necessarily gravitates, from engendering antipolitical forms of resentment, anger, and cynicism is thus a crucial task for those still captured by the radical promise of democratic politics as robustly participatory and egalitarian, as a politics in which the people rule themselves more often and more deeply than the mere practice of elections allows.

For such a form of politics to be at all possible, it would be especially important to develop strategies able to respond to the division and uncertainty within the individual self and its identity that follows from the experience of debate and contestation over the meaning and norms of the democratic "we." For the openness that is so essential to democratic community and its identity extends to those of individual citizens as well. Indeed, democratic speech and action place the identity of the self at risk in the most general sense in that, even in liberal and individualist forms, it involves a direct (if generally unacknowledged) engagement with our radical intersubjectivity. Central to the democratic experience, that is, are those ways in which the citizen is dependent on — although never simply determined by — her fellow citizens for her identity and highest values, as all together construct who they are through the never-ending process of one person speaking in the name of others and of having others, in turn, speak for one in one's (collective) name.

Although something like this goes on in even the most everyday political discussions, such a process is particularly apparent, and can be particularly disturbing, in cases of claims to new rights (e.g., claims for equal treatment and respect across differences of gender, "race," and sexual preference) that speak in the name of an as-yet (for most) unrecognized (and often seemingly unrecogniz*able*) "we." If "they" are like "me," deserving of the same rights, treatments, and possibilities, then I am no longer like myself. To accept previously excluded groups into the circle of the "we" is to transform the "we" and with it all the "I"'s that identify with it and draw sustenance from it. The challenge that such claims pose to both collective and personal identity can be so powerfully disorienting, even frightening, then, in part because they bring out the contingent nature of identity itself.[50] They bring out the fact that "I" don't have to be who and what I am now, even raising the possibility that I *shouldn't be* the way I am (that perhaps some of the possibilities I have repressed or rejected were in fact preferable).

Conflict, uncertainty, and ambivalence within the self are thus constitutive of the kind of universalist, egalitarian, reciprocal politics characteristic of democracy. To engage in the kind of politics of "enlarged mentalities" and "reversibility" that Castoriadis, Benhabib, and other radical and/or deliberative democrats quite rightly (as democrats) champion is to be thrown into a situation of confusion and vulnerability (however productive the end results might be).[51] The "space" of democratic citizenship is thus always a difficult one to be in, all the more so the larger and more inclusive one wishes the space to be. The questions all this raises are whether and how such processes can be more easily endured — how to create the openness to hear the claims of others, claims that call into question one's own identity and commitments, even as they are made in the

name of what "we" are all already supposed to share? How best to negotiate the uncertainty of self and of community that is so constitutive of
democratic culture, and the insecurities that come with democratic dialogue, argument, negotiation, and shared action, so as to foster the general willingness to orient oneself toward, and take the risks of engaging,
democracy's "enlarged mentality?"[52] Indeed, perhaps the central challenge facing democratic politics today is that of developing more effectively "open" forms of identification and social spirit, ones that allow
both an active, participatory, orientation to what we share in common
while also respecting the constitutive uncertainty of the common that
comes precisely from its being the *whole* community's *shared* creation.

Especially from the perspective of those who still wish to respect and
give full reign to the radical nature of democracy's demand that the
people rule themselves, the democratic logic of *moral* argument and justification thus needs to be supplemented with what might be called a
democratic ethos, one that works to enable democratic energies and
involvement by making more bearable the experience of conflict, uncertainty, mistakes, unexpected consequences, and feelings of self-contradiction or division that are constitutive of democratic action. Amounting to
an alternate set of nonrational jump-starts to the people's political
"rationality," designed to facilitate the positive experience of democracy's
burdens, such forms of civic virtue would amount to the cultivation of a
different relation to democratic universals, one that tries to facilitate an
engagement with democratic ideals through an initial recognition of the
impossibility of ever simply achieving them and an acceptance of the burdens of acting in their name.

Central to such an ethos would be the development of democratic languages of compassion and forgiveness, designed to release citizens from
the unintended and unpredictable pain and suffering that accompany
political action and that come with the failure to be able to honor fully
the whole range of democratic values. As Hannah Arendt writes in *The
Human Condition*, "trespassing is an everyday occurrence which is in the
very nature of action's constant establishment of new relationships within
a web of relations, and it needs forgiving, dismissing, in order to make it
possible for life to go on by constantly releasing men from what they have
done unknowingly." As Arendt explains, "in this respect, forgiveness is
the exact opposite of vengeance, which acts in the form of re-acting
against an original trespassing, whereby far from putting an end to the
consequences of the first misdeed, everybody remains bound to the
process, permitting the chain reaction contained within every action to
take its unhindered course."[53] A democratic language of compassion,
together with other practices of forgiveness — and, more generally, the

kind of compassion that seeks to respond to present injustice and suffering by understanding their sources in a chain of previous injustices and
suffering — would aim to break, or at least soften, the dangerous cycles of
recrimination and counter-recrimination that are born of the endless
resources for resentment that democratic politics provides. By offering a
mode of what Arendt calls "mutual release" from the trespasses and failures of political action, they would also hold out the hope of freeing up
democratic energies and enthusiasm that otherwise would be blocked on
the one hand by resignation (in the face of democratic deficits) and withdrawal (from the burdens of challenging or negotiating those deficits), or,
on the other hand, by the cynicism of realpolitik and "decisionism."[54]

In the final chapter, I explore at greater length why such ethical and
rhetorical practices are especially needed under present conditions of
widespread disenchantment and cynicism about the possibilities of democratic politics and begin to sketch out what such practices might look
like. I focus in particular on the political possibilities that might lie within
a language of political engagement that avoided the dangers of resentment and cynicism through a compassionate understanding, rooted in a
democratic critique of self-identity, of the inevitable trespass, failure,
impurity, and incompletion that characterize political action. Through an
engagement with Michael Sandel's contemporary reworking of the civic
republican tradition we have just encountered in Rousseau, I explore how
such a language of political engagement might foster a form of civic virtue
that would make possible more effective democratic identifications, even
as it respects the openness and uncertainty of democratic politics and
identity.

To deepen our understanding of the paradoxes and dilemmas of democratic freedom, however, we investigate in the intervening chapters two
further theoretical attempts to take account of the questionable, non-
absolute character of political foundations and collective identity after the
"democratic revolution." The first of these attempts, and the focus of the
next chapter, is that of Hannah Arendt. For Arendt, the experience of
freedom — as an experience of contingency, plurality, and the possibility
of unpredictable, radically new beginnings — is the central experience of
politics. It is both the point of existing in political communities and the
model of action that makes those communities possible. Given that
democracy can be defined as the political practice built on nothing other
than the conditions of political freedom itself, I show how the nature of
democratic freedom and democratic political foundations is illuminated
in important ways in Arendt's work, especially in her discussion of the
complicated relationship of political freedom and political foundations,
which is the primary focus of the chapter. Indeed, I argue that the central

predicaments of democratic politics are revealed in a particularly acute way in the very collapse of the sharp distinction Arendt draws between political freedom (and the political) and the "nonpolitical" experiences of rule and forceful closure. For that collapse — and the new, more complicated vision of freedom that emerges out of it — offers further evidence of the nature, and severity, of the paradoxes that afflict political theory and the dilemmas that face democratic practice, once absolute, unquestionable foundations have disappeared and the people are left to rule themselves.

CHAPTER TWO

Promises, Promises

*The Abyss of Freedom and the Loss of the Political
in the Work of Hannah Arendt*

The effort to recapture the lost spirit of revolution must, to a certain extent, consist in the attempt at thinking together and combining meaningfully what our present vocabulary presents to us in terms of opposition and contradiction.

—Hannah Arendt, *On Revolution*

Have you ever asked yourselves sufficiently how much the erection of *every* ideal on earth has cost? . . . If a temple is to be erected *a temple must be destroyed*: that is the law — let anyone who can show me a case in which it is not fulfilled!

—Friedrich Nietzsche, *On the Genealogy of Morals*

"The periods of being free have always been relatively short in the history of mankind," Hannah Arendt reminds us, in her difficult essay "What Is Freedom?"[1] In recognition of the ease with which freedom is lost or forgotten, Arendt devotes considerable attention in her writing to the foundation of political communities, most directly in her interpretation of the American and French Revolutions in *On Revolution*. The founding of a new political body is a particularly privileged instance of human freedom for Arendt: it asserts the freedom to bring something new into the world, the ever-present possibility of what Arendt calls "beginnings," *and* it establishes the public or political realm itself, which she defines as the very realm of action and freedom. Such moments of foundation are essential to both politics and freedom, because freedom, although inexhaustible, is limited to the moment of its being put into action: "the appearance of freedom . . . coincides with the performing act. . . . To *be* free and to act are the same" (WF 152–53). As a result, freedom is always threatened with loss and oblivion; "without a politically guaranteed public realm, freedom lacks the worldly space to make its appearance" (WF 149). The importance of the act of founding the political realm lies in the need to make possible the continuation of what can never be absolutely secured, to "guarantee" a space for the appearance and possibility of the most transient and fragile of human experiences, freedom itself.

One of the central difficulties that confronts Arendt's theory of freedom (as well as any analysis of it), however, is the tension that exists within her work between the temporal and the political aspects of freedom. Arendt's political theory, which is at its heart a theory of freedom, is deeply indebted to her understanding of time as radically open to new possibilities; yet politics for her is clearly not only a matter of time. This tension becomes particularly acute when the issue at hand is the foundation of political bodies, or the constitution of the political realm itself. If the political is valuable for Arendt as the space for, or the mode of, the appearance of freedom, which is itself inseparable from a particular aspect of time, then the act of founding the political "realm" must be consistent with that free temporality. But the political realm needs the stability of foundations precisely because freedom cannot simply be left up to time; for freedom to be active and effective as a force in the world, it requires the *continuous* support of political foundations.

Foundation, then, is a hinge word in Arendt's texts, turning (and torn) between the openness of *beginning* and the demand that something be begun and then maintained; like "the political" itself, "foundation" is caught between the "free" logic of time, with its possibilities for new beginnings, and the requirement that the realm of freedom be given *lasting* support. In this chapter, I explore this tension — whose parallels with the tensions between openness and closures in the previous chapter become clear as we proceed — and Arendt's attempt to come to terms with it. In particular, I focus on her idealization of "mutual promising" as the means by which the freedom found in political action can save itself by granting itself its own, free, foundation. I argue that despite Arendt's trust in the promise as a means to preserve freedom and its political realm, neither freedom nor foundation can survive intact the deep interdependence that Arendt so carefully elaborates. Although Arendt seems, in *On Revolution*, to recognize the inability of promising to found a realm of political freedom, her eventual turn in that text to the notion of authority as a process of "augmentation," in the hope that it will provide the same combination of freedom and foundation that mutual promising has failed to give, repeats at a new level the dilemmas contained in her extraordinary claims for promising.

Reading on the basis of Arendt's own formulation of the relation of
freedom and foundation, and yet against Arendt's desire to "save" the
free and open space of the political by walling it off from the realm of violence and rule, I argue that the political realm and the freedom it houses
can only be found by accepting their inevitable "loss." However hard
Arendt tries to separate freedom and political action — defined by their
contingency, plurality, and openness — from the violence and closures
associated with sovereignty and political rule, freedom's very need for
foundation inevitably entangles it in just such "nonpolitical" activities.
Seen in this light, "freedom," "action," and "the political" take on new,
more complex meanings, according to which they can never be entirely
detached from those qualities Arendt repeatedly posits as their opposites.
Far from implying the simple "death" or absence of either freedom or the
political, however, the recognition of the impossibility of arriving at a
political realm purified of nonpolitical or unfree elements is instead, I
argue, a means to take up the challenge of freedom and political action in
a different way, one commensurate with the difficulty and complexity of
Arendt's own analysis of political foundation.

As the previous chapter suggests, to do so would be to find oneself not
merely within the realm of politics and freedom but firmly within the
space of *democratic* politics and freedom. Indeed, it will be immediately
clear as we unpack the difficult relationship in Arendt's work between
freedom and foundation that we are once again amid the dilemmas and
paradoxes of democratic politics that we analyzed in the preceding chapter. Readers of Arendt have, of course, noted the strong connections
between democratic politics, with its logic of equality and collective
autonomy, and Arendt's understanding of freedom as the shared experience of new beginnings and the collective creation of a common space for
deliberation and action among equals.[2] The central democratic task of
instituting and maintaining a practice of politics that keeps the community open to question and never *finally* determined is seen clearly in
Arendt's project of finding a foundation that makes possible, rather than
interferes with, the experience of freedom. That both projects turn at
times to the figure of the promise makes this connection all the more evident. Yet at the same time, other commentators have noted Arendt's indif-
ference, and at times even hostility, to democracy, at least in its modern
form. Her definition of "the political" — the realm of freedom — as distinct from "the social" — the realm of need and necessity — and of freedom as separate from sovereignty have seemed to place her squarely at
odds with much of what is taken to define modern democracy, indeed,
with the very idea of the "rule" of "the people."[3]

Rather than focusing on Arendt's own opinions and analysis of democracy, however, I use Arendt's reflections on political freedom to illuminate further the dilemmas of democratic politics.[4] That is, given what we have seen is the central role in democratic politics of collective self-constitution, and the plurality and openness it involves, Arendt's analysis of freedom as an experience of contingency and plurality offers a particularly acute description of the conditions of political action after the democratic revolution, once all "natural" or absolute grounds of law and judgment have lost their validity. More specifically, by making clear the resistance of freedom to any absolute, or singular, ground, her work helps explain democratic autonomy as the process of constant foundation and refoundation of the always "promised" people. Arendt's reflections on freedom's need for foundation are particularly instructive for thinking through the difficulties and uncertainties of democratic politics, regardless of any particular argument she makes about the nature of democracy (for instance, her sharp critique of Rousseau and the concept of the general will). To the extent that democracy is constituted around the *tension* within freedom between its openness and its need for a particular, closed, institutional form, the ultimate failure of Arendt's quest for a foundation that would guarantee an experience of freedom and the political cleansed of the "nonpolitical" sovereignty and rule, is itself best read as an effect and experience of the paradoxes of democratic foundation. The new, more complicated, senses of freedom, politics, and action that emerge out of that failure are, in the end, recognizably democratic ones.

Freedom without Sovereignty: The Paradoxes of Plurality and New Beginnings

Arendt's project of thinking through the complexities of freedom is part of an effort to resist the inevitable tendency to "forget" the experience of freedom and the political realm in which it is found. Yet Arendt is very clear that the forgetting of freedom is no mere accident that befalls us, or conspiracy on the part of the powerful. It is, instead, a danger built into the very structure of freedom itself: the most central aspect or source of freedom — the possibility of new beginnings — resists understanding and explanation. Since "beginning's very nature is to carry in itself an element of complete arbitrariness" (*LM* 207), its emergence can never be fully explained by any law of determination: it never *has* to happen (although once it has happened, it can never be undone). Freedom, as the capacity to begin, to bring something new into being, is structured like an "abyss." More precisely, "the abyss of freedom" is the hole formed when "an unconnected new event break[s] into the continuum, the sequence of chronological time" (*LM* 208). What begins, or what Arendt calls at some points "the event," is not only unpredictable, it is, strictly speaking, unimaginable and unknowable: it depends on "the freedom to call something into being which did not exist before, which was not given, not even as an object of cognition or imagination, and which therefore, strictly speaking, could not be known" (WF 151).

The arbitrariness and indeterminacy of the freedom lodged within the possibility of beginning make freedom hard to explain and hard to remember. For this very reason, freedom needs the support of political foundations in order to be more than an occasional or marginal occurrence; yet such foundations, unless they are somehow able to build within themselves a respect for the fragile, unpredictable temporality of freedom, threaten to assist in its forgetting. The resulting "riddle of [political] foundation" amounts to the problem of "how to re-start time within an inexorable time continuum" (*LM* 214) while still respecting freedom. How can a political entity be brought into being in a way that *founds* a new identity and history ("re-starting time") without denying the arbitrary and contingent nature of that beginning? For Arendt, the greatest example of an encounter with the riddle of political foundation is the American Revolution. The American founders knew

> that an act can only be called free if it is not affected or caused by anything preceding it and yet, insofar as it immediately turns into a cause of whatever follows, it demands a justification which, if it is to be successful, will have to show the act as the continuation of a preceding series, that is, renege on the very experience of freedom and novelty. (*LM* 210)

The "founding fathers" knew that to establish a space of political freedom required an act that was itself entirely free, one that could have no immediate cause or higher power that commanded it. Yet they also knew that for the founding to be successful, to begin a new collective endeavor and bring a new public space into existence, it would have to be the impetus, even cause, of a whole chain of events that were to follow. It would therefore find itself caught up in a chain of cause and effect, which would in turn implicate it in the structures of "justification" or authorization that the free act *essentially contests*. Which explains why, when they were "called upon to solve . . . the perplexity inherent in the task of *foundation*" (*LM* 211), the American founders chose to retreat from their own practice and experience of freedom by imagining that they were founding a new Rome and by generally relying on the Roman tradition (which itself saw all beginnings as re-beginnings). Thus, "the abyss of pure spontaneity . . . was covered up by the device . . . of understanding the *new* as an improved re-statement of the old" (*LM* 216).

How *is* it possible to think the fact of *beginning*, especially the beginning of a political community, without reducing it to something secondary, to the effect of what preceded it in a temporal continuum? It is no surprise that those, whether philosophers or political actors, who have tried to think the fact of freedom have found themselves tempted by explanations and absolutes, by ways of explaining away the "abyss of pure spontaneity" with solutions that make of beginnings only the effects of some previous event or some higher law. But this is so not only because the temporality of freedom is abyssal and thus resists straightforward accounts, but for the related paradoxical reason that "nowhere does man appear to be less free than in those capacities whose very essence is freedom" (*THC* 234).[5] For the temporality of political action, of the freedom to begin something new, being an action of absolute contingency carries with it an inevitable "burden of irreversibility and unpredictability": what is freely done can neither be predicted beforehand nor undone once started; it can never even be known, much less understood, until after its completion. (Which is to say that it can never *fully* be known: "the reason why we are never able to foretell with certainty the outcome and end of any action," Arendt explains, "is simply that action has no end" [*THC* 233].) Because it is essentially incomplete, action is also necessarily plural: it requires the assistance of others to be completed; its "authors," finally, because of such plurality, must remain anonymous as well. All in all, to accept the burden of freedom is to be thrown into an abyss of uncertain relationships and to be carried to unknown and unknowable destinations. The result is

that he who acts never quite knows what he is doing, that he always becomes "guilty" of consequences he never intended or even foresaw, that no matter how disastrous and unexpected the consequences of his deed he can never undo it, that the process he starts is never consummated unequivocally in one single deed or event, and that its very meaning never discloses itself to the actor but only to the backward glance of the historian who himself does not act. (*THC* 233)

The fact of this "simultaneous presence of freedom and non-sovereignty, of being able to begin something new and of not being able to control or even foretell its consequences" (*THC* 235), means that freedom, as a matter of possibility, requires the presence and interaction of others, and thus a common space of appearance and action. Put more simply, freedom, because it can only be found in the midst of plurality, is essentially political. In this regard, Arendt praises the American founders for their recognition that "political freedom is distinct from philosophical freedom in being clearly a quality of the I-can and not of the I-will." It is something possessed only by the citizen, not by humanity in general; it can be had only in communities, since "political freedom is possible only in the sphere of human plurality" (*LM* 200).

Yet the freedom that can be experienced in political action, and most particularly in the foundation of the political realm, has, according to Arendt, been repeatedly ignored or covered over by theories that locate freedom in the *will*. Whether they understand the will to be an "inner" space of freedom, or a capacity for collective "sovereignty," such theories fail to face up to the complexities of political freedom. For as Arendt puts it, "public debate can only deal with things which — if we want to put it negatively — we cannot figure out with certainty. Otherwise, if we can figure it out with certainty, why do we all need to get together?"[6] The political — the plural and uncertain, which is to say nonsovereign — nature of freedom has been particularly resisted by many supposedly political thinkers. As a result, the frustrations of freedom have led to destructive dreams of sovereignty, where political action is converted into a process of making or fabrication, and plurality is reduced to the singularity of "one-man rule" (whether that of the individual monarch or the collective identity of a single political or national body). Born out of the frustrations inherent to political freedom, the "sovereign" will desires control and rule: control over the effects of its action into the future, and ultimately rule over others. To understand freedom as "sovereignty, the ideal of a free will, independent from others and eventually prevailing against them" (WF 163), is to try to dodge the plurality and irreducibly complex temporality of political freedom: it rests everything on the singularity of the willing agent and the *present moment* of the willing act. The dream is of a will that can fully inhabit the present in such a way as to control the future, and all alterity, from within it.

According to Arendt, the master of this antipolitical fantasy was Rousseau, who "conceive[d] of political power in the strict image of individual will-power . . . [and] argued . . . that power must be sovereign, that is, indivisible, because 'a divided will would be inconceivable'" (WF 163). The disastrous irony is that theorists of sovereignty, imagining it possible to rule from the position of an undivided, present moment of the will, in fact invent worlds without freedom and without politics. For "the famous sovereignty of political bodies has always been an illusion, which, moreover, can be maintained only by the instruments of violence, that is, with essentially nonpolitical means. . . . If men wish to be free, it is precisely sovereignty they must renounce" (WF 164–65).[7]

Those who desire sovereignty fail to realize that the attempt to escape from the essential incompletion and unpredictability of all free action is in fact doomed to paralysis — a paralysis of power that then requires a supplemental dose of violence to shore things up. "In reality," Arendt writes, "Rousseau's theory stands refuted for the simple reason that 'it is absurd for the will to bind itself for the future' [quoting from *On the Social Contract*]; a community actually founded on this sovereign will would be built not on sand but on quicksand" (WF 164). The sovereign dream of ruling from within the undivided presence of the will guarantees ineffectiveness: to inhabit fully the present moment guarantees isolation from, rather than control over, the future. Indeed, central to Arendt's argument is that the political present, the "gap between past and future" that so fascinates her and that is the time of freedom, only emerges in relation to the future (and thus, as we see later in this chapter, to the past as well).

Freedom and its political burdens cannot be taken up by retreating into the present of the will but only by recognizing the necessity of the future to the present, a recognition performed in the act of *promising*. "All political business," Arendt explains in response to Rousseau,

is and always has been, transacted within an elaborate framework of ties and bonds for the future — such as laws and constitutions, treaties and alliances — all of which derive in the last instance from the faculty to promise and to keep promises in the face of the essential uncertainties of the future. (WF 164)

Instead of yielding to the temptations of the will and the desire to *rule*, a properly *political* response to the experience of freedom — as an experience of being out of control — is contained in the faculty of promising. Promising remedies unpredictability:

binding oneself through promises, serves to set up in the ocean of uncertainty, which the future is by definition, islands of security without which not even continuity, let alone durability of any kind, would be possible in the relationships between men. (*THC* 237)

Unlike sovereignty, which wants to eliminate the future through the hegemonic rule of the present will, the political strategy of relying on promises rests content with merely establishing "certain islands of predictability" and "certain guideposts of reliability" (*THC* 244). The force of promise is so strong, though, that it can in fact grant the otherwise "spurious" sovereignty "a certain limited reality." Such sovereignty

resides in the resulting, limited independence from the incalculability of the future. . . . The sovereignty of a body of people bound and kept together, not by an identical will which somehow magically inspires them all, but by an agreed purpose for which alone the promises are valid and binding . . . [results in] the capacity to dispose of the future as though it were the present, that is, the enormous and truly miraculous enlargement of the very dimension in which power can be effective. (*THC* 245)

By contrast with sovereignty, promising takes into account the nature of political power, which Arendt defines as the "power generated when people gather together and 'act in concert,' which disappears the moment they depart" (*THC* 244). It is the "force of mutual promise or contract" that "keeps them together," Arendt explains, in a crucial stipulation, "as distinguished from the *space of appearances* in which they gather and the *power* which keeps this public space in existence" (*THC* 244–45). In the recognition that neither the necessity of the future to all action nor the essential *plurality* of action can ever be eliminated but only managed politically through the act of mutual promising, a "force" is generated that "keeps together," and even "enlarges," the "space" maintained by power, by speaking and acting together.

Mutual Promises:
Constituting the Open Space of Speech and Action

Arendt's ideal of mutual promising would play a crucial role, then, in preventing the realm of the political from being lost to sovereignty, with its confusion of freedom with the will, violence, and rule. Whether Arendt's promising can actually escape the difficulties that plague Rousseau's notion of sovereignty is the focus of the concluding section of this chapter.[8] But to get there, we must first consider in detail just what makes promising so important in Arendt's quest for a *free* political foundation. On the one hand, Arendt has argued that the freedom found in "speaking and acting together" (which might be abbreviated as *speech-action* and which defines for Arendt the political itself)[9] can never be guaranteed, since it exists no longer than its actualization, than its existence *in* and *as* action. Yet to the extent that freedom is valued as what is most properly and gloriously human, the space for the appearance of freedom must be preserved, or given life beyond the fleeting moment of its initial appearance. How can something that rejects all substantialization or reification, that resists the very logic of time as a continuum, be given any duration or afterlife? "The force of mutual promise or contract" suggests a way out of the difficulty: by respecting both the plurality of those who inhabit the political realm and the uncertainty introduced into political life by the future (and the possibility of new beginnings that it contains), promising can act as a foundation for the political realm while remaining true to the logic of freedom essential to it.[10]

How exactly promising performs this function, however, requires explanation. In her description (in the passage just cited) of the centrality of promising to the foundation of political communities, Arendt is careful to distinguish three apparently separate stages of political freedom: "the space of appearance in which [people] gather"; the "power generated when people gather together and 'act in concert,'" which "keeps this public space in existence"; and finally, "the force of mutual promise or contract," which "keeps them [the gathered people] together." According to this model, promising would merely shore up — by formalizing — the power and freedom already alive in the political community. Arendt cannot allow the appearance of freedom — as the power of the beginning, the power of an "unconnected" event erupting into and disrupting the continuum that has preceded it — to *depend* on the prior existence of a formally constituted political space. The constitution or foundation of that space must itself *follow* the logic of freedom.

Yet without the duration that promising gives, freedom is caught in its own evanescent, insubstantial temporality, doomed to a fitful, primarily "hidden" existence. By holding the actors together into the indefinite future, promising transforms freedom from the simple possibility of new beginnings into "worldly," *political* freedom.[11] Even as it follows the appearance of freedom in the world, promising gives freedom the "space" for its "fully developed" political existence.

How is it possible, then, to accept the centrality of promising to the developed, stable, political existence of freedom without losing the undetermined, "beginning" quality of the freedom that needs to be secured? In the section of *The Human Condition* titled "Power and the Space of Appearance," Arendt presents a "solution" to this question that helps clarify her assertions about the founding power of promising. She argues at first that the polis, as the space of freedom's appearance, is free from the need for any institutional support:

the space of appearance comes into being wherever men are together in the manner of speech and action, and therefore *predates all formal constitution of the public realm* and various forms of government, that is, the various forms in which the public realm can be organized. Its peculiarity is that . . . it does not survive the actuality of the movement which brought it into being, but *disappears not only with the dispersal of men . . . but with the disappearance or arrest of the activities themselves.* Wherever people gather together, it is potentially there, but only potentially, not necessarily and not forever. (*THC* 199, emphasis added)

There is a clear priority of freedom over "formal constitution" in this definition of the political realm. Yet that priority of freedom still leaves the political dangerously "potential"; the public realm would then be subject to repeated loss, to being forgotten as soon as men cease their political activity. That this "potential" nature of the public realm of freedom is a problem requiring some solution can be seen in Arendt's almost immediate qualification that such a space of appearance is itself in need of the support of *power*. "Power," she explains, "is what keeps the public realm, the potential space of appearance between acting and speaking men, in existence. . . . What first undermines and then kills political communities is loss of power" (*THC* 200).

Yet power, too, is subject to the same problem that plagues freedom: it "cannot be stored up and kept in reserve for emergencies, like the instruments of violence but exists only in its actualization." Indeed,

the word itself, its Greek equivalent *dynamis*, like the Latin *potentia* with its various modern derivatives or the German *Macht* (which derives from *mogen* and *moglich*, not from *machen*), indicates its "potential" character. Power is always, as we would say, a power potential and not an unchangeable, measurable, and reliable entity like force or strength. . . . [It is] dependent upon the unreliable and only temporary agreement of many wills and intentions. (*THC* 200–201)

It would seem, then, that there is no plausible explanation for how the public realm, by its nature radically potential, could ever be maintained beyond the sporadic moments of its actualization, since its reliance on power is in fact only a reliance on another form of potentiality. It would seem doomed to a mere chance existence, to come and go as people happened to rediscover it after previous neglect or forgetfulness.

Unless — in the only possible solution to the challenge posed to Arendt's theory of political foundation by her own theory of freedom — such potentiality were somehow able to operate as its own guarantee. Were it able to act as its own support, keeping itself alive between the moments of its actualization, across the gaps of its being mere "potentiality," the danger of its being forgotten would diminish, and the *foundation* of freedom would once again be imaginable.[12] To suggest how such a solution might work, Arendt turns to Aristotle, whose notion of *energeia* or actuality, she claims, conceptualized the Greek experience of speech-action (and the political life it brought into being) as the highest possible human achievement. Central also to her own, non-instrumental conception of political action, *energeia*

designated all activities that do not pursue an end (are *ateleis*) and leave no work behind . . . , but exhaust their full meaning in the performance itself. . . . In these instances of action and speech the end (*telos*) is not pursued but lies in the activity itself which therefore becomes an *entelecheia*, and the work is not what follows and extinguishes the process but is imbedded in it; *the performance is the work*, is *energeia*. (*THC* 206, emphasis added)

The attractiveness of this idea for Arendt lies in the possibility of there being a "work," a tangible worldly entity, that is "embedded" in its own production — at once alive in its own right and yet entirely dependent on the moments of performance.

It is with this same understanding of performance — not only as its own end but also as its own *guarantee* — that Arendt claims one should read the words of Pericles, which

> are perhaps unique in their supreme confidence that men can enact *and* save their greatness at the same time and, as it were, by one and the same gesture, and that the performance as such will be enough to generate dynamis and not need the transforming reification of *homo faber* to keep it in reality. (*THC* 205)

The thought, so difficult to think, of an activity that can "save" (or remember) itself in "one and the same gesture" as its own performance — propelling itself forward and granting itself continued existence, without ever becoming an object separate from this performance — this thought is essential to Arendt's theory of political action (defined as a-telic, that is, without end other than maintaining itself). It also helps make sense of otherwise blatantly tautological statements. When Arendt claims, for instance, that "power" is "what keeps people together after the fleeting moment of action has passed (what we today call 'organization') and what, at the same time, they keep alive through remaining together" (*THC* 201), what first appears as disturbingly circular can instead be understood as an attempt to name the capacity of freedom and speech-action to generate their own substantialization or endurance. Arendt helps clarify this capacity when she explains that the activities of speech and action, "despite their material futility, possess an enduring quality of their own because *they create their own remembrance*" (*THC* 207–8, emphasis added): the possibility of maintaining freedom rests on the possibility of memory.

It remains fair to wonder how this might work, however. How could the most fleeting of activities be preserved even as they remain "materially futile" and have their "end" in the activity or performance itself? To think through what it means for speech and action to "create their own remembrance," we can reconsider now what Arendt argues about "the force of mutual promise." The promise extends power into the future, thus giving it duration. This extension into the future simultaneously gives power — and with it the political community — a past by giving it the time for memory; by opening the always fleeting freedom of action (and the power it generates) to the future, mutual promising grants the space for history and memory (and Arendt's frequently praised "immortality" of the public realm). Speech-action can "endure" in the form of "remembrance" only because of this "force" of promise. Promising is speech-action's way of remembering itself; it institutionalizes, or textualizes, the merely "potential" nature of free speech-action. Even when the act of mutual promising is not in fact written (although all of Arendt's actual examples of great political promises *are* written), it operates as a way of simultaneously constituting, and marking the constitution of, a new collective being. The *force* of promise lies in its ability to form a new political community, or "space," where none had been before, by deliberately leaving a trace or mark, in the present that immediately becomes past, on whose basis the identity and the freedom of the community can be measured.[13]

This returns us to the earlier suggestion that the promise plays an essential role in the constitution of a realm of political freedom: it is only on the basis of a promise that freedom can exist both "freely" and yet also with foundation, despite Arendt's initial presentation of promising as a merely secondary support for an already existing "space" of freedom. Freedom becomes more than sporadic only on the basis of the collective signature of the promise, the way in which the words of the promise mark off a site in which memory, and thus political action, can take place. The "speech-act" called a promise is a condition of possibility for the constitution of a space for "speech-action" in the broader sense.

Although Arendt details, and at times embraces, the way in which the constitutive power of the promise is essential to the emergence and preservation of political freedom, she nonetheless avoids exploring its more difficult implications. It is important to note, first of all, that to lay down the law of *freedom* — and remain consistent with Arendt's theory of political action as anti-instrumental, without end other than its own perpetuation — the promise can only be the promise of the political itself. What the promise promises is the establishment and continuation of a realm of politics: both the space of appearance (of freedom) and the power generated by common action. For that to be the case, the promise in fact only promises itself. When Arendt argues, for instance, that the "grandeur" of the Declaration of Independence lies "in its being the perfect way for an action to appear in words" (indeed, it represents "one of those rare moments in history when the power of action is great enough to *erect its own monument*"), that "action" turns out to be the "mutual pledge" that functioned as the "principle out of which the Republic eventually was founded" (*OR* 127). The action of promising promises action; the principle of free speech-action, which is enshrined in the promise as the essence of the political, turns out to be promising. The Declaration works as a promise of *freedom* only by the immediate memorialization or institutionalization of its action, by which it promises its own continuation, the continuation of joint action and mutual promising. Promises maintain the community of actors and promisors — they act as the foundation of freedom — only by their promising (and remembering) themselves.

To the extent, however, that promising is consistent with Arendt's logic of freedom and action, the foundation it provides the political realm is less than secure. To function, instead, as effectively *foundational*, political promises must limit all subsequent "free" acts, which are indebted for their very possibility to the space opened up and secured by the original promise. As Arendt herself argues, mutual promises are always specific: what holds together a people "bound" (or founded) by a promise is "an agreed purpose for which alone the promises are valid and binding." Thus the "law" of the promise, what gives it its foundational and "binding" character, is the particular purpose agreed upon by the community of promisors. But to the extent that the freedom of the political realm is founded on a *specific* project, it cannot be entirely free: the "space" for action opened up by such a promise will necessarily form boundaries to and limits on the possibility of new action that follows this founding moment and founding principle. Promising can effectively *lay down the law* of freedom only by immediately violating that same law: it is a free act that at once makes less than fully free all acts that follow its law and example.

Arendt's efforts to describe the political foundation of freedom thus remain caught between freedom and foundation, and the "mutual promising" that acts as the cement for the foundation of freedom oscillates *essentially* between these two poles. Even acknowledging the validity of Arendt's analysis of the extraordinary capacity of promising both to memorialize and continue the freedom of political action, we cannot be certain whether such promising can provide, in any simple or secure way, either freedom or foundation. This uncertainty, in turn, goes to the very heart of Arendt's efforts to uncover the means of securing, or founding, a realm of political freedom: if neither freedom nor foundation can survive their mutual dependence, any essential separation of the political realm from that of sovereignty, violence, and rule is impossible. Before addressing this danger directly, though, it is important to note one further attempt Arendt makes to avert it.

Authority: Memorializing the Principle of Promising and Common Deliberation

It becomes evident, in the course of the long comparison of the French and American Revolutions found in *On Revolution*, that Arendt herself accepts that the foundation of political freedom requires something more than promises. She argues that the experience of promising was central to the American "revolutionary spirit" and went a long way toward helping the Americans avoid the violence and instability of the French Revolution. Yet she makes it clear that promises were not enough for the *foundation* of freedom: that required something else, called "authority." Whether authority, in turn, proves to be strong (and supple) enough to solve the problems that undermine promises is a question to be taken up shortly. It is important, first, however, to clarify the precise character of promising's relation to authority, as Arendt describes it in the course of *On Revolution*.

The greatness of the American Revolution — and Arendt's appreciation of it — rests in large part on the way it (unlike the French Revolution) was able to circumvent the problem of the "absolute" — the apparent need for the act of constituting a new political body to be itself authorized or founded in some higher law or divine power. Although this basic "perplexity of foundation" plagued the leaders and theorists of both revolutions, the genius of the American founders was the way in which they avoided relying on the fiction of a "national will" (such as the *pouvoir constituant* of the French theorist E.-J. Sieyès), the "ever-changing" nature of which, Arendt argues, is such that "a structure built on it as its foundation is built on quicksand" (*OR* 162). The Americans were able to avoid invoking such a concept in part because the colonies were already organized into many different "self-governing bodies," or sources of power, and thus were never faced with the theoretical dilemmas of the state of nature; "there never was any serious questioning of the *pouvoir constituant* of those who framed the state constitutions, and, eventually, the Constitution of the United States" (*OR* 164). There was no need to "constitute" power; the already existing power, rather, had to be regulated and structured as the engine of foundation.

The power that flowed throughout the colonies was that power originally generated by acting together and maintained by a promise — specifically, the mutual promise of the Mayflower Compact. The original promisors on board the *Mayflower* had confidence

in their own power, granted and confirmed by no one and as yet unsupported by any means of violence, to combine themselves together into a "civil Body Politick" which, held together solely by the strength of mutual promise "in the Presence of God and one another," supposedly was powerful enough to "enact, constitute, and frame" all necessary laws and instruments of government. (*OR* 166–67)

The revolution merely "liberate[d] the power of covenant and constitution-making, as it had shown itself in the earliest days of colonization" (*OR* 167), which had thus, as an experience of the foundation of freedom, already been under way on the *Mayflower*:

binding and promising, combining and covenanting are the means by which power is kept in existence; where and when men succeed in keeping intact the power which sprang up between them during the course of any particular act or deed, they are already in the process of foundation, of constituting a stable worldly structure to house, as it were, their combined power of action. (*OR* 174–75)

Much of the revolution's work had been done even before the revolution itself occurred.

The Americans could avoid the vicious circles of *pouvoir* that plagued the French Revolution because power was already alive in the colonies and maintained by various forms of mutual promising.[14] Yet such power and promises were inadequate to the task of devising a lasting foundation — that is, an effective authority — for a new national political system:

Power, rooted in a people that had bound itself by mutual promises and lived in bodies constituted by compact, was enough "to go through a revolution" . . . , [but] it was by no means enough to establish a "perpetual union," that is, to found a new authority. Neither compact nor promise upon which compacts rest are sufficient to assure perpetuity, that is, to bestow upon the affairs of men that measure of stability without which they would be unable to build a world for their posterity, destined and designed to outlast their own mortal lives. (*OR* 182)

Despite her argument that promises move beyond the action and power that they institutionalize or memorialize, Arendt now argues that promises, like the power they maintain and preserve, are not strong enough to constitute a lasting foundation. The foundation of a republic, which would be the foundation of freedom, requires something more stable than power and promising. The American founders were finally able to avoid the violence and the instability that plagued the French Revolution only by deliberately separating the source of law and authority from that of power:

the framers of American constitutions, although they knew they had to establish a new source of law and to devise a new system of power, were never even tempted to derive law and power from the same origin. The source of power to them was the people, but the source of law was to become the Constitution, a written document, an endurable objective thing, which, to be sure, one could approach from many different angles and upon which one could impose many different interpretations, which one could change and amend in accordance with circumstances, but which nevertheless was never a subjective state of mind, like the will. It has remained a tangible worldly entity of greater durability than elections or public opinion polls. (*OR* 155–56)

Rather than put the source of law, or authority, in something as changeable as the people's will (assuming something like it could ever be found), or even their very real political power, the Americans placed authority in an entirely separate, and more reliable, sphere: it was located in a text — the Constitution — and an institution designed to interpret that text — the Supreme Court. The authority of a republican constitution lies in its resistance to change: it is *there*, a "tangible," unchanging artifact; it forms the boundaries for free action but is not itself, at least at this point in Arendt's argument, subject to the law of freedom, or the possibility of an absolutely new beginning. In other words, what such authority resists is *power*. Instead, the American republic has its foundation in the authority of a written text. That text can be interpreted, of course, but even the most radical reinterpretation would always be in the terms of the original document, and thus confined within certain boundaries, boundaries that act as a brake on the ever-changing expressions of the "will" or opinions, or even the power, of the political community.[15]

Although Arendt makes much of this separation of authority from power — for it is what grants authority a firmer foundation than promising — the relationship between the two is in fact significantly more complicated than the word *separation* might imply. For it is clear that authority's capacity to serve as a foundation cannot be entirely separate from the power maintained in promises (especially given Arendt's own claim that the foundation of American freedom was only the continuation of the experience begun with the power maintained in the Mayflower Compact). Instead, "authority" should be seen as Arendt's name for the next stage in the attempt to found freedom — another link in the chain — that begins with "the space of appearance," then goes on to "power," then to "the force of promise," and now finally to "authority." Although promising was supposed to enable power to "create its own remembrance," the stability thus lent to power and to freedom is insufficient for a sure *foundation*; the capacity of promises to "memorialize" power is not lasting enough. Authority, then, is called in to solve the problem now plaguing promising, which promising itself was to solve for power: it must somehow sustain the "free" and undetermined character of promising — and along with it, power — even as it gives them, and ultimately freedom, a lasting, durable foundation.

This solution was possible, Arendt explains, only on the basis of a radical insight into the nature of freedom and foundation reached by the men of the American Revolution. This insight was their realization that

> it would be the act of foundation itself, rather than an Immortal Legislator or self-evident truth or any other transcendent, transmundane source, which eventually would become the fountain of authority in the new body politic. From this it follows that it is futile to search for an absolute to break the vicious circle in which all beginning is inevitably caught, because this "absolute" lies in the very act of beginning itself. (*OR* 205)

In much the same way that promising — on the model of *energeia* — was said to be the way that power generates, out of its own free action, a means of self-remembrance, authority here finds its stability (or absolute) in the very activity of founding. Viewed from another angle, freedom can resist absolutes — foundations or sources or causes that violate its logic of beginning, contingency, and uncertainty — only by being itself "absolute." Arendt explains this in more detail:

what saves the act of beginning from its own arbitrariness is that it carries its own principle within itself, or, to be more precise, that beginning and principle, *principium* and principle, are not only related to each other, but are coeval. The absolute from which the beginning is to derive its own validity and which must save it, as it were, from its inherent arbitrariness is the principle which, together with it, makes its appearance in the world. The way the beginner starts whatever he intends to do *lays down the law* of action for those who have joined him in order to partake in the enterprise and to bring about its accomplishment. As such, the principle inspires the deeds that are to follow and remains apparent as long as the action lasts. (*OR* 214, emphasis added)

What lends the beginning — or constitution — of the new American republic its authority (or "validity") is the principle contained in that beginning, in the moment of foundation. But when it comes to the foundation of freedom, not just any principle will do. It has, of course, to be the principle of freedom: if freedom founds itself, it can only be on the basis of its own law. What then, is the law, or principle, of freedom in this case? Arendt explains that

the principle which came to light during those fateful years when the foundations where laid — not by the strength of one architect but by the combined power of the many — was the interconnected principle of mutual promise and common deliberation. (*OR* 215)

The principle that serves as the foundation for American authority and that saves the American foundation from vicious circles, absolutes, and quicksand is "the interconnected principle of mutual promise and common deliberation." The "authority" founded by the American Revolution, then, is something like the textualization, or institutionalization, of mutual promising. Promising is made lasting when it is transformed into the text of the Constitution and the institution of the Supreme Court. There, finally, promising (and along with it power and freedom) finds its remembrance: the law of freedom, as the practice of promising, is laid down.

The Force of Freedom's Foundation

Despite Arendt's argument that power and promising must be separated from law and authority, it turns out that, in fact, authority *is* based, in a certain way, on the "principle" of promising. Since Arendt's concern here is with the foundation of *freedom*, authority must remain true to freedom's logic of impermanence and "actuality"; it does so by acting as the institutionalization of promising, which is itself the self-remembrance or textualization of power and free action. As such, authority holds promising to its own law of *freedom*, continuing the *promise of* promising, rather than locking the promise into an unalterable form.

Yet it is clear that something happens in the move from promising to authority: the "principle" of promising, while obeying the fundamentally unstable temporality of all free action, is nevertheless supposed to possess, in the form of authority, a stability that promises alone have proven not to. Promising, as instituted in the form of authority, is different than promising *tout court*.

Arendt attempts to come to terms with, if not exactly solve, the seemingly paradoxical relation of freedom and foundation contained within "authority" by introducing the notion of "augmentation," derived from her reading of Roman *auctoritas*. Describing the influence of *auctoritas* on the American founders, Arendt explains that

authority in this context is nothing more or less than a kind of necessary "augmentation" by virtue of which all innovations and changes remain tied back to the foundation which, at the same time, they augment and increase. Thus the amendments to the Constitution augment and increase the original foundations of the American republic; needless to say, the very authority of the American Constitution resides in its inherent capacity to be amended and augmented. (*OR* 203)

Authority-as-foundation, as the text of the Constitution (or more generally, of the promise), cannot be separated from authority-as-freedom, as the possibility of revising the text, of adding to and reworking the clauses of the Constitution, the material out of which the political realm is made. The text (or foundation) grants the possibility of the political action (or freedom) of revision; freedom is only possible on the basis of this text, or contract, or institutionalized promise. But in the same way, such foundation, in order to be a *political* foundation, requires that it be revisable, that it be subject to the law of augmentation, rather than an absolute that lies beyond the freedom of political action. Authority, in short, is produced out of this interpenetration of freedom and foundation; it depends on the "coincidence of foundation and preservation by virtue of augmentation," in which "the 'revolutionary' act of beginning something entirely new, and conservative care, which will shield this new beginning through the centuries, are interconnected" (*OR* 203). Authority as augmentation, then, is another version of Arendt's ideal of *energeia*, in which freedom and foundation reside together and reinforce each other.

To the extent, though, that this process of "interconnection" and "coincidence" is understood by Arendt to preserve the independence and identity of the two terms involved ("beginning" and "conservation," or "freedom" and "foundation"), "augmentation" remains too simple a concept to describe the relation of freedom and foundation. Indeed, authority as "augmentation" attempts to have it both ways: to insulate the political from the threat that the "necessity" of foundation poses to freedom *and* from the loss threatened by its *lack* of foundation. Arendt's "augmentation," that is, presents as a smooth, evolutionary process what is instead a much less stable, even conflictual, relationship of freedom to foundation. And although the concept of augmentation might at first sight seem to be an example of her ideal of "thinking together and combining meaningfully what our present vocabulary presents to us in terms of opposition and contradiction," it actually smooths over the possibilities and difficulties that such a "thinking together" should provoke.

A theory of authority as augmentation, that is, takes no account of the way in which the political "space" marked off by the foundational promise always has both too much freedom and too much foundation (conditions that are, in fact, merely two sides of the same danger built into the nature of freedom). To the extent that Arendt's "authority" conforms to the law of freedom, the political realm that it "founds" must always remain only a *promised* realm, alive perhaps in the moment of action, but without security against future loss. Such a foundation can never guarantee the political realm against the dangers inherent to freedom itself: the danger of being lost, for example, through habit, insecurity, or forgetfulness.

But this same danger, in fact, is present in the very means Arendt suggests to alleviate it: to *lay down the law* of action, or promising, can only be to violate, in the very same gesture, the law of *action* (or freedom). Authority's institutionalization of the principle of mutual promising (just like promising's memorialization of power) must, in order to function as a foundation and a law, place limits on the freedom of all that follows it, on the very political action that it helps make possible. For it is always a *particular* law of freedom: authority, like the promise on which it is based, is always specific to "an agreed upon common purpose," whether this is enshrined in a verbal promise, a written compact, a founding "principle," or the text of a constitution. Freedom can only gain a foundation or a space, or become a law for a particular group of people, by taking on a specific, limited form; the foundation, in order to make certain options possible, must close down certain others: future possible new beginnings will be restricted and others ruled out entirely. And whatever "augmentations" that are made, in order for them to "augment" rather than *reject* the foundation, must take place within the limits set down in

the foundation.[16] The realm of freedom — seen as a logic of indeterminacy, openness, plurality, and the possibility of new beginnings — is
inevitably compromised in the attempt to found it, even as some such
foundation is necessary for its survival. (It thus should come as no surprise when, in the final chapter of *On Revolution*, Arendt explains that
even the American Revolution failed, in the end, to establish a lasting
foundation for freedom).

As a result of this paradoxical relation of freedom and foundation, the
loss of "the political" (as the realm of openness, plurality, and new beginnings) that Arendt regularly laments is a loss that cannot fail to happen.
The very means of saving it from being forgotten — the text of the promise or of authority — inevitably involves it in the workings of necessity and
nonfreedom against which its freedom is to be protected. Caught within,
and produced out of, a dialectic of freedom and foundation that leaves
neither term intact, the political can only be found within and through its
constitutive loss, within and through its fall into the nonpolitical. To
search for the political in light of the impossibility of sheltering it from the
"nonpolitical," however, requires accepting the political as itself a space
of conflict. Despite Arendt's efforts to wall off the realm of politics and
freedom from that of violence and rule, the way in which the political
space is constituted out of the conflict *between* freedom and foundation
has the effect of lodging conflict and violence *within* the heart of the political itself.

To defend this claim in the detail that it deserves would require a close
reading of Arendt's numerous discussions of violence, which is, unfortunately, beyond the scope of the present chapter. It can nonetheless be
shown, from within the terms of Arendt's own analysis, that in the face of
the openness and plurality of political freedom, the specific and limiting
nature of political foundations brings with it a constitutive threat of conflict and violence. One specific way this is so becomes apparent when we
examine more closely an aspect of promising about which Arendt has little to say: the fact that once it has been "performed" or agreed on, the
promise immediately becomes a text in need of interpretation.[17] As we
have seen previously, Arendt argues that promising is to be valued in part
for the way in which it protects the plurality of political action, refusing
to subsume all the promisors under a single *will*. Nonetheless, Arendt also
argues that it produces "a body of people bound and kept together . . . by
an agreed purpose for which alone the promises are valid and binding"
(*THC* 245, emphasis added); it holds together the power that is generated
out of the "temporary *agreement* of many wills and intentions" (*THC*
201, emphasis added). The promise can bind only because of the common
purpose that the promisors have agreed to pursue. Although Arendt

makes much of the way in which promises preserve the plurality essential to politics, she nonetheless treats each promise as if it were at all moments just a *single* promise. For the promise to function as the kind of foundation Arendt wants, its meaning, and the purpose with which everyone expresses their agreement through the promise, must in some sense be evident to and identical for all the promisors.

Arendt's assumption notwithstanding, what each member of the political body has "agreed" to in the mutual promise of foundation is never merely self-evident: for the promise to be "free," it too must be subject to the contingent play of political contestation that is the mark of freedom. Promises, that is, are subject to the law of freedom not only in their revision or augmentation over time but as texts whose meaning is found only in their interpretation, which renders them susceptible to as many potential interpretations as there are promisors. The freedom enshrined in the text of the promise, which makes it both so ideal as a *political* foundation and so unstable as a political *foundation*, can be found in the way in which the "single" promise serves as the common site for a multitude of different, potentially conflicting purposes. (There is no guarantee of unanimity, for instance, about what counts as "augmenting" or "continuing" the founding act and the principle[s] it enshrines.) A promise, like any agreement, is at best a point of conjuncture, a site at which conflicting goals, intentions, forces, and projects find a common expression or formulation but never an identity of meaning. To assume the founding promise can be limited to a single, fixed, meaning would be to deny an aspect of the interpretability that is at the basis of Arendt's own ideal of augmentation. Indeed, for a promise to be truly an agreement, for it to be free, it must emerge out of, and continue to be threatened by, the possibility of real *dis*agreement, of a real "differend" that has no guarantee of peaceful resolution.

Thus, whatever foundational support the promise itself offers (whether directly or in the form of Arendt's "authority") comes from the single, *authoritative* interpretation that must at certain crucial moments be established, more or less forcefully. To argue that the promise offers a site for competing interpretations, and thus for a certain form of freedom, in no way reduces the extent to which the promise also serves to limit the very freedom it enshrines. Although the necessity that the promise be interpreted opens the space for a plurality of interpretations, it also involves the opposing necessity of deciding on one interpretation rather than another. (It is this requirement of deciding between interpretations that transforms their plurality into *conflict*.) Rulings about how the law is to be interpreted, about what counts as "augmenting" or continuing the founding principles of a document like the Constitution, or other such collectively binding decisions that rework the meaning of the "agreed upon purpose" of the mutual promise (and with it the identity of the "body" of promisors), are all integral aspects of the *freedom* of any political community.

But this means, in turn, that its very role as a foundation lodges within the promise a certain kind of forcefulness (a forcefulness, however, that is inextricable from freedom itself). Despite Arendt's desire to banish from the political realm the violence involved in *ruling* (since it substitutes the singularity of a command or decision for the plurality of the moment of promising), ruling is nevertheless both unavoidable and fully political. A political community founded on promising cannot avoid such moments of decision, in which the promise that *all* make and to which *all* are bound is given an inevitably limited, particular interpretation determined by only *some*. All pledge themselves — as members of the *one* "body of people" brought into being by the promise — to the "same" promise, or foundational law, even as the political decisions that specify the scope or application of the law redefine the (practical) meaning of the promise in ways *not* agreed to by all. By putting an end, at least temporarily, to the freedom found in the existence of varying interpretations of the founding promise, collective decisions bind members of the community to promises that they may not even agree they have made.

Rethinking the "Loss" of the Political: Toward a Theory and Practice of Democratic Impurity

Accepting that the promise will always enshrine a particular purpose in need of interpretation involves recognizing that the promise is constitutively divided between plurality and singularity. This new back-and-forth of freedom and foundation renders the promise once again both less stable than Arendt would have it — since it is a site of conjuncture and conflict — and less free — since it functions as a foundation only to the extent that a single, limited, interpretation is imposed on it by some act of *decision*. As a result, it also entails recognizing once more that the political realm of freedom can never simply be separated from the "nonpolitical" realm of sovereignty and rule. As we saw in our earlier analyses of Castoriadis, Rousseau, and Benhabib, the very openness and freedom of the political realm ends up requiring their apparent opposites. The fact that the foundational promise is without self-evident meaning, independent arbiter, or any other absolute, and is thus subject to a multitude of possible interpretations and to the necessity of constant redefinition paradoxically leads to a continual process of decision-making, ruling, and closure that violates the political realm's own law of plurality, nonviolence, and openness. This tear in the heart of the political realm lies within the act of decision itself, divided as it is between the freedom of reconstituting the political realm by redefining the promise, and the violence of imposing that definition in ways that all do not accept and that exclude other possible communities and other possible futures.

The potential for conflict and violence that comes with the need to decide on a single interpretation of the promise is, however, only one aspect of the force that attaches more generally to the particular and exclusive character of political foundations. Indeed, neither the foundation nor the force associated with the promise comes solely from the promise and its need for interpretation. As a performative speech act, the "founding" promise can be "felicitous" only to the extent that the community already exists in the form of shared goals, and common beliefs, assumptions, and practices. These not only limit disagreement but also allow the members of the community to know, at least provisionally, who they are and what their promise entails. The explicit act of founding is made possible, and effective, only by such prior work of foundation.[18] In this sense, Arendt can avoid reckoning with the forceful nature of foundations only by assuming that the political community is *already* fully formed.[19] For to the extent that the commonalities necessary to the successful promise do not exist, or exist only incompletely, the promised community will be less than fully formed, and the promise (with the law and authority attached to it) will act less as a foundation than as a particularly charged site for the repeated, conflictual, *re*foundation of the community. The political action that such a "foundation" makes possible, then, will consist in the community's continual re-creation of itself through the more or less forceful interpretation of the founding promise by some part of the community, in the name of all. The people of today, in turn, can re-form themselves only within the limits of that foundation, or through the more or less forceful rejection of it. All of which is to say that there are no absolutely new beginnings — the structure of the performative is such that all foundations are necessarily refoundations, and must themselves be repeated — but to the extent that such foundations *are* new, they inevitably have force attached to them. In this respect, Arendt's peaceful metaphors of building walls and making promises, together with the essential but never stated assumption that such foundation takes place in a vacuum, in an empty, not-yet-political space, deflect attention from the way in which the singular, limiting, and *decisive* nature of political foundation entails a more or less violent displacement of other, existing or potential, communities.[20]

The lesson here for democratic theorists and citizens alike is that to accept the possibilities contained within such free political action, one must also accept the costs that action entails for freedom itself. The particular complexity of the relationship between freedom and foundation that this chapter has explored should teach us that the democratic qualities of freedom and action that Arendt values most highly — those of openness, plurality, and lack of absolute ground — necessarily involve political action in some of the processes and actions that most endanger it. This refers not just to freedom's unavoidable reliance on foundations that will limit future freedom, nor just to the way in which the plurality and openness of action will always repeatedly culminate in (even as they continue to resist) singular and decisive acts of closure. Most important, instead, is how the very condition of freedom — the fact that foundations and decisions (in their singularity, limitation, and closure) are *free* acts rather than necessary ones, and that they take place, therefore, in the face of a plurality of opinions, perspectives, and criteria, without any guarantee of agreement or "absolute" to act as a ground — implicates political action in the supposedly "nonpolitical" world of sovereignty, rule, and violence. Those committed to more egalitarian and contestatory forms of democratic politics, then, must resist lamenting the repeated "loss" of the "revolutionary spirit" — when "freedom and power have parted company, and the fateful equation of power with violence, of the political with government, and of government with a necessary evil has begun" (*OR* 134) — as if one could someday resurrect an experience of democracy, or the political, free from that loss. There can simply *be* no political action free from the loss of the political and the tendency to forget the freedom that makes it possible.

Nor, for similar reasons, can either democratic or political action simply be equated with the work of *resisting* the inevitable loss of the political, with the constant effort to renew the spirit of foundation and to remember the freedom of beginning, as if the moment of action — of deciding, or founding, or resisting — could simply be separated from the moment when freedom is violated or forgotten.[21] As free acts, of course, promises and decisions are always provisional, and ways must be devised to continually reexamine the particular "promises" and decisions of a political community. But this reexamination cannot be performed as if it were a more pure act of political intervention, or in the name of a freedom or political practice somehow able to avoid its own fall into unfreedom, into the more or less violent closure, for instance, that comes with having to decide one way or the other, in the absence of unanimity or any absolute.

To argue, however, that within the very political action that freedom makes possible there is an unavoidable violation of freedom is not to argue for its simple impossibility or absence. It is, instead, to suggest that the promised, or free, character of the political can only be preserved by remembering its impurity and incompletion, and with it the fact that political freedom always comes at a cost — the cost of being implicated in various forms of forcefulness and unfreedom. To accept this condition would be to begin to negotiate the risks and possibilities of a distinctly democratic politics. To deny it would be to forget the freedom of the political in the name of another freedom, one so pure that it could never be enjoyed.[22]

Just what it would mean, and what it would take, to accept such conditions of impurity as necessary to democratic action is the central topic of the final chapter. There I investigate the possibility of developing forms of "civic virtue" that would aim to negotiate the constitutive "loss" of political freedom in such a way as to make it easier to take up its burdens. Such virtues would, I argue, aim to incorporate the kinds of "forgiveness" that we have seen Arendt herself argue are the necessary correlates of promising, given the inevitable trespasses and failures that accompany the unpredictable and unintended consequences of action. Chief among these practices, I suggest, should be a nonmoralistic, compassionate, language of democratic engagement and responsibility. Whereas Arendt offers a devastating analysis of the antipolitical effects of compassion in *On Revolution*, I argue that a different form of compassion, oriented toward the suffering experienced from the political condition itself — from its uncertainty, its plurality, and the impossibility of fully respecting its ideals of equality and openness — would offer powerful resources in support of greater, and more sustainable, political engagement. Although Arendt sees compassion as having no room for the persuasion, negotiation, and compromise that are the necessary effects of political freedom and plurality, I offer a beginning sketch of a form of compassion that acknowledges the suffering in oneself and others from the difficulties of trying to respect and live by these conditions of freedom and plurality.[23]

Before turning to these considerations, though, I first look at another theory of plurality, contingency, and openness — one that places these conditions at the center of both the experience and the value of a radically democratic form of politics. Once again, we'll see how even the most radical and open form of democratic politics — as theorized by Chantal Mouffe and Ernesto Laclau — is unable to avoid its "fall" into closure — and thus how important it is for those committed to such a form of politics to begin to think through what more effective responses to its inevitable difficulties and dilemmas might look like.

CHAPTER THREE

"Open Sesame!"

The Affirmation of Contingency and the Politics of Openness in Laclau and Mouffe's Radical and Plural Democracy

Once again we find the paradox dominating the whole of social action: freedom exists because society does not achieve constitution as a structural objective order; but any social action tends towards the constitution of that impossible object, and thus towards the elimination of the conditions of liberty itself.

— Ernesto Laclau, *New Reflections on the Revolution of Our Time*

The word people retained for them the meaning of manyness, of the endless variety of a multitude whose majesty resided in its very plurality.

— Hannah Arendt, *On Revolution*

For Ernesto Laclau and Chantal Mouffe, the theoretical analysis and political affirmation of the contingent and conflictual nature of all identity, both individual and collective, offer the resources for a radical extension of the democratic revolution. In their frequently cited book *Hegemony and Socialist Strategy*, and in a host of subsequent essays written individually, Laclau and Mouffe propose a project of radical democracy as "a form of politics which is founded . . . on affirmation of the contingency and ambiguity of every 'essence', and on the constitutive character of social division and antagonism."[1] Their elaboration of a "radical and plural democracy" can be seen as an effort to think through the difficulties and opportunities of democratic politics after the collapse, both in theory and in practice, of a unified sense of the people, and the growing uncertainty of all other forms of identity. They argue that the proliferation of new social struggles and identities and the generalized increase in sites of political conflict that follow from such a collapse offer possibilities for the expansion and radicalization of democracy.

To seize the opportunities that such developments provide for the construction of a new democratic community, they argue, we must recognize and affirm the constitutive nature of plurality, conflict, and ambiguity rather than lamenting them as obstacles to finding the true will of "the people." Situating their own theoretical work, and democratic politics more generally, squarely within the difficulties and tensions we first encountered in Rousseau, and have seen in a new form in Arendt's work on the foundation of political freedom, Laclau and Mouffe accept democracy as the form of politics in which the contingent, fully contestable status of all "grounds" becomes most clearly recognizable. Indeed, they argue that "democracy *is* the very placing in question of the notion of ground" (emphasis added).[2] Their work thus offers an opportunity to take up in a more concentrated way many of the most important aspects of democratic openness mentioned in the previous chapters.

Writing from within, but on their way out of, the tradition of socialist and Marxist thinking, Laclau and Mouffe argue that proponents of left-wing and democratic thought must abandon many of the key tenets of their theoretical approach in order to understand and take advantage of the opportunities offered by the contemporary political and social situation. In particular, they argue for the rejection of the working class as the sole revolutionary agent, the party as its vanguard, and history as an inevitable march to socialism. For Laclau and Mouffe, the history of Marxist theory and practice has, in fact, been the story of the failure of its essentialist, antipolitical approach. Classical Marxism has found itself unable to found a successful democratic struggle and equally unable to explain the source of its difficulties. Yet its very failure has produced within Marxist discourse a rogue element — the notion of hegemony — which increasingly served to fill in for the inadequacy of its essentialist categories. "Hegemony" has functioned in particular to explain how certain social groups could take up political tasks that were not assigned to them as their own by Marxism's "necessary" historical laws. Reaching its most elaborated and central role in the writings of Gramsci, hegemony described the role that contingent political organizing, definition, and persuasion could play in the construction (rather than the discovery) of a radical, democratic "collective will."

Much of *Hegemony and Socialist Strategy* focuses on the slow and difficult emergence of the concept and experience of "hegemony" within Marxist theory and political organizing, and their theory of radical and plural democracy is in many ways a continuation and further radicalization of the logic of hegemony. Its fundamental claim is that only by finally and fully abandoning essentialist and a priori thinking can the left seize the radically democratic potential of contemporary political developments. The constitutively open, or "unsutured," quality of what Laclau and Mouffe call "the social" must not only be recognized but affirmed. This involves affirming the relational and contingent character of all identity — the fact that the meaning of any identity or political struggle only emerges from its relations with other identities and struggles, which thus leaves it open to constant rearticulation. Particular political forces and identities have no necessary meaning, and their development in any particular political direction can in no way be guaranteed since it depends entirely on the form of their political articulation. Because there is no ultimate foundation that secures the shifts in relation and meaning of the various fragments of the social — because the only ground is "plurality" itself — whatever stability exists is the partial and fully contingent product of a hegemonic articulation.

Although these conditions in some ways render democratic politics more difficult than the classical left understood it to be, Laclau and Mouffe nonetheless argue that a new, more "radical and plural" form of democracy is made available through the very *affirmation* of such contingency. This chapter seeks to clarify the character of that new democratic politics by examining the exact nature of that affirmation and the specific effects that Laclau and Mouffe claim to follow from it. Part of their argument is that the knowledge of the contingent nature of identity and social relations reveals the entirety of the social and political world as open to political struggle and achievement. Indeed, as Laclau writes in an essay of his own, the contingent, or "dislocated," character of social relations is "the very form of freedom" (NR 43, 44). The contingency, or dislocation, of the social order provides, then, the space, or possibility, for politics: for the active intervention into and reconstruction of social structures and identities.[3]

The recognition of contingency is important for Laclau and Mouffe, not just because it encourages the expansion of struggles against inequality and oppression of all kinds but because the general *extension of the field of politics* is itself democratic. More and more social relations are seen as *political*, and thus as spaces for autonomy — for seizing control of the forces that shape people's life — and the claiming of new rights. According to Laclau and Mouffe, the challenging, and eventual destruction, of supposedly natural hierarchies, a process we have earlier seen to lie at the heart of the "democratic revolution," allows for the simultaneous expansion of equality and of liberty, through the expansion of the political realm itself.

Central to Laclau and Mouffe's argument, in turn, is the claim that the new form of democratic community that the affirmation of contingency promises is only possible through the abandonment of all substantive notions of the good and essential notions of collective identity. Instead, through the process of "hegemony," a new "we" can be built out of the very plurality of the different struggles and "subject positions." The discursive logic of "equivalence" offers in particular, they argue, a way of respecting the plurality and autonomy of the different struggles, even as it links them together as "equivalent" struggles, as parts of a common democratic project that seeks liberty and equality for all. By refusing the demands for a natural, or substantive, form of commonality, radical and plural democracy makes possible a "common bond" in which the constitutive nature of difference and uncertainty is accepted. In doing so, it simultaneously expands the spaces of equality and liberty.

To the extent, however, that radical and plural democracy is defined simply as the extension or expansion of the democratic logic of autonomy, I argue that it quickly reaches an impasse. For there is within autonomy a built-in tension between liberty and equality, or between the equal liber*ties* of all. The extension of autonomy in one sphere will ultimately limit, or be limited by, autonomy in another sphere. Given the radical contingency and plurality from which Laclau and Mouffe begin, there can be no preexisting commonality between *different* demands for autonomy, and no essential definition of equality, that would allow us to find, or recognize, the proper balance between different claims when they overlap.

As a result, the attempt to bring into being a radically and plurally democratic community will face its own versions of Rousseau's paradox of effect and cause (made more severe, in some ways, by the need to respect, rather than reduce, the differences between democratic struggles and identities). To understand the specificity of Laclau and Mouffe's democratic project, then, one would need to know the particular strategies that radical and plural democracy might use to negotiate (without ever fully overcoming) such paradoxes and construct politically sustainable democratic identifications. Without specific claims about the best way to negotiate the otherwise conflicting identities and interests, or a sense of what the "common concern" might be that could form the basis for a new democratic "we," the fact that such differences *can*, in theory, be made compatible is not enough to define a radical and plural form of democracy. "Equivalence," in this case, would simply offer a formal notion of commonality in place of the discarded substantive sense of the good.

I argue, then, that in the form in which Laclau and Mouffe often present it, radical and plural democracy can only describe, and affirm, the condition of doing politics after the "democratic revolution" and its "dissolution of final markers," when freedom and politics invade, at least potentially, every social sphere and contest all "natural" categories and arrangements. Without a sense of the particular meaning and importance it gives to the different democratic identities and struggles, or the particular interpretation it gives of "autonomy," radical and plural democracy would seem only to be a description of the general structure of democratic politics rather than itself constituting a specific version of it.

At other points in their writing, Laclau and Mouffe do recognize the inevitable existence, even within radical and plural democracy, of a tension between liberty and equality, and, within the struggle for radical democratic hegemony, between the autonomy of its different struggles and the necessity of articulating them together. Indeed, their response is to locate much of the specificity of radical and plural democracy in the very recognition and even enhancement of such tensions. *Affirming* the way in which democracy is constituted around a tension that is impossible to reconcile fully or finally, radical and plural democracy would be the name for a politics of openness, questioning, and contestation, struggling against all forms of political closure.

Although such an affirmation of openness lends some greater specificity to the project of radical and plural democracy, radical and plural democracy cannot simply be *equated with* the affirmation of openness. For the political practice of remaining open to difference, to otherness, and to competing conceptions of the "common bond" is itself a *particular* one, with its practice requiring a significant degree of equality and sense of commonality. And given that such an attitude is only one possible response to the conditions of contingency and conflict that Laclau and Mouffe describe so well (resentment, cynicism, and the demand for increased "security" being other likely possibilities), it requires particular forms of closure, or institutionalization, in order to be more than just an idiosyncratic accomplishment of unusually generous individuals.

In other words, there remains a tension within radical and plural democracy between the more or less substantive project of constructing a new "common bond" and the practice of keeping open the tension within democracy between liberty and equality and affirming the impossibility of their final reconciliation. Although the goal of such a form of democracy is to produce a community in which the sense of common identification with a "we" is experienced differently — more openly, less substantively — and one therefore in which the demands of foundation are compatible with those of freedom, I argue, much as I have in the previous chapters, that the two sides of the tension nevertheless continually interfere with each other. Fundamental to any practice of radical and plural democracy, then, would be the question of how its citizens might best handle this tension and the dilemmas it poses. What forms of political engagement, modes of rhetorical appeal, or psychological strategies might best allow one to accept the openness and uncertainty of the democratic "we" in productive, sustainable ways, even when so much of democratic politics is necessarily oriented toward establishing particular, more or less established, definitions of the political community?

Unfortunately, although Laclau and Mouffe accept the existence of such tensions in the abstract, they give little or no consideration to the limits such conditions pose — in the sense of practical difficulties they cause and the questions they raise — for their own politics of radical and plural democracy. Because any form of openness requires some degree of closure, and because, as we have seen throughout the book, neither democracy nor the affirmation of the condition of contingency can furnish a rule to judge the proper weight to be given to their competing demands, a politics of questioning and openness is burdened by the necessity of making contingent, often risky political decisions about its specific forms of openness *and* closure. How exactly do Laclau and Mouffe see those decisions being made and their burdens handled in ways that would sustain, rather than undermine, radical and plural democracy? For such a radical and plural form of the democratic "we" to be more than a theoretical possibility, that is, it requires not only specific attempts at forging a common democratic project and bond out of the plurality of democratic struggles and identities, but also particular strategies for handling the inevitable *inadequacy* of all such attempts as well as the risks and burdens involved in making such decisions in the absence of clear answers and secure visions of the "we." Until there is some clarification of the characteristic strategies that would enable a *sustainable* radical and pluralistic response to the democratic paradoxes and dilemmas we have seen throughout the book, there is only a limited sense in which Laclau and Mouffe's radical and plural democracy is clearly distinguishable from democracy in general, or from the particular forms of it that are presently with us. In their general failure to address these questions, Laclau and Mouffe imply, at least, that the simple knowledge and affirmation of democracy's constitutive conditions can by itself lead to a new form of democratic politics. It is at the point of contingent political practice, however, that the theoretical affirmation of contingency finds its greatest challenge.

From the Contingency of the Social to a Radically Democratic "We," via Hegemony

Following Tocqueville, Laclau and Mouffe situate the start of the ongoing democratic revolution at roughly two hundred years ago, arguing that it consisted in the "decisive mutation in the political imaginary of Western societies" that came when "the democratic principle of liberty and equality . . . impose[d] itself as the new matrix of the social imaginary," or in the more technical theoretical language that Laclau and Mouffe often employ, when "the logic of equivalence was transformed into the fundamental instrument of production of the social" (*HSS* 155). Before this, they argue, society was understood as a stable, hierarchically structured totality, centered around the body of the king (which was itself ultimately grounded on divine power). Individuals were largely confined to fixed social categories, and history was experienced primarily as continuity and repetition. With the eruption onto the political scene of the force known as "the people," with their claims to legitimate authority and their "Rights of Man," there emerged

the discursive conditions which made it possible to propose the different forms of inequality as illegitimate and anti-natural, and thus make them equivalent as forms of oppression. Here lay the profound subversive power of the democratic discourse, which would allow the spread of equality and liberty into increasingly wider domains and therefore act as a fermenting agent upon the different forms of struggle against subordination. (*HSS* 155)

The "democratic principle of equality and liberty," then, is intimately connected from the very first with the destruction, or subversion, of the image and understanding of society as a fully grounded, centered, and *natural* order. The demand for equality progressively (although not always with full success) penetrated into new social relations, as more and more inequalities were seen as artificial and fully human products, and illegitimate in equivalent ways as those inequalities already done away with.[4]

Laclau and Mouffe can thus argue that the process whereby "the arbitrary character of a whole set of relations of subordination" have been increasingly "laid bare" in the postwar West opens up fertile ground for the extension of the democratic logic of equality and liberty for all. As they put it, "the terrain has been created which makes possible a new extension of egalitarian equivalences, and thereby the expansion of the democratic revolution in new directions. It is in this terrain that there have arisen those new forms of political identity which, in recent debates, have frequently been grouped under the name of 'new social movements'" (*HSS* 158). Included within this very broad category, in Laclau and Mouffe's definition, are feminism, movements for racial, ethnic, and national minorities, lesbian and gay rights, environmentalism, and a host of other "antiauthoritarian" and "anticapitalist" struggles.

The importance of the new social movements for Laclau and Mouffe's overall argument, and for their conception of radical and plural democracy, can hardly be overstated. The interest they hold for Laclau and

Mouffe lies in "the *novel* role they play in articulating that rapid diffusion of social conflictuality to more and more numerous relations which is characteristic today of advanced industrial societies" (*HSS* 159–60). They are important not only because they extend the democratic revolution into "a whole new series of social relations" by "call[ing] into question new forms of subordination," but also because, by doing so, they point up the "multiplicity of social relations from which antagonisms and struggles may originate . . . [and which] constitute terrains for the struggle against inequalities and the claiming of new rights" (*HSS* 161). The democratic potential of the new social movements, then, is not limited to the fact that they challenge forms of subordination, in the name of equal rights and power. They are also democratic in the way they expand the space of autonomy and freedom by expanding the number of social relations (and subject positions) that are understood to involve power and thus to be at least *ideally* open to political contestation and negotiation.[5]

The meaning of this doubly democratic aspect of the increased politicization associated with the new social movements is clarified when we turn to Laclau and Mouffe's argument that these new struggles bear a close relationship to the decentered nature of subjectivity. They argue that the external multiplicity of sites for political argument and activism that these struggles exhibit corresponds to the radical diversity *internal* to each individual, to the way in which "the subject" is constructed at the point of overlap of multiple discourses, without ultimate center or ground.[6] "The plurality of the social, and the unsutured character of all political identity," they write, is "the very terrain which made *possible* a deepening of the democratic revolution" (*HSS* 166). It is thus that Laclau and Mouffe can argue that

the critique of the category of unified subject, and the recognition of the discursive dispersion within which every subject position is constituted, therefore involve something more than the enunciation of a general theoretical position: they are the *sine qua non* for thinking the multiplicity out of which antagonisms emerge in societies in which the democratic revolution has crossed a certain threshold. This gives us a theoretical terrain on the basis of which the notion of *radical and plural democracy* . . . finds the first conditions under which it can be apprehended. (*HSS* 166–67)

It is because each "individual" subject is in fact the site of address of multiple, overlapping discourses, which have no necessary relation to each other, that the numerous recent democratic antagonisms have been able to proliferate so rapidly. But in addition, an understanding of the essentially fractured character of the subject allows us to appreciate (to recognize and affirm) the radical *specificity* of each of the various struggles. Laclau and Mouffe write that the "radical" nature of the (political) plu-

ralism they argue for, which takes as its theoretical basis this constitutively multiple character of the subject, resides in the fact that the various

subject positions cannot be led back to a positive and unitary founding principle.
. . . Pluralism is *radical* only to the extent that each term of this plurality of identities finds within itself the principle of its own validity, without this having to be
sought in a transcendent or underlying positive ground for the hierarchy of meaning of them all and the source and guarantee of their legitimacy.

. . . And this radical pluralism is *democratic* to the extent that the autoconstitutivity of each one of its terms is the result of displacements of the egalitarian
imaginary. Hence, the project for a radical and plural democracy, *in a primary
sense*, is nothing other than the struggle for a maximum autonomization of
spheres on the basis of the generalization of the equivalential-egalitarian logic.[7]
(*HSS* 167)

The radical specificity, or "autoconstitutivity," of each term or aspect
of an individual's "subjectivity" is thus what allows the democratic revolution and its egalitarian imaginary to be radicalized and enter into more
and more domains. But Laclau and Mouffe are arguing, in addition, that
each struggle is also to be appreciated for its autonomy, and not merely
the fact that the struggle is carried out in the name of equality. Since, as
it will soon become apparent, the autonomy of the struggles based on
the diversity of identities and subject positions poses practical political
difficulties for a project of radical and plural democracy — difficulties
whose negotiation is central to the concerns of *Hegemony and Socialist
Strategy* — it is important to see why Laclau and Mouffe argue for the
necessity of "a maximum autonomization of spheres." More specifically,
because Laclau and Mouffe argue throughout *Hegemony* that the various
democratic struggles have to be "articulated" and coordinated with each
other into a hegemonic "bloc" — indeed, this process of strategic and
rhetorical coordination *is* the work of hegemony — it is not immediately
obvious why "the maximum autonomization of spheres" of struggle is
necessarily a positive goal. Another way of putting this is to ask: How
does the *constitutive plurality* of each subject and of the power relations
that produce them lead to the kind of "radical *pluralism*" that Laclau and
Mouffe advocate?

To understand why they argue that it does (which is not always clear
in their own account), one must understand the multiple meanings of
their claim that "each term of this plurality of identities finds within itself
the principle of its own validity, without this having to be sought in a
transcendent or underlying positive ground for the hierarchy of meaning
of them all and the source and guarantee of their legitimacy." The claim
is not merely a description of the radically contingent relation of each
subject position to those others that make up the same "individual." Nor

is it just the argument that every struggle for equality centered around one of these "terms" or "positions" will have a specificity that requires the attention of an autonomous political effort, rather than being reducible to an epiphenomenon of a larger, more "fundamental" struggle (which is generally the way non-class-based movements have been treated on the left). It also suggests that the autonomy of each subject position must be respected so as to respect the political autonomy and freedom of those involved in the struggles fought around them. That is, the recognition of the constitutive autonomy of each of the spheres must be matched by a recognition that these struggles are themselves struggles for self-determination, for the transformation of relations of subordination into ones that accept all involved as equal, autonomous agents, free to share in the creation of the terms of their involvement. It is thus that a *recognition* of the democratic nature of such struggles also requires an *affirmation* of their autonomy relative to other struggles — even though, as we will soon see, that autonomy will also be limited by the mutual implication of each sphere and each struggle in the others, which is itself the effect of the same underlying contingency involved in the irreducibly relational character of all identity.

Laclau and Mouffe's project of extending the democratic revolution that began with the fracturing of "natural" and hierarchical social structures and the growing signs of the contingent, decentered nature of the social itself thus has a dual character: they aim at a democracy that is both "radical" and "plural." Their claim is that both the expansion of egalitarian struggles and their growing autonomization find their condition of possibility in the contingent nature of identity and social relations. Even as, on the one hand, the increasing politicization that accompanies the recognition of this contingency holds out hope for the maximization of political freedom and self-determination, on the other hand, the seizing on the multiple and constructed character of the supposedly unitary subject simultaneously allows for the possible *reconstruction* of that subject and of the community as a whole in a democratic, egalitarian way.

The fact of contingency, however, brings with it difficulties as well as opportunities. Part of Laclau and Mouffe's critique of classical Marxist theory and the undue privilege that it gives to the working class is that Marxist theory assumes that the struggles of the working class have an inherent or "objective" meaning, which guarantees that they will operate in a politically "progressive" direction. But as Laclau and Mouffe argue throughout *Hegemony*,

all struggles [including those of the working class] . . . have a partial character, and can be articulated to very different discourses. It is this articulation which gives them their character, not the place from which they come. There is therefore no subject ... which is absolutely radical and irrecuperable by the dominant order, and which constitutes an absolutely guaranteed point of departure for a total transformation. (*HSS* 169)

It is partly on the basis of this claim that Laclau and Mouffe argue so strenuously for the importance of embracing the new social movements as a way of going beyond class as the necessary basis of a radical left politics. But as they realize, the fact that political struggles have no inherent meaning is also true of the antagonisms at the heart of the new social movements, which are thus not necessarily democratic. They are equally open to any number of non-, even anti-, democratic articulations. There are many different "feminisms," for instance, just as there are conservative, corporate, democratic, and anarchistic varieties of environmentalism. The fact that these and other nonclass antagonisms can all be said to be products of the extension of the democratic revolution means very little for the way they will be articulated in any given political context. This is because, as Laclau and Mouffe argue in an important point of clarification,

the democratic revolution is simply the terrain upon which there operates a logic of displacement supported by an egalitarian imaginary, but ... it does not predetermine the *direction* in which this imaginary will operate. ... The discursive compass of the democratic revolution opens the way for political logics as diverse as right-wing populism and totalitarianism on the one hand, and a radical democracy on the other. (*HSS* 168)

The democratic revolution, that is, names the process by which the constitutive openness of the social — the absence of final grounds and the contestability of all relations of power — becomes more and more extensively and explicitly the condition for political life. But how that "radical unfixity" of the social is given, as it must be, some provisional order — the particular answers that are given to democracy's questions, the kind and degree of equality that is institutionalized — is the result of contingent, more or less explicit, political battles.

The work of providing order to the fundamentally unfixed domain of the social, and of giving particular political meaning to its always "polysemic" antagonisms, is what Laclau and Mouffe call *hegemony*. The meaning of each antagonism, they argue, is fixed "only to the extent that the struggle moves outside itself, and through chains of equivalence, links itself structurally to other struggles" (*HSS* 170). Feminist struggles, for example, take on a corporate political direction when the general demand for equal treatment is understood in the register of (or articulated with the demands of) meritocracy, efficiency, and rationalization; the "same" demand for equality becomes a radical and democratic one when its achievement is seen to entail significant rearrangements in the structures of power throughout the society, affecting groups other than women. The contingent and relational character of identity and meaning, then, on the one hand renders impossible the quest for a single ground or center of the social, since such a ground is always in need of some other force or identity with or against which it takes on its own identity and meaning, thus forfeiting its fundamental or originary status. Nonetheless, the same logic also rules out the possibility of any of the fragments or elements of the social being absolutely autonomous: they are what they are, and they mean what they mean, only because of the existence and meaning of factors outside of them. As a result, Laclau and Mouffe's project for a radical and *plural* democracy, with its emphasis on the specificity and autonomy of the different struggles that need to be won, is faced with the equal necessity of articulating those different struggles together as part of a *common* hegemonic strategy. It is this logic of equivalence, where feminist demands for equality and autonomy are seen as *equivalent to* (implicated in and dependent on the success of) the demands for equality made by ethnic, racial, and sexual minorities, those for control over the production process by workers, those for ecological sustainability, and so forth — it is this relationship of equivalence that defines a specifically *democratic* politics (and the more extensive the chain of equivalences, the more "radical" is the politics).[8]

The question that is immediately raised, then, is how such hegemonic articulation can be compatible with "the autonomization of the spheres of struggle and the multiplication of political spaces" that Laclau and Mouffe argue are "preconditions of every truly democratic transformation of society" (*HSS* 178). Laclau and Mouffe themselves ask if there isn't an "incompatibility between the proliferation of political spaces proper to a radical democracy and the construction of collective identities on the basis of the logic of equivalence" (*HSS* 181). Although they accept that the logic of equivalence and the logic of autonomy point in different directions — the one toward unification, the other toward diversity — they also argue that the two are never simply separable from each other. Because there is no ultimate ground of the social, because of its constitutively open or unsutured character, neither the logic of equivalence nor that of autonomy ever reach completion: there can never be complete unification and identity of all the different political spaces, nor can they ever fragment into absolutely discrete elements. Since the ultimate moment of closure imagined, in their opposite ways, by both of these scenarios, can never come to pass, Laclau and Mouffe can argue that "the incompatibility between equivalence and autonomy disappears" (*HSS* 183). In other words, while we are still faced with competing "social logics, which intervene to different degrees in the constitution of every social identity, and which partially limit their mutual effects," we are never faced with a simple choice between one or the other, since both logics are in fact at work at all points and in all political situations. Indeed, autonomy is always relative to and the product of a particular hegemonic formation, just as that hegemony can only be built on the basis of discrete antagonisms.[9] It is thus theoretically consistent for Laclau and Mouffe to argue for the possibility of a democratic project that simultaneously multiplies the sites of what are irreducibly specific struggles and attempts to construct a unity between them through the process of hegemonic articulation.

However, Laclau and Mouffe argue, for such a project to be successful, its struggles must be carried out on the basis of a specifically *democratic* form of articulation. This requires, they argue, more than the simple multiplication of demands for equality, or what they call "the mere displacement of the egalitarian imaginary." Given that the demands of various groups are not only different but frequently incompatible, simply multiplying demands for equality does not necessarily lead to any "real equivalence between the various democratic demands" (*HSS* 183). For that to happen, for there to be a truly democratic form of "equivalence," they argue that one must construct

a new "common sense" which changes the identity of the different groups, in such a way that the demands of each group are articulated equivalentially with those of the others — in Marx's words, that "the free development of each should be the condition for the free development of all." That is, equivalence is always hegemonic insofar as it does not simply establish an "alliance" between given interests, but modifies the very identity of the forces engaging in that alliance. (*HSS* 183–84)

In the absence of this identity-transformative politics, one is trapped in a zero-sum game of competing rights claims in which the demands of each group are made without "respect for the rights to equality of other subordinated groups" (*HSS* 184).

To ensure that the formation of such a hegemonic bloc and its "common sense" respect — as they argue it can and must — both the plurality of political spaces and the liberal defense of "the liberty of the individual to fulfill his or her human capacities," one must produce "*another* individual, an individual who is no longer constructed out of the matrix of possessive individualism" (*HSS* 184).[10] In fact, Laclau and Mouffe argue that the very relation of individual to community needs to be radically rethought:

the idea of "natural" rights prior to society — and, indeed, the whole of the false dichotomy individual/society — should be abandoned, and replaced by another manner of posing the problem of rights. It is never possible for individual rights to be defined in isolation, but only in the context of social relations which define determinate subject positions. As a consequence, it will always be a question of rights which involve other subjects who participate in the same social relation. It is in this sense that the notion of "democratic rights" must be understood, as these are rights which can only be exercised collectively, and which suppose the existence of equal rights for others. (*HSS* 184–85)

This critique of a hyper-individualized understanding of rights, and of the sharp distinction between public and private on which it is founded, follows the same logic as their earlier deconstruction of the apparent contradiction between autonomy and hegemony. The rights of an individual are not gained in isolation from the community and the existence of others' rights; far from being "natural" or prepolitical, the individual and her rights are fully political products. Individuality and liberty are always won in and through community. There is, then, no essential incompatibility between the realms of public and private. Democratic rights are, in turn, those rights constituted explicitly on the recognition of the equal rights of others: for rights to be democratic, they must be constructed only in relation to the equal rights of others; they cannot come at the expense of other members of the community of equals. The democratic individual is one whose identity, rights, and interests are explicitly open to those rearticulations that make her particular demands compatible with (though not identical to) those of her equals.[11] Just as the project of radical and *plural* democracy consists in the preservation of the autonomy and plurality of the different struggles that must be articulated together in a common movement, so the establishment of democratic rights requires the simultaneous affirmation of the equivalence and the specificity of the different rights involved.

Beyond the Liberal–Communitarian Debate: Toward an Egalitarian and Plural *"We"*

Fundamental to the argument of *Hegemony and Socialist Strategy*, then, is the claim that the constitutive *condition* according to which the individual is always already political and communal *makes possible* the democratic political project of articulating otherwise competing rights in a way that provides for equality and liberty for all. This raises an immediate theoretical difficulty, however. Given that the overlap between the individual and the community is *constitutive*, and not something one can accept or reject, and given that what constitutes "liberty" and "equality" (or "compatibility") is entirely interpretive, virtually any political program would seem to be able to meet the criteria for having "democratic rights." The "other individual" whose job it is for radical democracy to construct is, in this sense, already with us. What specific characteristics distinguish radical and plural democracy from other forms of politics after the democratic revolution would remain, at least at this point, unannounced.[12] This blankness at the heart of radical and plural democracy leaves us, in turn, with the difficulty of actually moving from the constitutive *possibility* to the *practice* and *achievement* of specifically "democratic rights" (here understood in their "radical and plural" form). The theoretical possibility of articulating a series of autonomous struggles and rights claims in a way that nonetheless preserves their democratic autonomy, precisely *because* such a process rests on the *contingency* of the identities involved, can guarantee nothing in the way of its practical achievement. The work of democratic politics, in other words, remains to be done: the construction, with and against the desires of others, of the particular form of community within which one wishes to live as a free and equal member.

How to rethink the process of constructing a radically democratic political community — whose "we" would also preserve the specificity of the different democratic identities and their struggles — is taken up as the explicit topic of a series of more recent, post-*Hegemony*, essays by Chantal Mouffe. Most helpful for our purposes is the essay "Democratic Citizenship and Political Community," which investigates the effects that a revised conception of citizenship would have on the prospects for a radical and plural democracy.[13] In particular, Mouffe tries to reconstruct a sense of citizenship from out of the false and sterile divide between "liberalism" and "communitarianism" (or "civic republicanism"), drawing on both traditions in order to "combine their insights in a new conception of citizenship adequate for a project of radical and plural democracy" (DC 72).

Mouffe argues that the liberal tradition has reduced "citizenship to a mere legal status, indicating the possession of rights that the individual holds against the state" (DC 72), and has thus lost any ethical sense that the use of such rights should be directed toward the public good. Nonetheless, she sees liberalism as having made a "crucial contribution" to democracy. "The defense of pluralism, the idea of individual liberty, the separation of church and state, the development of civil society, all these [liberal ideas] are constitutive of democratic politics" (DC 72), Mouffe writes. So, too, more generally, is the liberal sense that "principles of justice must not privilege a particular conception of the good life." "Modern democracy," Mouffe writes, referring to the work of Claude Lefort, "is precisely characterized by the absence of a substantive common good" (DC 73–74). Thus, even as contemporary communitarians are right to criticize the way in which, in contemporary liberal society, "all normative concerns have increasingly been relegated to the field of private morality . . . , and politics has been stripped of its ethical components," their desire to resurrect the civic republican tradition, characterized by a single substantive idea of the common good, threatens to destroy "the novelty of modern democracy" (DC 74–75).[14]

Mouffe's aim to find the kind of political community that allows for the "articulation between the rights of the individual and the political participation of the citizen" (DC 73) continues the critique launched in *Hegemony* against the public–private distinction. The goal is to achieve an effective "ethico-political bond" — a shared, public identity — that nonetheless allows large amounts of room for the plurality of moral perspectives, fully respecting "the priority of the right over the good." The "solution" Mouffe proposes comes in the form of the "grammar" of principles. "What we share and what makes us fellow citizens in a liberal democratic regime," Mouffe writes,

is not a substantive idea of the good but a set of political principles specific to such a tradition: the principles of freedom and equality for all. . . . To be a citizen is to recognize the authority of those principles and the rules in which they are embodied — to have them informing our political judgment and our actions. (DC 75)

To explain in more detail what it means for a political community to be regulated by nonsubstantive principles, Mouffe turns to the work of Michael Oakeshott, and in particular his idea of political community as *societas*. For Oakeshott, Mouffe writes,

societas or "civil association" designates a formal relationship in terms of rules, not a substantive relation in terms of common action. . . . [It is] a relation in which participants are related to one another in the acknowledgment of the authority of certain conditions in acting . . . , the authority of the conditions specifying their common or "public" concern, a "practice of civility." (DC 76)

In such a regime, individuals' "allegiances to specific communities are not seen as conflicting with their membership in the civil association" because the latter is not a purposive but rather a formal, procedural, or "grammatical" one. As Mouffe describes it, "to belong to the political community, what is required is to accept a specific language of civil intercourse, the *respublica*." Rather than requiring specific actions to be performed or ends to be sought, the rules

prescribe norms of conduct to be subscribed to in seeking self-chosen satisfactions and in performing self-chosen ends. The identification with those rules of civil intercourse creates a common political identity among persons otherwise engaged in many different enterprises. . . . [The] community is held together . . . by a common bond, a public concern. (DC 77)

Unlike the liberal rule of law, whose supposed neutrality is an instrumental one, designed to facilitate the achievement of self-interest, Oakeshott's "civility," in his words, "'denotes an order of moral . . . considerations, and the so-called neutrality of civil prescriptions is a half truth which needs to be supplemented by the recognition of civil association as itself a moral and not a prudential condition'" (DC 77).[15] Yet because the "morality" embodied in such rules involves the "conditions" or forms of action rather than specific actions themselves, it allows for the coexistence of a wide range of purposes, ends, beliefs, and values, rather than enforcing any single common purpose or good.[16]

The appeal of such a conception of political association for Mouffe's goal of a refigured ideal of democratic citizenship should be clear. It promises the reconciliation of equality and difference, public and private, identity and plurality that the project of radical and plural democracy requires. Citizenship based on the identification with the *respublica*, the bond produced by the "common recognition of a set of ethico-political values," is neither just one identity among others (liberalism) nor the overriding identity (communitarianism), but "an articulating principle that affects the different subject positions of the social agent . . . while allowing for a plurality of specific allegiances and for the respect of individual liberty" (DC 79).

But the reconciliation of equality and difference at the formal level is not enough for Mouffe. As the example of Oakeshott itself attests, the *content* of the principles of any given *respublica* can turn out to be far from democratic. The liberal-democratic interpretation will, in Mouffe's vision, supply the principles of "equality and liberty for all," so that "the conditions to be subscribed to and taken into account in acting are to be understood as the exigency of treating others as free and equal persons."[17] But this, too, can be interpreted in different ways, and more or less radically. And with this, we are back in the terrain of *Hegemony and Socialist Strategy*. Mouffe explains that "a radical democratic interpretation will emphasize the numerous social relations where relations of domination exist and must be challenged if the principles of liberty and equality are to apply" (DC 79). By constructing a chain of equivalence "among the democratic demands found in a variety of different movements: women, workers, black, gay, ecological, as well as in several other 'new social movements,'" a new "we" (with its new democratic "citizens") can be formed out of the common identification with the radical democratic interpretation of the principles of "liberty and equality for all" (DC 79–80).

Built on the "recognition among different groups struggling for an extension and radicalization of democracy that they have a common concern and that in choosing their actions they should subscribe to certain rules of conduct" (DC 79), the construction of a common political identity as radical democratic citizens is — repeating the argument from *Hegemony* — "a matter not of establishing a mere alliance between given interests but of actually modifying the very identity of these forces" (DC 80). Yet, for Mouffe, the new *identity* that is formed is not, strictly speaking, a matter of being *identical*. For although all actions must conform to a certain "grammar" of action, the liberty of the private realm, and difference more generally, is still respected. Although "private" spheres and the relations of domination that exist within them are open to political challenges aimed at forcing them to meet the requirements of the grammar of liberty and equality for all, Mouffe claims, nevertheless, that since "the rules of the *respublica* do not enjoin, prohibit, or warrant substantive actions or utterances, and do not tell agents what to do . . . we are not dealing with a purposive kind of community affirming one single goal for all its members, and the freedom of the individual is preserved" (DC 81).[18]

When one begins to press on the claims outlined above, things turn out to be not quite so simple, or so hopeful, as they might appear initially. It is important to see, first of all, that if one accepts Mouffe's own arguments for the constitutive openness and contingency at the ground of the social, then, as Laclau and Mouffe argue in *Hegemony and Socialist Strategy*, there is no possibility of either a fully "sutured" community, with a *single* substantive good, or its opposite, a "community" composed only of wholly autonomous elements. Neither of the two positions that Mouffe is trying to steer her way between is a viable option (nor, therefore, can either be a danger).[19] Instead, every community will be a combination of both aspects. This is, in fact, the very point of the deconstruction of the public–private (or society–individual) distinction that Laclau and Mouffe offer in *Hegemony and Socialist Strategy*. But that critique, however valuable as a counterpoint to certain theoretical claims of liberal individualism and communitarianism, does not translate by itself into a critique of liberal or communitarian political positions or into proposals for radical democratic alternatives. The real problem with communitarianism for Mouffe, then, is not that it would impose a single substantive good and allow no room for any differences — since that is impossible — but rather that it would not allow room for *enough* or for the right *kinds* of differences. (And the reverse for liberalism: it would not foster the right kind, or degree, of public, ethical spirit.)

A closely related point can be argued from a slightly different angle. Despite Mouffe's suggestion that the formal nature of the rules of the *societas* is valuable for the way it makes possible a common (equal) bond that also respects individual differences and plurality, nevertheless, even the most formal or "grammatical" of rules impose substantive (and often substantial) restrictions on individual actions. Even when such rules do not explicitly prohibit (or enforce) particular actions, their goal of fostering norms of "civil" conduct has the necessary effect of disallowing certain actions and allowing others. That is the whole point of *rules*. This is especially the case when the "civility" being enforced requires that "a concern for equality and liberty should inform one's actions in all areas of social life" (DC 81). The enforcement of a scheme of equality and liberty for all, in other words, requires making (nonneutral) choices that restrict the freedom of all, and of some more than others.[20]

Indeed, to argue that even the most formal of rules produce substantive effects — as they are interpreted in a way that produces a particular, exclusive political identity — is, in one sense, to restate the criticisms that Mouffe herself lodges against Oakeshott's particular brand of conservative "civility." According to Mouffe, Oakeshott's notion of politics is flawed to the extent that it has no place for the constitutive nature of division and antagonism and thus for the way in which the *respublica* itself is the contestable "product of a given hegemony, the expression of power relations." The rules of political association do not merely create a space for politics but are themselves crucial sites of political struggle, precisely because they make possible certain modes of action and disallow others. Politics is about "the construction of a 'we' in the context of diversity and conflict," Mouffe writes, a "we" whose existence depends on the frontier that differentiates it from the excluded "they." "Therefore, while politics aims at constructing a political community and creating a unity, a fully inclusive political community and a final unity can never be realized since there will permanently be a 'constitutive outside,' an exterior to the community that makes its existence possible" (DC 78). Antagonism, division, conflict are not temporary limits to an ultimate harmony but are constitutive of political life, even that of radical democracy, whose agreements can be no more than partial and provisional. Even the most radically democratic regime of liberty and equality for all is established on the basis of a particular and exclusive version of those principles/practices.

All of this is to argue, then, that there can be no final harmony between liberty and equality: from any particular standpoint, an increase in equality will mean a decrease in some form of liberty, and vice versa. Indeed, Mouffe argues as much herself. In a slightly surprising conclusion to an essay devoted to exploring a conception of citizenship that would allow for the coexistence of (public) equality and (private) liberty, she writes in the final paragraph of "Democratic Citizenship and Political Community" that there is a *"permanent* tension that can *never* be reconciled" between one's public "duties as a citizen" and one's "freedoms as an individual." "This is," she adds, "precisely the tension between liberty and equality that characterizes modern democracy" (DC 81, emphasis added).[21]

If such a tension is in fact basic to democratic politics, then the radical democratic *hegemony* that Mouffe advocates would seem to require specific struggles over which liberties and which "equalities" to institute, and by what means — through which agents and institutions — rather than through the general principle of "liberty and equality for all." Mouffe, however, has very little to say about what choices would be required for the construction of a radical and plural democracy, other than to list the different struggles and identities that need to be articulated together in order to move toward a radical democratic hegemony. Mouffe's analysis of the contingent and discursively constructed nature of subjectivity and community certainly helps make clear how and why such articulations are possible. We are, however, still left with our original difficulty: how to ensure not merely that the principles of liberty and equality are *"understood in a way that takes account of* the different social relations and subject positions in which they are relevant: gender, class, race, ethnicity, sexual orientation, and so on" (DC 80), but that the "accounting" is a radically democratic one. For as Laclau and Mouffe's understanding of contingency mandates, one can "take account of" such struggles in radically *undemocratic* ways, ones that set different positions and identities against one another. Just what the "common concern" is that the different groups that make up the family of radical democratic agents are all supposed to "recognize" remains unannounced.

Reconfiguring Democratic Identities: A Difficult Labor

The point of drawing attention to the highly abstract character of Mouffe's radically democratic "common concern" is not primarily to criticize Mouffe for failing to provide the details of the "strategy" promised in the title of *Hegemony and Socialist Strategy: Towards a Radical Democratic Politics*. The more important and interesting problem is that Mouffe neglects to analyze the *difficulties* — strategic, rhetorical, psychological — that face the kind of hegemonic politics they propose — difficulties that emerge from the same "contingency" that Laclau and Mouffe suggest offers such hopeful possibilities. At the root of these difficulties is the way in which such a "common concern," like the political community itself, comes into existence only in and through the performative power of discourse and political action, and thus can be "recognized" only *after* it has been achieved. Given that Laclau and Mouffe's project takes as its starting point the lack of any essential commonality that might be shared by those involved in the democratic struggle and with it the absence of any telos to political struggle and change, any appeal (to potential radical democrats) to "recognize" "a common concern" must be an appeal to a *future* commonality, the commonality that demands to be constructed. The construction of a radical and plural democracy, that is, can rely on no other commonality than that *built out of* the plurality of autonomous demands and struggles — the only appeal Mouffe's analysis can suggest or allow is to our common sense of being those who accept the principles of radical and plural democracy.[22] For that reason, though, there can be no independent standard by which "radical democrats" of various perspectives and identities can recognize demands or struggles as compatible or incompatible with the goal of liberty and equality for all, for it is the very definition of those principles that they must forge through their common struggles, and across their present differences.[23]

As a practical matter, the danger is that the construction of a new political community will be blocked by the tenacity of the identifications of its constituent elements as they are *presently* constituted. One of the chief difficulties facing the kind of political project that Laclau and Mouffe propose is that the democratic demands and struggles posed by different subjects or identities must initially be based on interests and identifications as they exist or are understood from people's present position within the community. Thus many workers will want to save their jobs and the sense of identity that comes with them, even if that means building weapons or cutting down trees (activities that other members of the future democratic community will be actively trying to prevent).[24] Many who identify as ethnic and racial minorities seek to set aside resources or opportunities for their "own" members, so as to guarantee their equal representation, or what they consider their fair share — even if that causes tension with, or takes resources and opportunities away from, other groups whose assistance they need to construct a radical democratic community.

Although a process of dialogue and negotiation designed to reconfigure the identities and demands involved so as to make them mutually compatible is both necessary and possible, such reconfiguration must at a certain level be antagonistic, given that, as Mouffe puts it in her critique of liberal pluralism, "some existing rights have been constituted on the very exclusion or subordination of the rights of other categories." The extension of the sphere of democratic rights to groups and struggles hitherto excluded cannot simply be a smooth one of progressive inclusion, then, since identities as they are presently constructed "must first be deconstructed if several new rights are to be recognized" (DC 80).

Although liberty and equality are not incompatible *as such*, the recon-struction of liberty and equality that is part of radical democratic politics will nevertheless require the rearrangement of power and freedom in such a way that some "lose," at least according to present standards, while others "win." Precisely how the overall scheme of rights will be rearranged, and whose liberties are reduced so as to make possible the "equal" liberty of others, will be the subject of intense political struggle.[25] And because this struggle is a fully *contingent* one, it must be undertaken in the absence of any neutral calculus for balancing the competing claims: any sense of what is equal, or common, or fair, will bear the particular traces of one of the positions being "compromised." There is thus no guarantee that a common sense of the community's "common concern" can be reached (although there is also nothing that rules it out). Standards that would be acceptable to all parties involved — which is the ideal role for the principles of radical and plural democracy — are themselves one of the crucial things that need to be constructed.

Thus although the contingency of identity makes hegemonic struggle possible, it also makes it particularly hard to convince different groups/identities to enter into a hegemonic project with others precisely *because* that overall struggle will require them to change "who" they are now. Often a terrifying prospect in itself, such change is particularly risky in the absence of any guarantees that the situation a person will ultimately find herself in will be an improvement over her present state. (From the per-spective of Laclau and Mouffe's discourse theory, there can be, strictly speaking, no way even to judge this issue, given that the very standards of measurement will themselves have undergone transformation.) In the name of what, then, are those who are presently in some way advantaged by, or psychically and materially invested in, their present location in the community discursively repositioned so as to sacrifice their present selves and reimagine themselves instead under the form of a new, not yet fully defined, democratic citizen? (Although it applies to all potential radical democrats, the problem obviously grows more difficult the more inclusive the movement tries or needs to be, as it extends to those who are more secure, or have a greater stake, in the present configuration of their "sub-ject positions.") Although a discourse of equality and justice is clearly necessary to persuade people to accept such risks, what justice requires can itself only be judged from some particular vision of the community, and thus its effectiveness as an appeal to a new democratic future requires something of the sense of trust and commonality whose "foundation" is exactly what must be built. To make matters even more difficult, that trust is complicated, if not threatened, by demands that stress the auton-omy and particularity of separate identities, especially to the extent that they consist in demands to make up for past inequality and injustices, demands whose satisfaction would necessarily impose "unequal" costs on other parts of the community.

We are, at this point, back to Rousseau's paradox of democratic foundation, where the people would have to be *before* the law (in this case, the "law" of radical and plural democracy) what they can only become *after* receiving it. Only now this paradox is in some ways exacerbated by the fact that the content of the "law" involves the demand that certain differences be affirmed, rather than overcome in a "general will." As we have seen throughout the preceding chapters, there is no way around this paradox. It is, in different ways, constitutive of democratic politics. Missing from Mouffe's (and Laclau's) analysis of the prospects for radical democracy, though, is a sense of the specific forms that this paradox takes in contemporary politics — in particular, those forces and pressures that keep people attached to their identities as separate, inviolable things, thus blocking the sacrifice of those old selves and the creation of new, more radically democratic ones.[26]

More important, there is no sense of how such problems — the difficulties of overcoming such obstacles and of determining which transformations and tradeoffs must be made to push forward the movement for radical democracy — have their basis in precisely those "permanent tensions" that make up the principles of radical democracy — tensions between liberty and equality, and between autonomy and hegemonic articulation.[27] For much of the difficulty, if not the impossibility, of reaching a truly *common* understanding of the "common concern" that ties democratic citizens together lies in the fact that moving toward that future point requires the *violation* of the principle of autonomy of the separate democratic struggles that is the very lifeblood of radical and *plural* democracy. The necessity of articulating together the multiplicity of struggles requires the re-creation of present (partially democratic) forms of identity, in order to make each identity more compatible with the others and thus truly democratic. Although the ultimate goal of this effort is to produce a network of plural and autonomous identities, groups, and political sites, from the point of view of the presently constituted identity the effect of democratic hegemony is its *destruction*.

Radical and plural democracy, then, provides us with a set of principles whose demands are, in any *particular* case, in conflict, even as they each must be respected: affirm the plurality and autonomy of the struggles based on different subject positions, and yet transform those struggles, and the identities they are based on, so as to fit them together. Or, in a more classically (and juridically) liberal form of the dilemma: affirm individual liberty and private freedom while simultaneously limiting the actions of individuals to those that don't harm the equal freedom of others. The point of this is not to accuse Laclau and Mouffe of self-contradiction. Indeed, as they themselves argue, any judgment one made in a particular case about how to balance the competing values would necessarily in some sense respect each value. That, however, only brings us to another side of the same dilemma: given the condition of contingency — the absence of any prepolitical ground for determining the meaning of either liberty or equality — what social arrangement could *not* be said to satisfy the demands of radical and plural democracy for plurality and equality? Radical and plural democracy, at least to the extent that it is understood no more specifically than as the "extension" or "radicalization" of the principles at the heart of the democratic revolution, merely presents us with two competing values, both of which must be respected. It can thus by itself offer no guidance for knowing the proper, or acceptable, balance between them. There is, in other words, a certain blankness at the heart of radical and plural democracy: it sets the terms, or the *form* of the problem — we must respect the democratic demands and autonomy of the plurality of new social movements and articulate them together to form a new hegemonic bloc — but offers no suggestions for negotiating it, or even for distinguishing better negotiations from worse ones.[28] By refusing to leave the theoretical heights so as to offer a sense of the particular arrangements and negotiations of democracy's tensions that might today help constitute the "common bond" of radical and plural democracy — suggesting instead in various ways that it emerges out of the conditions of contingency itself — their work will remain primarily a description of the constitutive democratic dilemma rather than a strategy for hegemonic political reconstruction.

Antagonism, Power, and the Affirmation of Democracy's Permanent Incompletion

Although they fail to make clear the particular ways of negotiating democracy's constitutive tensions that would promote a contemporary project of radical and plural democratic hegemony, Laclau and Mouffe are, nonetheless, well aware of the general form that these democratic dilemmas take. And it is in response to them that they introduce an additional argument central to specifying their notion of radical and plural democracy. This move marks an important turn in their argument, shifting the thrust of their analysis away from the initial project of hegemonic political reconstruction and toward a different, "second-order" model of radical democratic politics.

In the closing pages of *Hegemony and Socialist Strategy*, they directly acknowledge that the hegemonic project for a radical democracy can only begin from the elements at hand, however unevenly developed and imperfectly suited to the task they might be: such a project will always be faced with certain "structural limits" posed by competing "social logics" (*HSS* 190). More generally, they argue that the utopian dreams of a fully transformed and egalitarian society that are basic to a project of radical democracy will always be limited by the same conditions of contingency that make such dreams possible, conditions in which "compromise, the precarious character of every arrangement, . . . [and] antagonism are the primary facts" (*HSS* 191). The same contingency and constitutive plurality responsible for the autonomy of the different democratic demands and the possibility of articulating them also put limits on how complete such articulation can be. As a result, the struggle for "a maximum advance for the democratic revolution in a broad range of spheres" must remain in an "unstable equilibrium" with "the capacity for the hegemonic direction and positive reconstruction of these spheres on the part of subordinated groups" (*HSS* 189).

Faced with this "tension" between the "radical imaginary" of a fully reconciled plurality of democratic struggles and the necessity of "managing" the "impossibility of a transparent society," Laclau and Mouffe do not simply argue in a resigned way for the acceptance of the tension. They argue, instead, that it "should be *affirmed* and defended" (*HSS* 190, emphasis added). In fact, "this moment of tension, of openness, which gives the social its essentially incomplete and precarious character, is what every project for radical democracy should set out to institutionalize" (*HSS* 190). The "openness" that democracy must institutionalize includes, then, not only the openness we have already encountered in the form of liberty, plurality, the autonomy of struggles, and so forth, but also the tension within democracy *between* this openness and the forms of closure it both requires and resists. As Mouffe puts it at the conclusion to "Democratic Citizenship and Political Community," the tension between the claims of liberty and equality is "the very life" of modern democracy (81).

Indeed, despite the apparent optimism of that essay's initial promises of constructing a practice of democratic citizenship able to bring together the claims of liberty and of equality and reconcile the variety of radical democratic demands, Mouffe accepts in the end that any such reconciliation will be at best temporary and imperfect, thwarted by the "permanent tension" at the heart of democracy itself. Rather than something to be lamented, though, the lack of fit between the competing values and demands of democracy becomes its own democratic value to be *affirmed*.

"Any attempt to bring about a perfect harmony, to realize a 'true' democracy, can only lead to its destruction," Mouffe writes. "This is why a project of radical and plural democracy recognizes the impossibility of the complete realization of democracy and the final achievement of the political community" (DC 81).

Given that democracy is constituted around the impossibility of any particular political arrangement ever satisfying entirely and simultaneously the values of liberty and equality for all, democratic politics requires "recognizing" this incompletion, and renouncing any claims to be able to achieve a "completed," fully reconciled society. For such a recognition to take place, any particular relation of openness and closure that has been achieved must itself remain in *tension*, always open to challenge and reconstruction. "The tension between [liberty and equality] has to be acknowledged," Mouffe writes in another essay, "and a radical and plural democracy rather than trying to resolve it should *enhance and protect* it." Thus, Mouffe argues not simply that "between the democratic logic of identity and equivalence and the liberal logic of pluralism and difference, the experience of a radical and plural democracy can only consist in the recognition of the multiplicity of social logics and the necessity of their articulation." Mouffe must also add that "this articulation should always be recreated and renegotiated, and there is no hope of a final reconciliation. This is why radical democracy also means the radical impossibility of a fully achieved democracy."[29] In fact, it is *because* there is "no hope of a final reconciliation" between the multiplicity of social logics that every particular arrangement of them must be open to revision. Even as one struggles to get the articulation "right," one must respect what is lost. Democracy, as the political regime of the contingent and inessential, can never offer a final answer but must always remain questionable.

But why exactly is such incompletion irremediable, and what exactly is entailed in its "recognition," or in the "affirmation" of democracy's constitutive "tensions"? A better sense of this is provided by Mouffe's essay "Democracy, Power, and 'the Political'." In this essay, she argues that radical democratic politics begins from the acceptance that no collective identity can ever be fully inclusive, given that every identity is made possible only by the existence of a "constitutive outside." For Mouffe, what is distinct about "radical and plural democracy" is its realization that the constitutive plurality — or "irreducible alterity" — out of which any particular social arrangement (precariously) emerges "represents both a condition of possibility and a condition of impossibility of every identity."[30] All identities, both individual and collective, are fully relational; they are contingently and always provisionally constituted through the exclusion of other identities. "Antagonism" is thus fundamental, and power ineradicable: rather than being an external relation between preconstituted identities, Mouffe argues, power is what constitutes the identities themselves. Any "social objectivity" or identity, then, will show "the traces of the acts of exclusion which govern its constitution; what . . . can be referred to as its 'constitutive outside'" (DP 21). In Mouffe's vision of radical democracy, "pluralism implies the permanence of conflict and antagonism" (DP 33).[31]

The exclusion of an "outside" is thus necessary for the constitution of even the most democratic and egalitarian of communities. The specificity of radical and plural democracy, Mouffe argues, rests in its *affirmation* (or "enhancement") of this condition and the impossibility of a fully inclusive community. In contrast to other projects of radical or participatory democracy, especially those "informed by a rationalistic framework," Laclau and Mouffe's radical and plural democracy "rejects the very possibility of a non-exclusive public sphere of rational argument where a non-coercive consensus could be attained" (DP 33). Instead, radical and plural democracy "acknowledge[s] the existence of relations of power and the need to transform them, while renouncing the illusion that we could free ourselves completely from power" (DP 22). The revelation that such perfect consensus is "a *conceptual* impossibility," Mouffe argues, far from threatening the democratic ideal, actually "protects pluralist democracy against any attempts of closure" and thus helps keep its dynamics alive. Although modern democratic politics, "linked as it is to the declaration of human rights, does indeed imply a reference to universality," Mouffe writes, "this universality is conceived as an horizon that can never be reached." In the name of the ideals of inclusion and universality themselves, one must relinquish all claims to have achieved them and pretensions to being able to achieve them in the future, as such claims work to cover over, and thus further entrench, the exclusions all arrangements necessarily involve. Given that power and exclusion are constitutive features of the democratic community, "every pretension to occupy the place of the universal, to fix its final meaning through rationality must be rejected. The content of the universal must remain indeterminate since it is this indeterminacy that is the condition of existence of democratic politics."[32] A society is democratic, then, only to the extent that "no limited social actor can attribute to herself or himself the representation of the totality" and "no social agent [is] able to claim any mastery of the *foundation* of society" (DP 21–22). Rather than consisting of the absence of domination and violence, "the specificity of modern pluralist democracy . . . reside[s] . . . in the establishment of a set of institutions through which they can be limited and contested" (DP 22).[33]

The incompletion that necessarily haunts democracy is rooted, then, in the constitutive nature of plurality and in the antagonism and power that it lodges at the heart of all identity. Laclau and Mouffe's "affirmative" response to the tensions within democratic politics that such unavoidable antagonism brings with it consists, in turn, of two related responses: first, abandoning all claims to represent (even ideally) a universal position or perspective (and challenging any attempts to do so); and second, making possible the questioning and contestation of the exclusions and violence on which all collective identities and political arrangements depend. In short, the "openness" that is the (non)ground of politics, identity, and community finds its democratic response in the second-order "openness" of contestation and questioning, designed to keep a community's political arrangements from closure.

In other words, given that, as a democrat, one accepts the goal of universality — of equality and inclusion — an understanding that its full realization is impossible produces the obligation to be honest about, and thus to argue for and to leave open to revision, those exclusions one's particular arrangements depend on. No decision is truly final, then; there must be no attempts to "fix" the universal. And because one must guarantee that one's own beliefs and political institutions are questionable, one must refuse the practice of defending one's exclusions on grounds that they are "natural," or "necessary," and thus beyond argumentation.

The Limits of Theoretical Critique

Although some degree of "openness" — in the sense of the possibility of questioning a community's decisions and institutions — must certainly be ensured for a community to be called democratic, it is, nonetheless, not so clear how Laclau and Mouffe's principle, particular to radical and plural democracy, of affirming (or "enhancing and protecting") democracy's constitutive tensions, would require much in the way of changes from present "liberal-democratic" practice. For as we have seen in the preceding chapters, the principle of openness, even one grounded in an analysis of certain ontological conditions of identity, can by itself provide little sense of what "being open" means in practice, of the kind or extent of "questionableness" or actual revision that is necessary to satisfy it, or of how, in any particular case, one might best adjudicate between the demands of articulation and those of openness and questioning.

Knowing when questioning and openness are being adequately respected is complicated in part simply because, as Laclau and Mouffe both argue at times, some "ground," in the form of assumptions, beliefs, values, or institutions, must be in place in order to question others: not everything can be open, or questioned, at once.[34] What's more, politics, including democratic politics, necessarily involves the making of decisions and the closing down of certain possibilities, at least temporarily. Part of the purpose of political action is to establish certain things as *decided*; even someone committed to the value of robust debate and the possibility of future reconsideration nonetheless struggles to see that those rights, principles, and institutions she believes in are "entrenched," placed at least to some extent off-limits to further critique and negotiation. One tries, in other words, to win and preserve victories. Such past decisions, however firmly established, then go on to help set the frame for future action, questioning, deciding. Indeed, the principle and practice of "openness" and questioning must themselves be established, or "institutionalized," as Laclau and Mouffe put it. That is one of the primary goals of the project for radical democratic hegemony. Yet, from the other side of the coin, what further complicates efforts at determining what "openness" should mean in practice is the fact that for the "law" of making things questionable to be *democratic*, it, too, is, and must be, questionable — open to interpretation and contestation. There can be no absolute, a-contextual, sense of the kind of openness, questionability, or questioning necessary for a community to be democratic. It, too, must be included in the list of topics for debate and can be determined only on the basis of a particular, situated, judgment rather than an abstract principle separate from the political situation itself.

In short, the principles of radical and plural democracy inform us only that both closure and openness are necessary; but there is nothing in democracy itself — or in the value of universality combined with the knowledge of its always limited nature — that can tell us the form or degree of openness that is appropriate in any particular occasion. As a result, given that some closure and some universal claims are necessary in democratic politics (and yet also impossible to achieve fully), it isn't so obvious how different the ("provisional" and "questionable") closure characteristic of radical and plural democracy is from the illicit, unquestionable, universalizations that Mouffe finds and criticizes in other nominally liberal or democratic programs. In fact, it is not so clear just which contemporary liberal-democratic political programs — as opposed to certain *theoretical* projects — could be said to include attempts to "fix" the final meaning of universality. What would such "fixing" look like? Few if any claims are made, at least in present political situations, to have arrived at the universal, nonviolent, non-exclusive regime itself. Instead, specific claims are made that some things should be excluded and other things should not, claims that, as we have seen, radical democracy cannot do without.[35]

At the very least, then, the injunction to keep the universal open, and to resist claims to define and speak for it perfectly, once and for all, without remainder, has a limited *practical* value: given that some sort of closure is both necessary and desirable, the toleration of *any* form of discussion, debate, or disagreement would seem to be enough to disprove the charge that one was engaged in an antidemocratic practice. As long as there was some structure or process of questioning a community's exclusions (thus meeting the criteria of openness Mouffe sketches out), one's criticisms would have to be directed at the particular forms of power that are sheltered from critique (or perhaps simply ignored), rather than at the denial of power as such. Any debate that then ensued would turn on the *particular* exclusions established and the kind and extent of questioning allowed. Mouffe's argument for the importance of affirming a community's constitutive openness, then, seems an accurate description of that wide range of possible political projects that can be called democratic, to the extent that such projects allow for some contestation of political power. However, her argument cannot function, as Mouffe seems to want it to, as the kind of imperative or guide to action ("we *must not* fix the universal") that defines a new, radical, and plural form of democracy.[36] As a radical democrat, Mouffe clearly thinks that present-day "democracies" are neither equal nor open enough; but within such a context, a new, radical, and plural democracy will be brought no closer to existence from the invocation of the democratic imperative of keeping the universal unoccupied.

Mouffe's critique, then, is perhaps best understood as directed not so much at self-professed democratic political *institutions* as at the effects on democratic political practice from those *theoretical* approaches that hold out the ultimate possibility of a fully rational and inclusive consensus. Such theories, Mouffe argues, "by searching for an argument beyond argumentation and by wanting to define the meaning of the universal, make the same mistake for which [they] criticize totalitarianism: the rejection of democratic indeterminacy and the identification of the universal with a given particular."[37] Even though such approaches aim to lay the basis for the widest political discussion and the most inclusive political community possible, their effort to find a single universal language whose rationality will ensure the absence of coercion paradoxically involves its own brand of more or less violent exclusion. The identification of a single acceptable form of argumentation as the guarantee of the perfectly inclusive community would radically limit the acceptable language games and the range of political discourse. What's more, by presenting such "rationality" as a neutral, universal language (as language or rationality itself), it also denies that any real exclusion has taken place (and without any other defense than the circular one of their lack of "rationality"). The rhetorical force of the ideal of rationality and a noncoercive discursive situation, through its antidemocratic denial of its own contestability, only compounds the power and exclusions built into the particularity of all discourses.

Democratic openness, then, demands not only that there be the possibility of presenting arguments that run counter to those presently dominant, but also that different *types* of arguments, or a plurality of "language games," be recognized as at least potentially legitimate modes of engagement. It is this latter possibility, Mouffe argues, that is restricted by theories that identify the universal with the rational, a loss that is then compounded by the claim that because "the rational" is truly universal, it is the only appropriate or necessary language, and thus involves no loss.

Despite the value of Mouffe's critique, however, it is important to see the ways in which it, too, must face the limits described by her *own* argument for the impossibility of a fully open form of political discussion. The knowledge that any form of discourse carries with it constitutive exclusions, or blindnesses, can indeed make one more open to recognizing other discourses as possible bearers of legitimate claims or insights. Yet such "openness" cannot itself be total. Given that discourses are *constitutive* of the problems, objects, or worlds that they make visible, being attentive to the existence of, even actively searching for, other discourses and perspectives can offer no guarantee of success, or even that one will notice when one is *failing* to notice certain "voices" or arguments or "realities" — precisely because they fall outside the boundaries of what one's discourses make it *possible* to "see" or "hear." The radical democratic argument against the undue closure of the universal, then, because it has no truly universal form of discourse to substitute for the false universal of "rationality," always works within some limited number of discourses or language games. Radical and plural democracy will consist in an openness to hearing other voices and learning other languages, combined with the necessity of ruling some of them out of bounds. Neither Mouffe nor Laclau, however, offers any analysis of what it would mean in practice to be sufficiently, or effectively, open to other languages. What strategies might one use, for instance, to be more alert to what exists "outside" the more hegemonic of our discourses?[38] Which kinds of language games might a more open, or plural, democratic discursive environment be more inclined to include, and which less so? Without even a provisional answer to such questions, it isn't clear how radical and plural democracy is different in practice from that informed by a "rationalist" theoretical perspective.

Perhaps, though, one could define the democratic affirmation of openness, paradoxically, as consisting at least in part of the deliberate *exclusion* of discourses that deny their limited nature, or that in some other way try to place themselves beyond critique and outside argumentation. One such discourse would be that which grounds a particular form of "universality" on a claim of "natural" identity and which argues that its exclusions and violences are "natural" or "necessary" given "who we are." To the extent that such racist (or nationalist, or sexist, or homophobic) projects do indeed rely on a belief in natural identities, they would certainly be threatened by the democratic law of questionability, and the critique of identity and essences at its base that radical and plural democracy highlights.

Here too, though, it is crucial to see the difficulty involved in trying to respond to the democratic principle of resisting discourses of natural or essential identity. For it is not always evident when an exclusion is based on a natural or essential category: categories that may clearly seem to be "essentialist" can be translated into much less obviously essentialist ones, as, for example, has recently been the case with the discursive move from "race" to "culture."[39] A claim, then, about who "I am" or who "we are" can be made with full recognition of the historical, contingent, and constructed character of the identity and yet still retain the rhetorical force of a natural, unarguable, claim. It is no easy task to distinguish between arguments that defend a category or exclusion as "natural for us," or "necessary given what we value," and "fully" essentialist claims in the name of "nature" or "necessity" itself. Indeed, much contemporary racism and nationalism are argued for on apparently prudential grounds: races and nations are to be kept separate because history has shown that they are not able to live together peacefully.[40]

In such cases, at least, the line is very thin (if it exists at all) between the kind of illicit dissuasion of criticism and questioning that comes with claiming a natural and necessary status to one's power arrangements and the kind of efforts that must be made, in the course of democratic politics, to protect one's achievements and values from attack and reversal. The difference would seem to turn on the *quality*, or extent, of the closure involved, rather than on its simple presence or absence. In any case, it is far from clear that people will be convinced to change such attitudes on the strength of a theoretical critique of identity or essentialism, however philosophically powerful. Instead, arguments must be made for the destructive effects of present exclusions, and hegemonic strategies must be devised whose rhetorical force is strong enough to produce new, less exclusive, collective identifications. A theoretically informed analysis will make sense and be persuasive only to the extent that it can suggest, and/or help bring into being, other practices or forms of community that can

generate identifications powerful enough to be maintained even as they
are more fully open to challenge and change. Investigating what such
forms and practices of community might look like, though, is unfortunately not part of Mouffe's theorization of radical and plural democracy.

Mouffe is thus certainly right to argue that democracy requires bringing "the traces of power and exclusion . . . to the fore, to make them visible so that they can enter the terrain of contestation" (DP 34). It is
nonetheless the case that such a politico-ethical principle leaves many of
the most difficult and important democratic questions unasked and unanswered. How, for instance, are democratic citizens to learn how to engage
in and sustain the difficult — threatening, burdensome, painful — practice
of challenging the "traces of power and exclusion" that help constitute
their own individual and collective identities? What are the rhetorical and
psychological characteristics best suited to enabling such practices of self-
critique? More concretely, just how visible must the exclusions be made?
How frequent and extensive is this "making visible" to be? What form is
it to take, who is in charge of the process, who is to decide what counts
as an exclusion worthy of contestation? Much of what will be distinctive
about a project for a radical and plural democracy will depend on how
these questions are answered in specific political situations, rather than
on the general demand that exclusions be made visible.

From the Knowledge of Democracy's Paradoxes to the Expansion of Democratic Contestation

Although there is nothing in the radical democratic principle of affirming
the impossibility of perfect universality that by itself fills out the very
broad parameters of the injunction to challenge exclusions, there is nevertheless a very strong sense in Mouffe's essay — and throughout Laclau
and Mouffe's work as a whole — that making exclusions visible and thus
contestable should be done as frequently and extensively as possible. The
affirmation of openness that is central to radical and plural democracy
involves more than just providing some means for the questioning and
revision of past decisions and institutions; it is also a matter of the *active
highlighting* of the relative, contingent, and limited nature of one's universals (and one's identity and beliefs more generally), all in an effort to
render them fully contestable. "The relation between social agents
becomes *more* democratic," Mouffe argues, "*only as far as* they accept
the particularity and the limitation of their claims" (DP 21, emphasis
added), and with that, in turn, a sense of the questionable nature of all
such claims.[41] Democratic openness would, on this reading, form the

basis for an ethical politics of self-limitation, of increased willingness to entertain other viewpoints, and ultimately to change: the knowledge of the partiality and limitedness of one's perspective would bring with it the obligation to restrain and question oneself, and encourage others' questioning. The recognition of the limits, gaps, dislocation, and openness that constitute the general *field* of politics, that is, is understood to produce a new, more democratic *practice* of politics, where the urge to win, to impose one's will on the rest of the community, is limited by a recognition of the contingent, relative, and "transitory" nature of our identities and of any claim to speak for the interest of the community as a whole.

Such a politics, with its deliberate and systematic emphasis on the provisional, contingent, and revisable nature of our identities and institutions, would have the additional benefit of ensuring that nothing ever gets *too* decided or *fully* institutionalized. This, in turn, as we have seen above, is valuable to the extent that the openness it preserves provides the space for the experience of freedom itself, for the making of ourselves and our world that is both the gift and burden of freedom.[42] Affirming the contingent nature of our identities and political arrangements reminds us of our freedom to create and re-create, and helps resist claims that we are locked into certain patterns naturally, or out of necessity. At the heart of Laclau and Mouffe's argument is the claim that politics is the privileged realm for this experience and that it is through the affirmation of the constitutive openness of the social that "the field of politics can be extended" (NR 51).

Yet the "field of politics," understood here as that portion of the social world not yet decided or determined, cannot be total. Laclau himself accepts that democratic politics, and freedom itself, necessarily involve closure, determination, and decision as well as openness, incompletion, and contestation. "To avoid any misunderstanding," he writes,

> we must once again emphasize that the dislocation of a structure does not mean that *everything* becomes possible or that *all* symbolic frameworks disappear, since no dislocation could take place in that psychotic universe: a structure must be there for it to be dislocated. The situation of dislocation is that of a lack which involves a structural reference. There is a widening of the field of the possible, but this takes place in a *determinate* situation: that is, one in which there is always a relative structuration. (NR 43)

Certain things must be in place for other things to be questioned or made "possible." "Possibilities," as specific forms of openness, only arise in specific situations, against a background of closure.

What's more, as Laclau also recognizes, politics and freedom inevitably involve projects directed toward particular ends (if only the preservation of their own conditions), and thus efforts to close down certain possibilities (precisely so as to open up other ones). Laclau chooses to figure this structure as "the paradox dominating the whole of social action." "Freedom exists because society does not achieve constitution as a structural objective order," Laclau writes, "but any social action tends toward the constitution of that impossible object, and thus toward the elimination of the conditions of liberty itself" (NR 44). And as he immediately adds: "This paradox has no solution." Further on he writes, "political victory is equivalent to the elimination of *the specifically political nature* of the victorious practices" (NR 68, emphasis added).

In short, even as Laclau insists on equating the "specifically political nature" of an action or practice with the condition of being open, in the sense of not-yet-decided, he also argues that political actions are nevertheless necessarily directed toward the closing down of future freedom. To the extent that politics is a matter of struggles and demands aimed at the achievement of some new arrangement of the community and its relations of power, it aims to settle things, to close down certain options. Part of the essence and value of freedom itself is taking action that results in certain things being decided.[43] Going against the drift of much of the rest of their argument, Laclau's own description of the situatedness of dislocation and possibility, and the paradox of freedom, suggests that there can be no general increase in the constitutive or ontological openness (indetermination) of a society.[44] Particular institutions, decisions, or assumptions can be challenged, destabilized, called into question in such a way that they are available for radical reconstruction, but the production of such spaces of freedom and uncertainty depends on the existence of other "spaces" (beliefs, practices, institutions) that remain more or less stable, even taken for granted.

The claim that it is impossible to achieve a general increase in freedom as such (in the sense of a society less determined in an absolute sense) does not, however, require one to dismiss the possibility of political consequences resulting from the recognition and acceptance of contingency and constitutive openness. For the affirmation of openness promoted by Laclau and Mouffe might indeed lead to a greater awareness throughout the community of the not-fully-determined nature of society and the historically specific nature of its values and institutions, which might, in turn, bring with it, as a response, an increase in political activity, in the sense of debate, argument, questioning, contestation, and so forth. The affirmation of openness, that is, might mean that people are *generally more likely* to interrogate certain claims and categories, given the denaturalization those categories undergo in light of the knowledge of their contingency. It might also involve a general increase in the amount of questioning or the number of things questioned. Or it might mean that decisions are made with greater awareness of, and perhaps also efforts to preserve, their provisionality. All these are, in fact, basic goals of the project of radical and plural democracy.[45]

Nonetheless, for any of that to be the case — for the *knowledge* of contingency to lead to the practice of more questioning, or a deliberate heightening of the provisional nature of political decisions and institutions — certain conditions must first be met. One must, for instance, first argue, and convince others, that there is a *value*, both in general and in any particular political situation, to spending more time questioning, or being more likely to question and more open to being questioned. For even as an increase in questionability and/or in questioning may well allow for greater political involvement, which is a democratic value in itself, and even as it can open up particular democratic political possibilities, it can also pose risks to those democratic decisions and values that have been or should be instituted. Deciding on the proper kind and extent of questioning and questionability can only be a contingent and strategic act, one that takes into account the *risk* of particular questions and the answers, or revisions, they might generate in a given political situation, as well as the risk of a general loss of control over the political agenda and the threat that might pose to the achievement of a radical democratic hegemony.[46]

In addition, even if one endorses the value of an increase in either questionability or questioning, this does not mean that anything in particular should or will be revised. Given the absence of any noncontingent, universal set of political arrangements or practices available for substitution, actually challenging and changing those that do exist would require specific arguments about the problems with those claims and categories, and not just the general recognition of their contingent, and thus contestable, nature. Indeed, radical and plural democracy aims to achieve a new, improved design of the political community, one that will presumably have *less* (or at least less of basic importance) about it that should be changed or contested, at least for the time being. Even as it recognizes the impossibility of achieving a universally satisfying articulation of liberty and equality or a fully inclusive collective identity, and even as it responds to this condition with the institutionalization of some means of contesting its choices and exclusions, it still hopes to provide better solutions, and thus ones less in need of questioning, than what presently exists. The recognition of its nonuniversality and exclusionary nature does not by itself endanger the strength of one's attachment to it.

Nor, for these same reasons, is it possible simply to equate democracy with the presence of conflict, as Mouffe suggests is the case when she writes that "in a democratic polity, conflicts and confrontations, far from being a sign of imperfection, indicate that democracy is alive and inhabited by pluralism" (DP 34).[47] Even if one accepts the value of affirming freedom as openness and accepts the claim that democracy has a particularly close relation to its experience, the simple fact that there are "conflicts and confrontations" tells us nothing in itself about the state of "a democratic polity." The existence of conflicts would indeed be a sign that the polity is "inhabited by pluralism," which, to the extent that it refers to the availability of different perspectives and political positions, is indeed a fundamental democratic value. In a strictly formal sense, then, the presence of such pluralism would be a sign that "democracy is alive." But to argue that one shouldn't hide the exclusions and violences necessary to one's social and political arrangements, that they should instead be open to challenge, is not the same as arguing that the more challenging there is the better, or that democracy is strengthened or improved through the existence of conflict and confrontation.

Put most simply, not all signs of pluralism, and certainly not all conflicts, are to be welcomed, even in a democratic polity: it would make little sense, for instance, to say that the conflicts resulting from a coordinated attack on the achievements and supporters of radical democracy "indicate that democracy is alive and inhabited by pluralism." To equate an increase in conflict as such with an increase in democracy would be to mistake one side of democracy with all of it. Democratic politics requires and imposes closure (a point, as we have just noted, that Laclau himself argues), for it requires certain things being achieved, the most important being equality (in part to assure the possibility of challenging decisions). Democratic politics, then, is found on both sides of the openness/closure division, not only on that of openness and conflict. Thus the aspect of democratic politics that resides in the *process* of questioning and making contestable — and the conflict that often brings with it — will always remain in tension (and at times actively at odds) with the *content* of any particular definition of democracy — with the fact that for democracy to mean anything (and especially for it to be "radical"), certain things have to have been decided. Even in a politics that deliberately "affirms" "openness," then, one will want some decisions, beliefs, laws challenged, or reopened, and others left closed. The most radical and plural of democrats will still be within the general domain of politics, faced with the necessity of specific choices about the amount of questioning, the number of things decided, and the particular freedoms decided on.

From the point of view of radical and plural democracy — understood as something more than just a description of the formal requirements of democracy in general — what counts for a judgment of democratic vitality cannot, then, be the mere existence or the *amount* of conflict. Instead, three issues must be considered. First, whether the *possibility* of disagreeing, reconsidering, and questioning is accepted and established to the right degree; and second, *which* established modes are challenged and in the name of what sort of alternative: are the conflicts over the denial of voting rights and the growth of unaccountable corporate or state power, or are they over the threats that "radical feminists and environmentalists" pose to traditional values and cultural norms, or the dangers of "class warfare" waged by those arguing for a more progressive rate of taxation?

Third, and most difficult: for contingency to be experienced in a way that is conducive to the openness and questioning that is fundamental to radical and plural democracy, specific political, rhetorical, and psychological practices must be established and maintained. Without hegemonic efforts to structure and interpret the experience of contingency in particular ways, that experience is just as likely, within a political context informed by the democratic demands of liberty and equality, to produce antidemocratic forms of politics. When faced with the finitude (in time, resources, knowledge, strength) that is an essential aspect of contingency, for instance, the democratic ideal of equal freedom is as likely, by itself, to lead to resentment at all the many ways one is neither equal nor free as it is to lead to a politics of self-limitation and respect for difference. So, too, without institutions in place that make possible effective political involvement, the inevitable failure of democratic politics to live up to its own ideals can produce disappointment and cynicism about the very possibility of community and public life. Or, finally, to the extent that the fragmenting and destabilizing effects of contingency are experienced by people as insecurity, they will be less likely to risk the change in identity that is demanded by radical and plural democracy — whether in the form of a general increase in flexibility, or as part of the process of identifying with a new radical democratic "common concern." Instead, their sense of identity is more likely to harden, and their identifications to be with the "threatened" communal body (e.g., of the nation, race, or culture) and those who speak in its name and claim to "protect" it and its members. For the *affirmation* of contingency and democratic incompletion to pave the way for a more fully democratic and pluralistic experience of politics, then, it must be more than theoretical. To be meaningful, such affirmation must instead be embodied in specific practices — specific forms of *civic virtue* — that are able to structure the uncertainty of identity and political action so that citizens are more, rather than less, able to take up the risks of democratic contestation and questioning. The following chapter examines in more detail what such a suitably radical and plural form of civic virtue might look like under present conditions.

Negotiating the Practical Difficulties
of Democratic Openness

At crucial points throughout their writings, then, Laclau and Mouffe's argument relies on the following implicit claim: because radical and plural democracy is based on the affirmation of the constitutive openness and incompletion at the heart of the social, and with it the ineradicable presence of antagonism and conflict, then questioning, challenging, revising, and maintaining the awareness of such openness are to be valued in themselves and pursued as often as possible. Their argument thus frequently moves from the formal level (in this case, the way in which democracy involves pluralism and questionability), which is supported by a theoretical analysis of constitutive conditions (the antagonistic or conflictual nature of identity), to a particular substantive understanding of radical and plural democracy (the presence of conflict and questioning is to be affirmed and valued), understood as a regime that is supposed to rest on the recognition of this condition. In other words, the theoretical analysis of the ontological conditions of identity and political existence, if properly embraced, is meant to push us along in a direction that radicalizes certain formal characteristics of democracy — questioning, the plurality of identities and viewpoints, the de-naturalization of social relations, equality. Their theoretical, conceptual, ontological analysis, then, is offered as support for a particular political practice.[48]

The problem that we have encountered repeatedly, however, is that at both the constitutive, ontological level and the level of a formal analysis of the elements of democracy, the demands of "openness" cannot be met without also meeting the demands of some form of *closure*. Radical and plural democracy, understood as a particular program that aims to increase the level of questioning, contestation, and the provisionality of decisions and institutions, cannot flow directly from the affirmation of the constitutive conditions of contingency and openness, since those conditions, as Laclau's own analysis of the paradox of freedom shows, always involve us in both openness and closure. There can be no experience of the one without the other. For that reason among others, a whole range of different political programs (all of them, broadly speaking, democratic) can be said to emerge out of the "affirmation" of those conditions. The acceptance of constitutive openness that Laclau and Mouffe argue is central to radical and plural democracy has no *necessary* connection to any specifically radical and/or plural practice of democracy. This does not mean that there is no need in contemporary democratic politics for more questioning and critique, or a greater number of viable political positions. But if that is what the affirmation of contingency and openness particular to radical and plural democracy amounts to, then it requires arguments made on the basis of *contingent* political considerations (which involve arguable ethical and strategic claims), not in the name of necessary ontological conditions (or even of democracy itself). The meaning of radical and plural democracy, like any other form of democracy, can only be determined by its specific answers to the demands its principles (of liberty, equality, openness, and closure) pose in specific situations.

All of which is to say that trying to "follow" the principles of democracy, and of radical and plural democracy in particular, places one in a particularly *difficult* position. This is in part simply because, as with all general principles, the rules of democracy can never by themselves determine actions, since they only come into existence, they only become "themselves," as they are interpreted from a particular perspective and according to the demands of the specific situation at hand. This "open" character of rules — the way in which a rule is transformed in each encounter with a particular case — is in fact affirmed by the democratic law of freedom: the authority of rules is entirely provisional; they are rules only to the extent that they are endorsed, and only in the form in which they are understood, by and in the name of the present community. The difficulties this raises are, in turn, exacerbated by the fact that the "rule" of democracy is itself constituted by competing principles, each of which poses a *condition* and a *risk* to the other. The demand that things be kept open to contestation poses a risk to what has been decided, including the values of radical and plural democracy and its particular articulation of liberty and equality. And as the requirement of renegotiation places democratic achievements at risk, so the need to defend such achievements requires that one cut short the process of debate and reconsideration. Not merely are questioning and contestation fundamental democratic principles, but they themselves are "questioned" and "contested" by the competing principle of decision and closure. As we began to see in the first chapter, then, the "rule" of democracy is particularly difficult to follow, given that in the moment of action or decision, it points us in two different directions, with each side of the rule producing the critique of the other.[49]

Given this sense of its constitutive openness, democracy is better defined as a set of *questions* than as an answer or a guide to action. The principles of democracy pose problems in need of resolution — Is there enough liberty? Enough equality? Is the correct interpretation of liberty and equality at work? Are the appropriate institutions in place for questioning and contestation? — rather than solutions to those problems, or guides to acting in response to them. Politics is democratic, then, when democratic questions are being answered, and not other questions ("Who are the real members of the nation, or race?" for instance, or "How can we ensure that the right people rule and the others obey?"). One of the paradoxes involved, of course, is that the different answers to democracy's questions — answers that define the competing versions of democracy — all claim in some way or another to be the *right* answers, and thus to define the "correct" version of democracy "itself." In this sense, then, the "unruly" character of democratic politics is simply a more pronounced version of politics in general: the fact that the "ground" (or rule) that is to be followed is constructed in the act of claiming to follow it produces a political practice of argument and contest without any final, or absolute, rule that could determine which version, or interpretation, of democracy is the right one. "Democracy," then, exists in the tension between its formal, quite general requirements (the questions it asks) and the particular concrete claims (or answers) about what it means in a given situation — claims that can refer back to no neutral version, or "rule," of democracy itself.

But to take seriously the incompletion, contingency, and openness that democratic politics is supposed to affirm — to really affirm it — involves accepting not only that democracy offers a particularly acute experience of the *unruly* character of politics but also that it offers no secure place from which to *affirm* this situation. Given that its two central principles are at odds with each other, there is no political position external to its tensions and difficulties from which one could affirm them without also being subject to, and thus torn by them. Although one can produce a general, theoretical, affirmation of the open, incomplete nature of democratic politics, any real such affirmation from within the moment of action and decision will include a recognition of the *loss* that accompanies democracy's incompletion and openness. To affirm openness, that is, requires accepting what is lost when democratic values fail to fit together harmoniously, as well as the risk that being open to renegotiation poses to past and future democratic achievements, and not merely looking toward the future possibilities latent in its openness. The conditions of freedom and contingency cannot truly be said to be affirmed without the pain and suffering being affirmed too — the pain not only of the losses and exclusions necessary to any decision or institution but also of the fact that the contingency of political victories means none is ever secure, that one always has to fight the same fights again and again, and that the necessity of making one's decisions and victories questionable — which is itself part of the required affirmation of democracy's openness — only adds to these dangers. The democratic affirmation of contingency and openness must include the affirmation of this painful, agonizing aspect of having to do politics while realizing all that is lost and endangered by the very need to be true to one's own values.

The affirmation of openness, in short, will never release one from democracy's constitutive dilemmas, as Laclau and Mouffe seem to suggest at times. At best it offers a way of negotiating them in more, rather than less, productive ways.[50] For the promise of a democratic politics based on the knowledge and affirmation of contingency to come to fruition — to make the difficulties and losses of democratic politics more *bearable* — one must, then, go beyond a *theoretical* affirmation of openness. For a new radical and plural interpretation of the principles of democracy to become a viable practice, specific strategies are needed to navigate the difficulties and dangers posed by the contingency of democratic politics. For the knowledge of contingency to be liberating or otherwise politically positive, and for a democratic politics of freedom, self-limitation, and identity transformation to be possible and effective, rhetorical and psychological resources must be found, and practices of "civic virtue" developed, that are able to structure the experience of contingency in democratically supportive ways. Without such resources, cynicism, resignation, resentment, and the demand for security are all more likely responses to democracy's constitutive dilemmas and difficulties than are the openness and self-critique necessary to radical and plural democracy. In the following chapter I begin to explore some of the rhetorical and ethical strategies that might assist in such a democratic structuring of contingency, especially in the present context of widespread cynicism and disenchantment with the very realm of politics itself.

Rather than affirming the increase in freedom and politics that accompanies the extension of the logic of "dislocation," then — as if the close connection between democracy and contingency made such an increase in dislocation necessarily positive — the project of radical and plural democracy needs to offer specific strategies for installing what might be called the "ethical" attitude of self-limitation, generosity, and questioning in politically effective, rather than self-defeating, ways.[51] What is needed, in other words, is a new response to Rousseau's paradox of democratic foundation, updated in a radical and plural form: how to forge a new common identity as democratic citizens who affirm and institutionalize freedom and plurality even in the face of the political pressures that arise from the antidemocratic exploitation of precisely those conditions of plurality, conflict, and the lack of any neutral ground. What, in short, are the most appropriate and promising forms of *civic virtue* for today's difficult political conditions? The provisional answers, if they are out there, can only be found within the contingency of democratic politics — not as it is "affirmed" in principle or theory, but rather as it is experienced and practiced.

CHAPTER FOUR

Generating a Virtuous Circle

*Democratic Identity, Moralism, and the Languages
of Political Responsibility*

Paradoxically, while hardly anyone questions that the self-styled "advanced industrialized democracies" really are democracies, fewer still care to argue that "the people" actually rule in any one of them, or that it would be a good idea if it did. For in societies where managerial rule is widely practiced, democracy appears as inherently crude and hence unsuited for the task of governing complex and rapidly changing societies. At the same time in those quarters, it is often declared that democracy demands such a high level of political sophistication from citizens as to make it doubtful that it can be mastered by Third World peoples. Thus democracy is too simple for complex societies and too complex for simple ones.

— Sheldon Wolin, "Fugitive Democracy," in *Democracy and Difference*

Where the will to power is in charge, the higher the ideals, the lower the results. Try to make people happy, and you lay the groundwork for misery. Try to make people moral, and you lay the groundwork for vice.

— Lao-tzu, *Tao Te Ching: A New English Version*, trans. Stephen Mitchell

Throughout the preceding chapters, we have explored the conceptual and practical difficulties that accompany the experience of democratic freedom and openness. Beginning from the most basic understanding of democracy as the rule of the people, we have argued that the precise contours of the people, and the meaning of the equality that all its members share, must, if their individual and collective freedom is to be respected, remain uncertain. We have tried to show that as a result of its constitutive openness, democracy offers a politics of never-ending contest and uncertainty, with the democratic "we," and the identities of its citizens, always in formation. This openness-as-contestability, however, is a product not only of the original freedom of the democratic community to determine itself but also of the very impossibility of that freedom being complete. For without any neutral, prepolitical ground from which to define the people or the terms of equal membership and participation, the democratic "we" must instead be created and re-created from less than fully open positions and with less than fully democratic means. Even as it aims at the openness of full and equal inclusion, then, the process by which the political community determines itself guarantees that its openness will always remain partial.

As we have seen in distinct ways in the arguments of Rousseau, Castoriadis, Benhabib, Arendt, and Laclau and Mouffe, democratic politics is thus defined both by the attempt to respect the fundamental equality, plurality, and uncertainty of political relationships and by the inevitable failure and incompletion of that attempt. Indeed, we have seen throughout the preceding pages that precisely for such openness and plurality to be experienced in *political* ways, rather than as mere chaos, there must be rules and structures in place whose relative stability and closure places limits on the very freedom and uncertainty being preserved. Democratic politics, we have argued, is thus built on a series of tensions — between equality and liberty, plurality and commonality, openness and closure — that can never fully be reconciled. The existence of such tensions, in turn, makes the experience of democratic freedom a particularly challenging one, for being *essential* aspects of the democratic condition, they resist all attempts to formulate clear theoretical rules that would guide democratic action. Instead, I have argued, democratic politics presents its citizens with a series of difficult and open questions, whose contingent answers can be found only amid the risks and uncertainty of democratic practice.

Yet even if theories of democratic politics are unable to answer democracy's questions, or eliminate its constitutive risks and dilemmas, could it nevertheless be possible to recognize and affirm the difficult experience of democratic freedom and openness in such a way as to *negotiate* such risks and dilemmas more effectively? Are there ways in which the democratic condition and the difficult questions it asks of us can be acknowledged and accepted so as to open up greater democratic space and energies, rather than shutting them down through exhaustion, or fear, or confusion, given the sizeable institutional barriers to effective participation that characterize politics today? This chapter investigates just what such an affirmation of democratic openness might look like under present conditions, with a particular focus on the state of democratic politics in the United States. How precisely might the affirmation of democracy as an experience of radical freedom — of contestability, of the lack of clear or final answers, of the perpetual questioning and uncertainty of our individual and collective identities — be used to expand democratic possibilities here, today, rather than rendering them more difficult, or amounting only to a theoretical gesture without practical effects?

Openness and the Challenge of Our Democratic Closures

Any such affirmation would seem to be a particularly difficult task today, given the severe democratic deficits that define American politics and the deeply entrenched obstacles these pose even for modest efforts at liberal-democratic reforms, much less attempts to deepen and radicalize the meaning and forms of democratic politics. To affirm and deepen the experience of the democratic community as open to question and contestation would seem a particularly fanciful project in a situation in which the very existence of democratic rule is itself in question. Signs of "democracy's discontent" are everywhere. Perhaps most striking, and frequently mentioned, are the significant declines in rates of voting and in other forms of political and civic participation (involvement in electoral campaigns, membership in political parties, attendance at town meetings, and so forth).[1] This is paralleled by a growing lack of even basic political knowledge among many citizens, and a striking correlation between levels of education and wealth, on the one hand, and political knowledge and participation (including financial contributions to electoral campaigns) on the other.[2] The range of democratic ideas and options open to debate has, in turn, been narrowed by a combination of factors. Most crucial here are changes in the nature of political campaigns, which increasingly rely on the use of expensive media forms (primarily television) to target the small minority of voters who are deemed most likely to affect the outcome,[3] the overwhelming influence of those industries and interests able to fund such media campaigns, and the increasing concentration of ownership in the industries of information that are the gateways for political ideas. The overall effect of such changes is to ensure that average citizens have increasingly less input into, effect over, and ultimately interest in political debates and decision-making.

Indeed, to the extent that one could make, with enough time and space, a persuasive case that (1) average citizens are largely unable to shape the political agenda or determine the polity's ultimate decisions except in limited, reactive, and sporadic ways; (2) those decisions in many basic areas fail to reflect their fundamental interests or opinions (thus the sharp increases in economic and social inequality over the past twenty years);[4] and (3) the society's fundamental political, economic, and social institutions and practices are not effectively open to debate and revision (in part because there isn't the kind of equality and social inclusion necessary for a diverse or representative range of voices to be heard) — to this extent, the concept of democratic questionability would take on a new, more bitterly ironic, meaning. For if constantly questioning who the people are and how they should rule their collective life is the hallmark of democratic openness, then today's democratic closures raise the different "democratic question" of whether the people can be said in any meaningful sense to rule at all.

The future of democratic politics in the United States is certainly questionable from the perspective of the kind of strongly democratic theory of republican legitimacy we first encountered in our analysis of Rousseau and Castoriadis. As elaborated more recently by Charles Taylor, for instance, such a "civic republican" approach argues that "a modern democratic state demands a people with a strong collective identity." For the collective self-rule of democracy to function, this line of argument goes, citizens must know and understand and listen to each other in such a way as to plausibly be said to form — and see themselves as forming — a *single* "body" or "personality."[5] And for the collective identifications necessary to this process to be in place, there must be some strong sense in which there are common purposes, or interests, or goods that all, or large and overlapping majorities, can see themselves as sharing. Only then can it be said to be *the people* who rules, rather than one (part of the) people ruling over another.

Updating an analysis first articulated by Tocqueville, Taylor argues that the roots of America's democratic "malaise" lie in what he calls "political fragmentation," a condition that "arises when people come to see themselves more and more atomistically, otherwise put, as less and less bound to their fellow citizens in common projects and allegiances."[6] In such a situation, some citizens do continue to work to protect or advance the interests or identities of smaller groupings, based on locality, or ethnicity, or a specific interest or allegiance, yet "the people" as a whole are nonetheless "increasingly less capable of forming a common purpose and carrying it out." Although some degree of recognizably political activity continues to take place, the particular kinds of politics fostered in such a situation — whether action oriented toward demanding and securing one's rights, frequently by judicial intervention, or attempts to promote specific interests or single-issue campaigns — are not, in the long run, democratically self-sustaining. By weakening collective identifications and common purposes, liberal rights-based and interest-group politics undermine both democratic legitimacy and the possibility of effective democratic action.

Most worrisome for committed democrats, however, is Taylor's argument that once such a process of "fragmentation" is under way, it takes on a "self-feeding" character as the result of the "failure of democratic initiative itself." As he puts it,

> Because the more fragmented a democratic electorate is in this sense, . . . the less possible it is to mobilize democratic majorities around commonly understood programs and policies. . . . The idea that the majority of people might frame and carry through a common project comes to seem utopian and naive. And so people give up. Already failing sympathy with others is further weakened by the lack of a common experience of action, and a sense of hopelessness makes it seem a waste of time to try. But that, of course, *makes* it hopeless, and a vicious circle is joined.[7]

As part of the critique of "liberal proceduralism" that he offers in his book *Democracy's Discontent*, Michael Sandel echoes Taylor's worry about what might be called the vicious circle of public disinvestment. In an important, although somewhat muted passage toward the end of the book, Sandel suggests that Rousseau's classic warning about the corrupting effects of large disparities of wealth on democratic legitimacy is now increasingly applicable to American politics. The difficulty, though, is that the antidemocratic effects of America's rapidly growing inequality of income and wealth would seem to be reversible only through an appeal to a national sense of mutual responsibility, which is precisely what can less and less be assumed: "As rich and poor gr[ow] further apart, their sense of shared fate diminishe[s], and with it the willingness of the rich to invest, through higher taxes, in the skills of their fellow citizens."[8] Helping to cement and propel the decline in shared identifications, Sandel suggests, are the increasingly separate lives lived by those with and without wealth. As the public sphere and its institutions suffer the effects of underfunding, those with enough money come increasingly to sequester themselves in private and privately funded spaces and activities, from health clubs and day-care centers to schools and gated residential communities. Public spaces and institutions, in turn, are left primarily to the poor and continue to decline in quality and attractiveness, thus further reducing the desirability and psychic investment in "public things" among all citizens. For Sandel, though, the casualties of this vicious circle of public disinvestment go beyond the shared sympathies necessary to a sustainable welfare state; equally important is the way in which the decline of public spaces and institutions erodes one of the richest sources of civic education and civic virtue. The fewer spaces in which people of all classes and backgrounds can meet and learn about and from each other, the less opportunity there is to "learn the habits of democratic citizenship" or to develop a sense of "civic identity, neighborliness, and community" (332).

Of course, in the American example that both Taylor and Sandel criticize, there are certainly powerful forms of collective identification at work — in particular, identifications, on the part of many of those of little or modest means, with the lives and values of the wealthy, or with an idealized middle class, identifications rooted in a belief in the American dream and the logic of free markets that ideally allow all citizens to improve their station in life through their own, rather than collective, or public, efforts.[9] From the perspective of republicanism, however, the democratic rights of citizens to manage and control their own lives are sustainable only through common action and the experience of public spaces and institutions, through which can be developed the habit of seeing oneself as an equal part of — both dependent on and a co-creator of — a larger democratic public.[10] Without these, the democratic "we" takes on an increasingly spectral form, with the predictable result that American political life as a whole has become the target of large amounts of cynicism and distrust, or simply lack of interest or concern.[11] In ways that we explore at greater length below, these forces go on to strengthen further the vicious circle of public disinvestment. Without the support of a strong lived experience of citizenship, common action, and public spaces and practices, even the public-spirited and those inclined toward strong democratic identifications begin to withdraw, as their trust in others, in public institutions, and in the possibilities of collective action is consistently disappointed. Hence the widespread loss of faith in — or simply memory of — the democratic promise of a political community in whose public institutions and practices all citizens can see themselves reflected and in whose construction all can be equally responsible participants.

The question this raises for those who still take this promise seriously and recognize the importance to healthy democratic politics of effective forms of public identifications is whether, and if so, how, the cycle can be transformed. Can it, in fact, be transformed into a "*virtuous* circle," or are we stuck in a contemporary version of Rousseau's paradox of the effect having to be the cause: unable to generate collective identifications with common purposes until there exist the vibrant public institutions and practices whose *own* existence depends precisely on such identifications and psychic investment? How, under conditions of public disinvestment, can a more vibrant democratic "we" be called into being, when both the language and the experience of democratic politics available to most people are so impoverished? More specifically, the question I pursue in the pages that follow concerns what languages of politicization democratically engaged citizens might speak today. It should be clear that one cannot *simply* intone the age-old democratic mantras — of equality, participation, civic virtue, the common good — and hope that if one does so loudly enough or to enough people, the vicious cycle will be reversed.[12] Implicit in both Taylor's and Sandel's analyses of the cycle of democratic disinvestment is the correct assumption that the belief in the *idea* of a democratic people requires for its sustenance some lived *experience* of the people or of the public. As the quality and frequency of that experience decline, something more than the mere repetition of the idea is needed. Indeed, with political fragmentation and the decline of public spaces and institutions has come a larger de-, even anti-, politicization, as the very forms and institutions of politics themselves seem increasingly disconnected from and distasteful to many citizens. If the vicious circle of public disinvestment is to have any chance of being reversed, then, what is needed is a language of democratic engagement and responsibility that is itself an effectively politicizing *practice*, able to make democratic identification and the practices it sustains less burdensome, the risks of reinvesting one's hopes and talents in the community less severe. The question to ask, then, is what kind of a language would make it easier for citizens to take up the risks and burdens of democratic identification and action, *given the particular conditions* of political fragmentation, disenchantment, and disconnection we suffer from today?

For Sandel, whose arguments in *Democracy's Discontent* are the focus of the first half of the chapter, the answer must emerge from a critique of the language and philosophy of what he calls "liberal proceduralism." Critical of its unduly truncated understanding of political freedom and its restricted sense of the debts that the liberal individual owes to the larger community, Sandel argues that the liberal vision and language of the democratic "we" must be challenged by a retrieval of the republican vision of political freedom and its corresponding practice of civic virtue. Although the general thrust of Sandel's critique of liberal proceduralism is powerful, and the case he makes for stronger forms of civic virtue than such liberalism can sustain is persuasive, I try to show nonetheless that jump-starting a *virtuous* circle of democratic identification requires a different understanding of virtue and its relation to democratic politics and "identity." More specifically, I argue that Sandel's vision of community and identity is insufficiently *political*, failing to pay sufficient respect to the internally complex and uncertain nature of democratic identity — both individual and collective — and to the constitutive difficulties of the democratic condition. As a result, Sandel's virtue and the languages of political responsibility that articulate it would all too easily take the form of *moralizing* calls to responsibility. By fueling the patterns of anger, resentment, and alienation that are important contributors to the vicious circle of public disinvestment, such moralizing ends up undermining the very democratic energies they aim to generate.

What is needed instead are forms of civic virtue that are built on a conscious recognition of the difficulties involved in democratic politics and that work to dislodge the overlapping forms of alienation that constitute so much of American political life. Crucial here would be languages of political engagement, born of a democratic critique of self-identity, that avoid the dangers of moralism and cynicism through a compassionate understanding of the inevitable trespass, failure, impurity, and incompletion that characterize political action. To the extent that such modes of rhetorical appeal are able to avoid the anger and cynicism that moralism so often generates, they would offer the possibility of simultaneously respecting the need for effective democratic identifications, on which the republican tradition places such importance, *and* the openness and uncertainty of democratic politics and identity, as advocated in their different ways by Laclau and Mouffe and William Connolly (whose own response to Sandel I briefly consider toward the end of the chapter). Indeed, my argument is that a compassionate, nonmoralistic language of civic virtue and responsibility has particular promise for opening up space for the democratic identifications necessary to building effective *opposition* to the political closures that are so powerful today. That is, for democratic citizens to be able to name and mount effective resistance to the powerful forces and institutions that currently close down so much democratic possibility, and to be able to re-work the identifications that sustain those closures, we need languages with which citizens can talk among themselves about power — including our differential implications within it and the injustice it often entails. Yet unless those languages are nondualistic, resisting the temptations of guilt-seeking and moralistic denunciation, they threaten to produce the anger and resentment that can push some citizens toward more privatized, or limited, forms of identification, or away from the political realm entirely. The wager made in this chapter — and in the democratic practice of virtue it advocates — is that by fully respecting the fact — and the value — of the *openness* at the heart of the democratic "we," and the difficulty and uncertainty of any politics oriented toward it, one might prepare in the very language of one's appeals the ground for more sustainable forms of democratic identification and political engagement.

The Democratic Deficits of Procedural Liberalism

For Sandel, the vicious circle of public disinvestment is a predictable effect of the decades of hegemony of the language and practice of "liberal pro-

ceduralism." The liberal vision and language of the democratic "we," in
his reading, have proved too weak to sustain its own treasured set of
rights, much less any more robust practice of democratic self-rule. As
Sandel puts it in the very beginning of *Democracy's Discontent*, liberal
proceduralism "cannot secure the liberty it promises, because it cannot
inspire the sense of community and civic engagement that liberty
requires" (6). The liberal proceduralist consensus that Sandel sees existing across much of the American political spectrum, including both welfare state liberals and market conservatives, is unable to address what
Sandel sees as the two fundamental political issues of the day: first, the
feeling that citizens have lost control over the forces that shape their lives,
and, second, the sense among many that community ties and the shared
moral fabric are eroding. These two fears — the loss of self-government
and the erosion of community — are deeply linked and together define
what Sandel calls "democracy's discontent." The feeling of disempowerment in the economic and political sphere helps fuel the sense that the
community is no longer one's own, and the experience of a rapidly changing, more atomized, and morally diverse community undercuts for many
the identifications necessary to active political engagement and collective
control over political and economic powers. By offering no language in
which to discuss and imagine freedom as self-government, and by remov-
ing any officially sanctioned discourse of morality and civic virtue from
law and politics, procedural liberalism undermines the sense of shared
identification and responsibility necessary to sustaining an active democratic "we" and feeds an increasingly bitterly divided, moralistic, and
cynical political life.

In Sandel's reading, procedural liberalism is rooted in a voluntarist
conception of freedom, which understands freedom as the capacity of
individual moral agents to choose their own ends. In its popularized
Kantian form, it involves the belief that "since people disagree about the
best way to live, government should not affirm in law any particular
vision of the good life. Instead, it should provide a framework of rights
that respects persons as free and independent selves, capable of choosing
their own values and ends" (4). Thus "its central idea is that government
should be neutral toward the moral and religious views its citizens
espouse." For Sandel, this idea is enshrined most clearly in American politics in the landmark Supreme Court decisions that established a woman's
right to choose an abortion, that strictly limit a community's rights to
police nonpolitical speech that runs counter to its moral sensibilities, and
that ban the expression of religious belief in schools and other public
institutions and spaces. At times such proceduralism is argued to be necessary to respect the inherent dignity of the freely choosing self to express

and/or fulfill itself. At other times, the proceduralism aims more pragmatically to achieve a workable, reasonable, political arrangement among people — all of them worthy of equal respect — who have widely divergent visions of the good life. In either case, the guiding spirit of procedural liberalism is to achieve a certain kind of neutrality through excluding as much as possible the use of people's particular, substantive moral beliefs as the basis for law and public policy.

Sandel accepts that the theory of the proper limits of government and law at the heart of the "procedural republic" has a powerful political and psychological appeal. Its vision of the individual as, at least in principle, unencumbered by moral or civic ties they haven't chosen suggests a powerful argument for equal treatment and nondiscrimination across differences of race, gender, sexuality, and so forth, which are now understood as morally irrelevant characteristics overlaying the universal being deserving of respect. The liberal understanding of the self also seems to open the gates to much greater freedom, as one is freed from the constraints of tradition and unconscious assumptions, ultimately capable of becoming one's own master. This vision of the individual as master of his or her own destiny thus holds out the additional promise of a much less demanding political practice — one centered on the state merely enforcing a scheme of equal rights that gives individuals the choice to live their lives as they wish.

Alas, recent American political history has shown these latter two claims to be false, Sandel argues. Far from being able to master her own life merely on the basis of the neutral enforcement of an equal set of rights, the individual in the procedural republic finds herself increasingly bereft of the political tools necessary to secure her own liberty. By not offering a place — either theoretical or practical — from which individuals can identify as active members of a larger political community in which they share both power and responsibility, procedural liberalism proves unable to generate the obligations necessary to sustaining either liberal rights (particularly in their more egalitarian, redistributive, form) or the larger democratic system of self-governance. The liberalism predicated on individuals with no other responsibilities than those they have explicitly chosen so weakens the claims and experience of community that it proves unable to generate the collective action and allegiance necessary to face and control modern forms of power. As a result, the democratic promise of collective mastery of the forces that control citizens' lives grows ever more disappointing, and something like the vicious circle of public disinvestment begins to take hold. Indeed, Sandel argues, liberal proceduralism has proven incapable of even *speaking* to the "widespread sense that common purposes and shared understandings were eroding" and that "individually and collectively, Americans were losing control of the forces that governed their lives" (275). The expression and analysis of this condition, instead, are left to conservative, often racist and xenophobic populists, who see "government regulations" and the self-righteous imposition of outside standards by "liberal elites" as the real source of people's disempowerment and loss of community.

In this phenomenon, we see what Sandel identifies as liberalism's two blind spots — its inability to address either the experience of collective disempowerment or the sense of community eroded — come together: having banished moral and religious argument from public life, the larger political sphere is impoverished, without the moral and civic resources, the sense of shared purposes and fate, or the "qualities of character" necessary for effective self-government. That is, both the language and practice of liberal "neutrality" undermine one of the primary sources of democratic identification by denying people the right to see themselves and their moral sensibilities instituted in their community's practices and institutions. In doing so, it further "creates a moral void that opens the way for narrow, intolerant moralisms" (24), which exploit the anxieties of a weakened citizenry and try to satisfy "the yearning for a public life of larger meaning" (322). The inability of procedural liberalism to "contain the moral energies of democratic life" simultaneously leads to a public discourse "riveted on the private vices of public officials" and "preoccupied with the scandalous, the sensational, and the confessional" (323), further weakening the sense of politics as a sphere of life worthy of respect, interest, and devotion of time and resources.[13]

The political dangers of the self-undermining character of liberal proceduralism rest, Sandel argues, not in its achieving the neutral procedures it seeks but in the particular way in which it *fails* to remove moral questions from law and policy. For its proceduralism is in fact always substantive and moral. This is true, Sandel holds, both in liberalism's weaker, "political" or "minimalist" version, and in its stronger, Kantian, form. In the first instance, Sandel argues that difficult political, legal, and/or constitutional questions require us to make judgments about the moral value of particular practices, whether these concern abortion, slavery, homosexuality, or morally repugnant speech. In the name of respecting the equal worth of those who hold diverse moral visions and in the name of keeping the social peace in such a context, minimalist liberalism "wants to separate the case for toleration from any judgment about the moral worth of the practices being tolerated. But this separation is not always defensible. We cannot determine whether toleration is justified in any given case without passing moral judgment on the practice in question" (19–20). Being neutral with respect to a difficult moral question — for

example, abortion or slavery — is a reasonable position only on a particular reading of the moral question, that is, only if one doesn't think abortion is murder, or that slavery is a deep moral wrong. As a result, "the
moral price of political agreement is far higher if abortion is wrong than
if it is permissible. How reasonable it is to bracket the contending moral
and religious views depends partly on which of those views is more plausible" (21). Indeed, Sandel shows that the Supreme Court's decisions in
the abortion cases actually presupposed an answer to the controversial
question of when life begins, despite the Court's denials. He also shows
convincingly that the argument for remaining content neutral in free
speech cases, for instance, makes less and less sense the more problematic,
either socially or morally deleterious, the content of the speech or action
is understood to be. In short, once the value of liberal proceduralism is
understood to rest on a pragmatic, consequentialist argument about the
(negative) role of religious and moral convictions in political life rather
than on a controversial conception of the human person as unencumbered, it is easy to show that at least sometimes the consequences of
allowing practices of which one does not approve are worse than the risk
of social conflict or the cost of disrespecting diversity.

Minimalist liberalism, in short, must forsake its own neutrality — either
to judge the relative weights of social peace and moral harm, or else to fall
back on the controversial conception of the unencumbered self that it
claims to do without. To the extent that procedural liberals choose the latter road and justify their "neutrality" on a particular vision of the self, its
moral character, and the kinds of obligation that can rationally be
expected of it, they fall into other difficult traps, argues Sandel. As Sandel
has argued in earlier writings, the vision of the unencumbered self simply
"cannot make sense of our moral experience, because it cannot account
for certain moral and political obligations that we commonly recognize,
even prize. These include obligations of solidarity, religious duties, and
other moral ties that may claim us for reasons unrelated to choice" (13).
Through an analysis of a series of Supreme Court cases determining the
extent of the Constitution's protection of religious liberty, Sandel shows
how proceduralist liberal arguments often "confuse the pursuit of preferences with the exercise of [religious] duties, and so forgets the special concern of religious liberty with the claims of conscientiously encumbered
selves" (71). Thus the Court has shown little interest in making legal space
for those practices required of religious believers by their particular creeds:

Protecting religion as a life-style, as one among the values that an independent self
may have, may miss the role that religion plays in the lives of those for whom the
observance of religious duties is a constitutive end, essential to their good and
indispensable to their identity. Treating persons as "self-originating sources of

valid claims," may thus fail to respect persons bound by duties derived from sources other than themselves. (67)

Sandel shows how the same logic affects other legal domains as well. In the case of divorce law,

by treating all persons as bearers of a self independent of its roles, the new law fails to respect mothers and homemakers of traditional marriages whose identity is constituted by their roles, who have lived their married lives as situated selves. (113)

The cumulative effect of this general transformation in family law is to

burden the practice of marriage as a community in the constitutive sense. By bracketing moral judgments, celebrating self-sufficiency, and loosening the relation between the self and its roles, the law is not neutral among competing visions of married life, but recasts the institution of marriage in the image of the unencumbered self. (115)

Establishing a particular conception of liberal freedom in the law, then, doesn't simply "enlarge the range of possible lives; [it] also make[s] some ways of life more difficult, especially those like traditional marriage that involve a high degree of mutual dependence and obligation" (114).

Our Overlapping Alienations

Given that establishing a particular conception of liberal freedom in the law necessarily makes some ways of life more difficult, it is no surprise that many Americans see the rules and practices of the procedural republic not as neutral means to expand everyone's range of choice and possibilities but rather as aggressive impositions of alien standards and ways of life. For as Sandel shows convincingly across a wide range of issues, procedural liberalism not only fails its own test of neutrality but in so doing also fails to respect its own key values of offering equal respect and fostering social cooperation in a context of social and moral diversity. The effective disrespect that liberal proceduralism shows those with encumbered selves, especially in the context of the vicious circle of public disinvestment, helps explain further the rise of intolerant moralisms among social conservatives.

Charles Taylor offers a helpful way of understanding the corrosive effects that this situation, and the political alienation it produces, can have on democratic discourse and legitimacy. In an essay responding to *Democracy's Discontent*, Taylor points out the dangers that arise when large numbers of citizens with shared political identifications come to feel that their views are not, and perhaps cannot, be heard by the rest of the political community and thus that they are not a part of the larger "people" for purposes of deliberation, or for purposes of legitimacy. The danger here, in Taylor's analysis, is that

the sense "we're not being heard" is close to the sense: "we can't talk to those people; we can only defeat them." People engage in politics on issues which have aroused this reaction rather as though they were engaging in a war. The other side has to be wiped out or totally neutralized. The goal is . . . somehow to root them out, or subjugate them, so that one does not have to deal with what they stand for anymore.

In such conflicts, each side "den[ies] the other a legitimate place in the deliberative community. . . . This kind of polarization can make it very hard to address, and build majorities around other important issues, because the potential majorities lie athwart the division which is being thus absolutized."[14] In this way, then, the political alienation that procedural liberalism (among other things) produces among social conservatives and others with "encumbered" or role-bound identities — their sense of being locked in a system that doesn't allow them to be heard — exacerbates the vicious circle of public disinvestment introduced earlier and further undermines the collective identifications necessary to effective self-government.

Of course, things are even more complicated than this argument might suggest. Just as procedural liberalism is not the only factor behind the political anger and alienation of social and religious conservatives, so, too, such conservatives are not the only groups in the American polity that are alienated in the sense Taylor describes. Indeed, one can argue that the landscape of American politics today is largely constituted by a series of distinct but interconnected forms of political alienation. Thus what in the 1960s and 1970s was a relatively hegemonic and arrogant discourse of liberalism has now become increasingly embattled and alienated, in response to the conservative "backlash" that began to take root in the 1970s and 1980s, as well as to the increasingly distorted distributions of power both nationally and globally that the backlash helped promote. Thus, if many social conservatives see themselves as besieged by a culture of immorality, perversion, violence, and disorder, many liberals, and even more so those further to "the left," see themselves and their ideals as besieged by a host of increasingly unaccountable and unmanageable forces. (The dominant languages of liberalism may not be able to speak clearly to the loss of effective democratic self-government, but many political liberals certainly see and struggle against its negative effects.) The list of concerns runs from global warming and other forms of environmental degradation, the growing inequality of wealth across nation and globe, and the host of other socially dislocating effects of increasingly unregulated global markets, to the growing appeal and often violent expressions of "racial" and ethnic chauvinism, the massive and often hidden political power of ever larger corporations, and the profit- and entertainment-centered media that make public knowledge and discussion of such political trends more and more difficult. For all these reasons, anyone who retains a strong attachment to the democratic ideals of popular participation, open debate, and equal dignity for all has serious cause for feeling on the defensive, if not for feeling outright despair. Indeed, some part of the dismissive attitude of the liberal left toward the concerns of social and religious conservatives is arguably due precisely to their own sense of being embattled. When one is part of a group that feels socially alienated and largely powerless to influence its immediate world, it is hard to see that others so different, with such opposing viewpoints, could have similar attitudes that need to be taken into account.[15]

Overlapping with left-liberal alienation, to some degree, is the obvious and historically long-standing political alienation of racial and ethnic minorities, most striking among them being that of many African Americans. In this instance the legacy of slavery, legally sanctioned discrimination, continuing patterns of segregation and unequal opportunity, and resistance from the larger community to efforts at rectifying the lingering social and economic effects of this history all combine to produce among many African Americans a shared feeling of alienation, of not having their voices heard; to a lesser degree, other Americans not of European descent may experience similar feelings.[16] To the extent that African Americans and other minority groups suffer disproportionately high rates of poverty, unemployment, and other disadvantages of class, a second, related, form of alienation identified by Taylor is activated. In this case, members of a group feel that the solidarity that is supposed to bind members of the people into a people does not extend to them: the community's "mechanisms of mutual aid and succor" are not felt to reach to them. The two forms of alienation can, of course, and in this case do, reinforce each other, because the actual fact of not having one's views heard means that one receives less solidarity from the larger community, while the fact of exclusion from the larger circle of solidarity makes it harder in a host of ways for one's voice to be heard politically.

Our map of overlapping experiences of political alienation would be incomplete, finally, without including the particular sense of alienation many white working-class men began to experience in the 1960s and

1970s, in response to the arrogant and unskillful attempt of a politically (if not socially) hegemonic liberalism to end the exclusion of various other alienated groups by rectifying past patterns of discrimination and unequal opportunity. As William Connolly describes the process in a particularly illuminating analysis, a whole series of social and political developments in the 1960s and early 1970s — ranging from the civil rights movement, middle-class feminism and environmentalism, the American defeat in Vietnam, and the loss of many well-paying industrial jobs — called into question the "ideology of sacrifice" central to the self-identities of many "white, male, married factory workers with children."[17] For many such men, Connolly writes, "their dignity was primarily defined by their role as 'head of household,' their freedom by a willingness to sacrifice personal pleasures now to insulate their spouses from the rigors of the workplace and to improve future prospects for their children." Despite the many shortcomings of such an ideology for all involved, "sacrifice through work was pivotal to the identity of this constituency and to the political loyalties it cultivated to welfare-state liberalism" (111–12).

In this context, a powerful set of social transformations came to be "experienced as attacks on the very fundaments of [many working-class white men's] identity" by jeopardizing the relations between dignity, freedom, and sacrifice that the sense of identity depended on. Thus, for example, in Connolly's words,

> if welfare programs appear to be extended to minorities on the grounds that they are not responsible for their dependencies, then white blue-collar workers are implicitly deprived of recognition for the jobs they have secured; if women and minorities are promised affirmative action in employment because they have been discriminated against historically while upper-class male professionals are assumed to merit the positions they hold, then white male blue-collar workers are implicitly told that they are the only ones in the country who deserve to be stuck in menial jobs; if environmental programs sacrifice luxuries of consumption most available to the working class, then they threaten one of the compensatory outlets available to it; . . . and if the connection between a high school education and a decent job is broken while the costs of higher education escalate, then new members of the working class are held accountable for their failure to land good jobs and their children are denied the future promise that once vindicated the ideology of sacrifice. (112–13)

Although such liberal initiatives aimed to solve very real problems, "the rhetoric accompanying the new initiatives accentuated threats to the self-identity of white workers even when the initiatives themselves failed to make impressive inroads into the real injustices they identified" — all the while ignoring a host of hardships that particularly affected white male workers. The result was to "set up this core constituency of the welfare state for a hostile takeover by the American right."[18] More generally, it helped produce a "subject-position of the white male blue-collar worker" filled with rage and resentment and tempted by an ideology of "hyper-masculinity." For "if boys in this class are inducted into a traditional code of masculine authority and gender responsibility, if they then find it increasingly difficult to get jobs that embody that ideal, if liberal rhetoric addresses this vulnerable condition in ways that assault that masculinity without opening up viable alternatives to it," it is not surprising that many white men would be tempted by an ideology that "belligerently assert[s their] primordial rights against women, gays, intellectuals, and African-Americans" (114). This anger and alienation feed into and support similar feelings among social and religious conservatives, even though they also remain distinct social groupings in many respects.

The democratic "we" is thus under pressure in multiple ways and from multiple directions. Our democratic discontents are not only the result of liberal proceduralism's neglect of civic virtue and strong public institutions and practices. The overlapping and interconnected forms of alienation quickly sketched out above are powerfully *depoliticizing* for many, convincing them of the futility of political action aimed at having their voices heard or building a more representative, just, or moral community. For others, they lead to a particular form of democratic politics that paradoxically works to undermine its own sustainability. By fostering, among those still politically engaged, mutually alienating modes of discourse and a winner-take-all mentality, it shrinks the imagined community to which one owes responsibility. This, in turn, further undermines the possibility of finding common ground in favor of public institutions and spaces that could pose some counterweight to otherwise unaccountable market and governmental forces. This helps shrink the political "we" in an additional way, by producing a bitter and divisive mode of political interaction that helps turn many less politically active citizens off of political activity per se, thus ceding further control to unaccountable forces unconcerned with the common good. Hence the vicious circle of public disinvestment is strengthened. In such a simultaneously depoliticized and hyperpoliticized context, what can civic virtue and an attachment to common things mean? Are there forms of democratic language and political activity that can help put the "we" together in ways that nonetheless respect its fundamental plurality and that make it possible for its constituents parts to struggle together in sustainable, rather than destructive, ways? Could there be developed forms of political engagement and politicizing language able to acknowledge and speak to one group's fears and suffering without alienating or disrespecting those of others?

Retrieving a Politics of Virtue

For Sandel, an effective response to democracy's discontent involves the revival, in a suitably pluralist form, of those forms of *virtue* necessary to democratic freedom and self-governance. This requires, in turn, that we remember and learn once again to make use of the republican, and not just the liberal, conception of liberty. As Sandel puts it, "republican political theory teaches that to be free is to share in governing a political community that controls its own fate. Self-government in this sense requires political communities that control their destinies, and citizens who identify sufficiently with those communities to think and act with a view to the common good" (274). How, though, to bring into being this kind of identification? The answer comes through virtue:

> to share in self-rule . . . requires that citizens possess, or come to acquire, certain qualities of character, or civic virtues. . . .
> . . . Insofar as certain dispositions, attachments, and commitments are essential to the realization of self-government, republican politics regards moral character as a public, not merely private, concern. In this sense, it attends to the *identity*, not just the interests, of its citizens. (5–6 and 25, emphasis added)

Such virtues are thus to be cultivated in part by recognizing and making use of those activities and attachments that encumbered selves see as essential to their identity:

> the republican tradition emphasizes the need to cultivate citizenship through particular ties and attachments. . . . Family, neighborhood, religion, trade unions, reform movements, and local government all offer examples of practices that have at times served to educate people in the exercise of citizenship by cultivating the habits of membership and orienting people to common goods beyond their private ends. (117)

What exactly "virtue" means in this context, though, remains tantalizingly uncertain in Sandel's analysis.[19] Put briefly, what exactly is the relation between *civic* virtue and virtue as such? To what extent, that is, does what we might call the "procedural" aspect of civic virtue — those attributes that orient one's actions toward the common good — depend on a more extensive, "substantive," conception about how to live a good, proper, correct life? What, in other words, is the relation between the "moral character" of a good citizen and that of a good person? How deep and how restrictive are the traits necessary to make one into a good "member" of the community? How "open" can Sandel's republican identifications be? Throughout *Democracy's Discontent*, Sandel seems torn between a fairly strong, basically Aristotelian, understanding of virtue and a more "proceduralist," self-reflexive, cosmopolitan variety.[20]

Recognizing in the abstract that the "formative politics" necessary for republican freedom makes it a "risky politics, a politics without guarantees" (321), Sandel explicitly refuses any direct endorsement of a particular conception of civic virtue. He argues, in fact, that the aim of a revival of the republican version of freedom is not to produce a more consensual form of politics but instead merely to shift the terms of political debate. Rather than arguments centered on "the meaning of neutrality, right, and truly voluntary choice, a political agenda informed by civic concerns would invite disagreement about the meaning of virtue and the forms of self-government that are possible in our time" (338).

Yet for this shift in the terms of debate to have the kind of practical meaning and impact Sandel and other republicans wish it to have, it would, of course, to some degree at least, have to open up greater room for community and/or state influence on individuals' behavior and choices. Thus Sandel feels compelled to address more directly the risks entailed by the formative nature of republican politics and to argue that the risks can be mitigated in a number of ways. First of all, he argues, character formation in healthy republican politics would draw from the lessons of Tocqueville rather than Rousseau. It would aim to develop "the habit of attending to public things," not a single identification with an unchallengeable general will. This habit would involve not merely a willingness and ability to feel attached to the common good, for instance, but also "the independence and judgment to deliberate well about" what that good is (320). As suggested by Sandel's various examples of "schools of citizenship" above, the habits of membership are also to be learned in a multiplicity of different sites and through a variety of practices. Deliberation about the common good, then, would generally involve much "clamour" and contentious debate. Hence, too, Sandel's advocacy of a more robust variety of federalism, understood as "a political vision that offers an alternative to the sovereign state and the univocal political identities such states require" and that believes "self-government works best when sovereignty is dispersed and citizenship formed across multiple sites of engagement" (347). In these various ways, then, the dangers of greater community involvement in the formation of personal character would be reduced, and the plurality and contestation necessary to democratic politics preserved.

According to Sandel, this particular mode of republican virtue politics would also require a corresponding conception — and practice — of the self: although this would be an encumbered self, which accepts that it can have obligations beyond those it explicitly chooses, it would also be a "multiply-encumbered" and reflective self. Its central quality of character would be "the disposition to see and bear one's life circumstances as a reflectively situated being — claimed by the history that implicates me in a particular life, but self-conscious of its particularity, and so alive to other ways, wider horizons" (16). Sandel is sharply critical of the cosmopolitan ideal of citizenship and its belief that abstract identifications with humankind as a whole can be politically efficacious, and that they necessarily take moral precedence over more particular ones. Yet while Sandel argues that all effective identifications are rooted in particular experiences and locations and the attachments they produce, he nevertheless accepts that these relatively local identifications can be more or less expansive and more or less open to challenge and reconfiguration. There is a need, that is, for a self whose identifications match the complexity and multiple layers that make up the globalized political landscape — we need not only to turn from Rousseau's republicanism to Tocqueville's but also to bring Tocqueville into the twenty-first century. And because the sites and forms of identification necessary to effective citizenship are now multiple — ranging from local neighborhoods to nations to the globe — political and social life will be filled with conflict both within and between selves. Indeed, one could say that the multiply-situated self is a dilemma- and conflict-ridden self, given that its various allegiances and identifications (religious, professional, gender, ethnic, national, ideological, geographic) and the multiple "common goods" these entail need to be balanced and chosen among constantly.

On the abstract level, Sandel recognizes the existence of such dilemmas. Not only do we "find ourselves claimed, at one time or another, by a wide range of different communities, some overlapping, other contending," but when their obligations conflict Sandel accepts that "there is no way of deciding in advance, once and for all, which should prevail." Those caught in such dilemmas can only do their best to decide according to "the content of the claims, their relative moral weight, and their role in the narratives by which the participants make sense of their lives" (343–44). Indeed, on the book's penultimate page, Sandel abruptly shifts his discussion of civic virtue from a concern with very particular, situated moral decisions to a new, meta-level of analysis. Thus, in Sandel's words, "the civic virtue distinctive to our time is the capacity to negotiate our way among the sometimes overlapping, sometimes conflicting obligations that claim us, and to *live with the tension* to which multiple loyalties give rise. This capacity is difficult to sustain, for it is easier to live with the plurality between persons than within them" (350, emphasis added).

About how to sustain this admirable capacity to live with the tension of multiple identities and multiple obligations, however, Sandel has little to say. He calls on us to recognize and avoid what he sees as the contrasting dangers that this condition characteristically produces: on the one hand, the fundamentalist intolerance of ambiguity and the desire for simple stories and identities, and, on the other hand, the formlessness of postmodern selves who have given up on achieving personal narrative coherence of any kind. But he is left with nothing to say about how to achieve this middle way, how to "weave the various strands of [one's] identity into a coherent whole" without falling into forms of fundamentalism — nor about how a sustainable political practice of the common good might emerge from the complexity of overlapping attachments and identifications within and between citizens. Instead, Sandel's insight into the need for a form of civic virtue specific to today's radically pluralist conditions remains largely a gesture of good intentions.

Not having the theoretical resources to pursue his pluralist insight further, Sandel is almost ineluctably drawn instead by the logic of his critique of liberalism toward a fairly strong, and democratically risky, mode of virtue politics. In following this path, he ignores crucial issues of political power, downplaying the concrete risks in republican formative politics that he abstractly recognizes. Particularly telling here is his support for the turn to "virtue" in debates over welfare, crime, and the breakdown of "family values." Without explicitly arguing for any particular set of policies, or proposing an overarching guideline for deciding such issues, Sandel clearly lends his sanction to a whole host of social policies that aim to police the personal behavior of individuals, especially those dependent on government support, in the name of "producing" "good" citizens. Thus he endorses the critique of welfare policy and the "nanny state" as having "bred dependence among recipients and rewarded immoral and irresponsible behavior" (325), and he praises efforts to "reorder the personal lives of the poor" now that the "connection between our deepest beliefs and our legislative agenda" is once again something that can be established in political practice (326). He quotes with approval one commentator's lament that "American political discourse 'fails to engage questions of personal morality,' of 'character and values. . . . The public debate gives only muted voice to the judgment that it is wrong to be sexually promiscuous, to be indolent and undisciplined, to be disrespectful of legitimate authority, or to be unreliable, untruthful, or unfaithful'" (327). Against these attempts to reinject moral judgments into those policies that affect individual behavior, Sandel juxtaposes — and impatiently rejects — what he calls "the nonjudgmental reflex characteristic of contemporary liberalism" that holds simply that "'everyone has different moral standards. You can't impose your standards on someone else'" (328).

Civic virtue as it is understood in this discussion seems very far removed from Sandel's ideal of those highly contestatory, reflective, self-critical abilities required to balance a citizen's competing identities and attachments. Instead, Sandel's text seems to endorse a model of the virtuous citizen as one who accepts the embeddedness of her identity within, and thus her debt to, the larger community by matching her personal behavior to the existing standards of what it means to be a good, decent, upstanding person. Here civic virtue is more a matter of following the guidelines the community gives you on how to live your life than it is of learning "the habit of attending to public things" so as to take on responsibilities larger than one's personal interest and be an active participant in collective decision-making.

Sandel's retreat from the more complex vision of the virtuous citizen to the more traditional and moralized one is due in part, I would argue, to the absence from his analysis of any sense of the political and power dynamics at work in the making and imposing of moral judgments about others' personal behavior, especially when those others are disproportionately poor and/or nonwhite. Thus when Sandel criticizes the liberal argument that "the attempt to regulate the moral character of welfare recipients [is] an unjust case of 'legislating morality,'" he slides quickly over one of the central claims of this position: that what is being imposed in such cases are "standards of morality which are a matter of free choice for other citizens" (286). In other words, some people are being made to follow rules that other "good citizens" with more money or political power can choose to ignore, and, what's more, they are often told to do so in the name of an ethic of individual "self-reliance" that Sandel would elsewhere be the first to challenge. Although Sandel recognizes in an abstract sense the dangers of formative politics, his actual analysis of contemporary American politics of virtue seems surprisingly unaware of the antiliberal and antidemocratic dangers such an approach can entail. His endorsement of personal virtue politics is in fact doubly depoliticizing: by ignoring the political and ideological agendas of the proponents of this sort of virtue, he implicitly endorses their turn away from political and social analysis of the sources of poverty, welfare dependence, crime, broken families. We thus end up with a conception of virtue miles away from the highly reflective, self-critical, generous-spirited one that Sandel would like, in principle, to endorse. We are also further away from the kind of collective self-awareness — for instance, of the causes and complexity of poverty and urban social dislocation — that is necessary for effective democratic self-rule.[21]

None of this is to argue that there is no room in democratic politics for analyzing and responding to the ways in which personal character traits can be implicated in entrenched social problems like crime, poverty, family dislocations, and so forth, nor that there should be no recourse to religious, or spiritual, or commonly held moral teachings and beliefs in addressing such problems. As we have seen earlier, Sandel shows convincingly that the law can never escape involvement in what he calls "moral" issues. This doesn't mean, however, that the law and policy require making the kinds of *moralizing* judgments of personal behavior that liberal voluntarists attack. Sandel slides from the one to the other, it seems, for two related reasons. First, because he assumes that the kinds of issues he calls "moral" ones can only be addressed through the enforcement of rules; and second, because he remains trapped in a vision of virtue and "morality" as residing either in the decisions of the free individual who chooses his own rules or in the community that imposes its rules on encumbered individuals. Sandel's attachment to these two assumptions forces him, once he has revealed the limits and inadequacies of the liberal voluntarist model, to turn back to the strong community-based model of virtue enforcement. Even more disappointing, though, is that he does so without any recognition of the personal and democratic costs of imposing such standards, much less any argument for why those costs — to personal autonomy, or to egalitarian principles — are outweighed by some greater benefit. All this is despite his own insight into the dilemma-ridden character of contemporary politics and civic virtue and the difficult nature of the situated judgments it demands.

Take, for example, his description of the 1943 Supreme Court decision that struck down state laws requiring children to salute the flag, a decision Sandel sees as a pivotal and exemplary moment in the more general midcentury shift from a republican theory of liberty to a liberal theory of freedom. According to Sandel's reading of the new liberal philosophy of the Court, "government could not impose on its citizens any particular conception of the good life: 'no official, high or petty, can prescribe what shall be orthodox in politics, nationalism, religion, or other matters of opinion.' Patriotism would now be a matter of choice, not of inculcation, a voluntary act by free and independent selves" (279). Here we see a particularly clear example of how Sandel's treatment of virtue remains overly rule-bound and locked within a false dichotomy of individual (choice) versus community (command). Sandel's critique of the Court's decision assumes that we face a choice between a process of "inculcation" that "prescribes orthodoxy" and a voluntarism of independent selves. But what about a form of "inculcation," or cultivation, that isn't a matter of prescription (or proscription) and that works with selves who have choice but aren't simply independent? The fact that the Court rules out those forms of inculcation that prescribe "orthodox" opinions doesn't mean that it has ruled out other means of instilling respect for one's political institutions or the cultivation of civic identification, and virtue. And the fact that the *freedom* of citizens to form their own minds on such issues must be respected doesn't mean citizens must be understood as fully *independent*. Why must our political discourse and imaginaries be limited to such stark choices? Indeed, throughout *Democracy's Discontent*, Sandel forces us into choosing either the free and independent self of Kantian voluntarism or the theory of an encumbered self whose moral and religious beliefs are so essential to and definitive of its "identity" that they must be allowed into democratic debate not merely as one element among many but as a proper basis for determining law and public policy.[22]

A crucial element here is Sandel's frequent — although not always explicit — reliance on a model of "identity" that sees it as existing before individual choice and beyond political negotiation. Criticizing procedural liberalism's consensus approach to free speech, for instance, Sandel defends the objections of the citizens of Skokie, Illinois, many of whom were Jewish survivors of the Holocaust, to permitting Nazis to march through their town. Defending the community's refusal to "bracket its abhorrence," Sandel argues that "given their shared memory and resolve to bear witness, the survivors could not bracket their view of the Nazis without destroying something essential to their identity" (85). Sandel's endorsement of conservative, often coercive, virtue politics, would, in turn, seem both to support and to be supported by this conception of identity. It would also, regrettably, seem to lend credence to many liberals' dismissive readings of Sandel. Thus the attack by the liberal philosopher Amartya Sen, who cites in particular an earlier text by Sandel in which he writes that "community describes not just what they have as fellow citizens but also what they are, not a relationship they choose (as in a voluntary association) but an attachment they discover, not merely an attribute but a constituent of their identity."[23] In response, Sen is quick to argue that claims by Sandel that identity is prior to choice ignore the ways in which all identities are ultimately *identifications*, and thus in principle open to critical judgment and reformulation. Sen and other procedural liberals can also point to the violence and antidemocratic dangers that accompany any form of politics that denies such reflection and choice.

This reading of Sandel's notion of the "encumbrances" of identity, however, is not the only one possible. To argue that one "discovers" the attachments one has to others as much as one chooses them, or that relations with others are "not merely" "attributes" but also "constituents" of identity, is fully consistent with accepting that choice can play a crucial role in identity. For "identity" need not be either fully chosen or fully "essential." In fact, the encumbered nature of the self, and Sandel's critique of voluntarist liberalism, is most powerfully understood as referring to the fact that any attachments or identifications one makes, while they can be both chosen and the product of serious reflection, are nonetheless always chosen against the background of other beliefs and assumptions that aren't themselves, at that moment of decision, open to choice, a background that is as, or more, definitive of one's "identity" as one's choices.[24] Indeed, this seems to be the basic thrust of Sandel's own argument for the "reflectively situated" nature of identity, in which I am "claimed by the history that implicates me in a particular way of life, but self-conscious of its particularity, and so alive to other ways, wider horizons" (16).

Unfortunately, Sandel's own, more frequent, insistence that we face a choice between a strong liberal theory of identity and morality and a strongly communitarian and essentialist one, an insistence that is ratified by his endorsement of conservative virtue politics, hides this other reading from view. This is particularly regrettable for those who haven't given up on the value of more participatory and contestatory forms of democracy, since it allows procedural liberals to ignore Sandel's critique of the theoretical inadequacies and negative political effects of their own "neutrality" and of the specific form of moralism *it* breeds. In particular, it allows a more psychological, more plausible, and more politically astute, understanding of Sandel's theory of encumbered selves to be lost from sight. In this alternate reading, Sandel's most interesting point would be that for large numbers of people, under particular, quite common, circumstances, certain identifications *feel* unavoidable, unchosen, as if they were natural and as if any attempt to change them would do great violence to their "true" self or identity. Regardless of how much one's sense of self and place in the world is in fact a matter of *identification*, and thus revisable, it often seems to many to be an *identity*. The political problem with procedural liberalism that Sandel points to, on this reading, is that it can only look down on such people, seeing their sense of encumbrance as a sign of moral weakness. Liberals are thus generally incapable of creating the conditions in which people would be more likely to approach their identifications in a more reflective, critical, experimental manner (or in which liberals themselves would be able to approach their own underlying assumptions in a similar way). The real disappointment of Sandel's argument is that his own text covers over this reading, and, except for occasional gestures toward a more complex understanding of identity and virtue, seems able to respond to liberalism's inadequacies only by arguing that the moral(izing) judgments of encumbered selves must be accepted as sources for our political and legal decisions.

The Virtues — and Limits —
of a Civic Pluralist Response

In part because of his own unnecessarily cramped understanding of identity, Sandel is forced into a deeply moralistic understanding of virtue. As a result, I am arguing, he is unable to pursue his own pluralist, "dilemma-conscious," insights into the requirements of civic virtue today. Because Sandel conflates morality and moralizing, or perhaps more accurately, because he defines virtue as a matter of following moral rules, he never takes *moralism itself* as his target. To do so would be to see that insisting on a choice between the dismissive moralizing of procedural liberalism and the conservative virtue politics that attempts to mold individual behavior to a majority's moral vision only ratifies the cycle of moralizing and countermoralizing that directly feeds the vicious circle of public disinvestment and its related forms of political disenchantment. In this sense it is what procedural liberals and virtue conservatives have in common that must be analyzed and challenged if one is to respond effectively to democracy's present discontents. In a recent treatment of *Democracy's Discontent*, William Connolly elaborates a similar line of criticism and begins to sketch the broad outlines of a more generous form of "virtue politics," one that might better resist the counterproductive moralizing of so much contemporary American politics.[25] Connolly's treatment of Sandel's turn to virtue and of the American liberal–conservative dialectic more generally is worth considering at some length, both for its insights into the dangers of too simple a "return" to republican conceptions of civic virtue and for what its own limitations imply about the kind of non-moralistic language of politicization that would best be able to navigate the particularly difficult waters of democratic politics today.

As is suggested by his analysis of the self-destructive nature of liberal disrespect of white working-class concerns, Connolly is in broad sympathy with Sandel's challenge to procedural liberalism. He also agrees with Sandel that liberal proceduralism is anything but neutral; indeed, he extends this challenge to liberal "neutralism" to include a critique of what he calls "liberal fundamentalism," by which he means the refusal of many liberals to submit their own fundamental beliefs to interrogation and their labeling of those who attempt such questioning as beyond the pale of "reason" or "reasonableness." He argues that the failure of many liberals to acknowledge that "the root assumptions of liberal dogma are anything but neutral, necessary, or incontestable" helps provoke rage and resentment among conservatives, who chafe at the imposition of "a liberal creed upon others in the name of a universal reason, a natural subject of rights, a neutral state, or a fictive contract conveniently skewed in favor of liberal presumptions and priorities" (FA 123). "When liberals remain deaf to charges of bias and hypocrisy leveled against them, they deepen and extend this rage. This is precisely how some versions of liberalism help to exacerbate the fundamentalist temper they set themselves against: they project fundamentalism solely onto the other and fail to recognize the strains in themselves" (FA 125).

Yet even as Connolly accepts much of Sandel's critique of procedural liberalism, he challenges Sandel's too easy adoption of the terms of many of its conservative critics. Connolly is particularly critical of the way in which Sandel misses the violence underlying the political vision of conservative virtue theorists like William Bennett, "skat[ing] too lightly over the connection between Bennett's quest to reinstate old unities and his conversion of republican virtues into contemporary weapons of cultural war in the domains of race, ethnicity, religion, gender, and sexuality" (CR 206). To Connolly's ear, Bennett's "endlessly reiterated phrase, 'the American people' . . . simultaneously summons a yearning for identity between individual and nation and identifies a diverse host of individuals, perhaps even a majority, falling below this threshold of tolerance in one way or another" (CR 206). Indeed, for Connolly, violence is built into the very republican imaginary, especially under conditions of globalization and the increasing pluralization of identities of all sorts. Despite Sandel's claims to mitigate the excesses of republican formative politics by relying on the thought of Tocqueville rather Rousseau, Connolly argues that "nostalgia for a republicanism of self-contained islands of political action cannot hope to consolidate itself today; such an ideal can only foster melancholy or the angry translation of traditional republican virtues into weapons of cultural war against vulnerable constituencies held responsible for failure to attain the impossible end" (CR 209). For Connolly, neither republicanism, organized around a single concept of the common good, nor the liberalism that tries to aggregate the divergent interests of ethically unencumbered constituencies, is able today to generate a sustainable form of democratic politics: "the former promotes cultural war between dogmatic contenders to occupy the cultural center while the latter fosters neglect of the mediating institutions upon which a robust pluralism rests. Such political action in concert emerges — if and when it does — out of a dense plurality in which many constituencies fold the cardinal virtues of civic pluralism into the relations they establish with others" (CR 210). "Civic pluralism" names here Connolly's deconstructive escape hatch from the dead-end conflict between republicanism and voluntarism.

Thus Connolly begins to explore what Sandel can only gesture helplessly toward: those "distinctive virtues needed to negotiate relations upon and between" the different "planes of action" along which "contemporary citizens are situated" (CR 210). In Connolly's civic pluralism, "sharing . . . commonalities between citizens" must be accompanied by "an equally important engagement of differences between them." Here he claims that what civic pluralism needs in order to flourish are "citizens who affirm comparative elements of contingency and contestability in those identities—those 'encumbrances'—that define them most dramatically; who establish relations of agonistic respect with faiths, even those of a philosophic and nontheistic bent, that challenge their own sources of moral inspiration; who cultivate critical responsiveness to surprising social movements that propel new identities into being out of old injuries, differences, and energies" (CR 210). Most crucial here is the argument that constructing the kind of common ground (however shifting and provisional) across diverse identities and constituencies that is crucial to democratic pluralism is more likely to be achieved "when none of these groups construct their identities through demonization of the other." When the engagement of differences

occurs without cultural demonization of either party by the other, each is *placed in an improved position* to appreciate elements of contingency (genetic, cultural, or both) in the organization of its own identity. This latter *experience disrupts* the destructive temptation to treat what you already are in each domain of identity as the paradigm of morality itself; *that effect, in turn, helps* you to cultivate the responsive civic sensibility needed for citizenship in a democracy marked by considerable diversity of class, region, religious belief, irreligion, ethnicity, sexuality, gender performance, and household organization. (CR 208, emphases added)

How, though, can this virtuous circle be gotten off the ground? This is the central question that even Connolly's compelling critique of traditional understandings of political identity doesn't quite address. One way of getting at this is to point out that it is not obvious that what Connolly here presents as separate steps or stages on the way to a democratic and plural form of civic virtue are so clearly separable. Isn't it more likely, for instance, that a true "appreciation" of "elements of contingency in the organization of [one's] identity" will have to precede, rather than follow from, a nondemonizing engagement with cultural and political difference? And isn't this appreciation just another way of describing what it is to have ceased to treat one's own "identity" as the paradigm of morality, rather than, as Connolly presents it here, a step on the way to this achievement? The crucial question remains, then, how to transform the appreciation of the contingency of identity from an idea, or ideal, into the actual "experience" that Connolly seems to imply will follow from the nondemonization of difference. How can "the responsive civic sensibility" Connolly wants to cultivate be translated from a theoretical recognition into an actual *practice* of identity? Although Connolly is persuasive in *naming* the virtues necessary to a sustainable form of democratic politics today, we are left without a sense of where their social or psychological sources might lie. In a sense, then, although at a different level, Connolly faces the same problem he diagnoses in Sandel: his approach works only if people are already generously inclined toward differences, yet there are few suggestions about how to get people to be generous or open in the ways required. And as Connolly himself recognizes at various points in his recent work, his challenge is made more difficult by the complex and entrenched cycles of public disinvestment and inequality we explored earlier. Being major sources of anger, fear, and resentment, these cycles act as powerful obstacles to generosity and openness of identity.[26]

A further problem follows from this. In his struggle to move from theorizing the virtues necessary to pluralist republican citizenship to suggesting how they might best be cultivated, Connolly, too — like all theorists of virtue, even those of the virtues of respecting difference and "otherness" — runs the risk of moralizing. That is, without augmentation, his argument threatens to boil down to chastising people like Sandel and Bennett — and, what is more important, those who find their arguments appealing — for not being generous or open enough to difference. Perhaps the most important task facing democrats of a radical and/or pluralist variety today is the very difficult one of being both politically and theoretically critical toward, and yet still generous with, the ungenerous (including those strains of nongenerosity in themselves). As I explore at greater length in the closing sections of the chapter, this mode of political engagement could be encouraged by a language that both accepts one's own implication in the actions and practices of identity that one is criticizing *and* appeals to the latent openness and possibility of transformation that reside in those one is criticizing. The danger here is that despite his best intentions, Connolly's position threatens to reproduce something very close to the liberal disrespect of cultural conservatives that Sandel and Taylor diagnose, only now in the name of a different, even more challenging democratic ideal of difference and openness.

To his credit, Connolly recognizes the dangers of moralism and the need for liberal and secularist democrats to build bridges to more conservative, religious, believers. This is possible, according to Connolly, only by taking up the challenge of what he calls postfundamentalism (his only slightly tongue-in-cheek reformulation of *postmodernism*), which takes as one of its central projects that of escaping the negative, and democratically speaking, self-destructive, dialectic of liberal and conservative fundamentalism. In his essay "Fundamentalism in America," Connolly explains that "a postfundamentalist liberalism would strive to expose and acknowledge the contestability of the fundaments governing *it*, including its governing conception of morality. It would struggle to introduce a new generosity into rivalries between alternative perspectives *based upon recognition of their reciprocal contestability* (FA 128, emphasis added). Postfundamentalism is built on the belief that one's ethical responsibilities can never be reduced to any general code of right and wrong, good and bad (or evil). Its guiding ethical spirit, then, is "to struggle against the temptation to allow an existing code of authority or justice to dominate the field of ethics entirely; the ethical idea is to maintain a critical tension between a congealed code of authority and justice and a more porous fund of critical responsiveness that might be drawn upon to modify it in the light of contemporary injuries it engenders and positive possibilities it ignores" (FA 127).

As one example of how the "cultivation of critical responsiveness to difference" might work, Connolly suggests that divergences between secular liberals and fundamentalist Christians on issues like abortion and feminism could be "phrased differently" to positive effect. Thus instead of insisting that a woman's right to choose an abortion is inviolate because "grounded in reason or the primordial character of the individual," liberals should highlight how "both this presumption and the opposing contention that a divine spark resides in life from the moment of conception reflect contestable dogmas of faith." And "since neither can be proven, since, surely, the state is incapable of doing so, abortion cannot be proved to be murder." If this is the case, then liberals can appeal to the Protestant tradition's own belief in "soul competency" (the ability of all persons to commune with God in their own terms) and its "respect for a diversity of faiths" as reasons to accept that "the particular faith of each adult should be determinative in exactly this territory" (FA 130). The hope here is that by presenting the liberal position as *one faith among many*, rather than the expression of reason or nature itself, and by appealing to, and thus showing respect for, the traditions of American Protestantism, liberals might generate in return at least some grudging "agonistic respect" from religious conservatives. The de-escalation of liberal rhetoric away from its fundamentalist temptation might work to reduce conservative defensiveness and fundamentalist aggression.

Although the basic rhetorical and psychological "logic" at work here seems sound, its limitations also seem severe. For it leaves unanswered the central question of how to get a politicized Christian to accept that her central beliefs — and the "fundaments of her identity" — are contestable. One could, of course, always try to offer a philosophical argument to this effect, but Connolly wisely refuses to go down this path, for the obvious reason that—except for those very few who might be persuaded to change their minds—it would appear as the imposition of a foreign, biased, mode of argumentation, one that the religious believer would be quick to reject as stacking the rhetorical deck against her. Yet in some ways, this is very close to the move that Connolly actually makes: for the crucial step in his hypothetical exchange over abortion is the acceptance by both sides that neither of their "faiths" can offer a definitive "proof" that abortion is murder. Yet what is the Bible to the conservative Christian but the carrier of God's own word and thus the highest possible form of proof (especially when it comes to issues of morality)? Doesn't Connolly's liberal–conservative dialogue depend on both sides accepting what is effectively a liberal secular standard of proof? How is this likely to succeed in moving a politicized Christian toward accepting the contestability of her faith? Indeed, rejecting use of the Bible's incontestable authority in one's engagement with politicized religious believers would surely be read by many of them as yet another attempt to surreptitiously dictate liberal modernist standards in the name of impartiality.

What I am suggesting here is that despite his persuasive analyses of the central role that identity concerns play in contemporary democratic politics, the strategies Connolly outlines under the names of "civic pluralism" and "postfundamentalism" seem in surprising ways to downplay the full power that existential, identity anxieties—reacting to and upon social and political factors—have to block the kind of generous, "open" democratic politics he promotes. Beginning, in however generous and self-critical a spirit, with a frontal assault on the contestability of people's fundamental faiths and on the contingency of their identities would seem likely to heighten precisely the kinds of fear and insecurity (at the threatened loss of certainty and control) that fuel so much of fundamentalist faith. It might, instead, be a wiser strategy first (or at least simultaneously) to recognize more directly the psychological power and even the legitimacy of the anger, fear, and anxiety felt by religious and social conservatives at what they see as the moral decline and loss of values that characterize today's society and culture. There is, of course, much that a good liberal democrat, especially of the postfundamentalist sort, can take issue with in the particular ways that many politicized religious and social conservatives frame the analysis of this condition and with the agents they locate as responsible—all of this Connolly does with particular subtlety in "Fundamentalism in America." Yet surely there is much room to acknowledge the sense of insecurity and anxiety provoked by the uncertainties that accompany the recent and deep challenges to traditional family, gender, and social roles and patterns that have occurred over the past three or four decades. It would then be crucial here to separate out these understandable, if politically regrettable, psychological and political reactions against challenges to tradition from the often quite legitimate concerns that social conservatives raise about the ways in which the liberal language of rights and self-expression interacts with the commercial aims of largely unaccountable media conglomerates to produce a society whose central public values seem to be greed, celebrity, violence, self-exposure, and ever more "extreme" forms of pleasure.

Indeed, some such acknowledgment would seem especially necessary for a project like postfundamentalism. For the social dislocations and instabilities, and the sense of powerlessness at stemming their tide, that provoke conservative fear and anger are easily interpreted as part and parcel of liberal, secular, modernity, of which the project of accepting the contingency and contestability of the fundamental aspects of our identity would seem merely another part. Connolly himself hints at these connections when he argues that conservative fundamentalism, hedonism, drug taking, and careerism are all divergent responses to the more general loss of faith in what he calls "the civilization of productivity," which continues to define (for lack of any viable alternative) "late modernity." As we saw earlier, Connolly makes central to his analysis the crucial role that the alienation of white working- and middle-class men has played in the decline of American liberalism and the need for any liberal-democratic project to address their legitimate grievances. He seems less concerned, though, with the need or possibility of reaching out in a similar manner to religious and social conservatives by recognizing the legitimacy of their fears and frustration, if not the wisdom of their preferred responses. Without such gestures, though, a political project based on the acceptance of contingency and contestability, and on the fostering of a radically open practice of identity, would seem guaranteed to appear to many as just one more manifestation of a society without clear values or beliefs, and thus to provoke more such fear and resentment.[27]

The very language of pluralist democratic engagement must, in other words, be infused with a large dose of compassion, with which one understands the sense of cultural dislocation felt by cultural conservatives and Christians caught in a liberal, highly sexualized, antihistorical, hypermodernized, consumer culture. This infusion might, to some small extent, open up space for greater political common ground between socially conservative and left-liberal critiques of the destructive effects of today's "hypermodernism." More important for my central argument, though, is that this form of compassion would allow liberals to see conservative fear and anger as rooted in processes of identification and identity formation in which all people are caught. That is, an effective language of democratic responsibility and civic virtue also requires some means of recognizing the common ground we all share in being subject to the insecurity, fear, rage, and resentment that are inevitable aspects of the experience of self-identity. The "appreciation" of the contingency of identity that Connolly wants to foster is likely to reduce demonization of the other and thus to increase the possibilities for new democratic alliances only to the extent that this *universal* experience of identity and its burdens is also publicly acknowledged in the very activity of political argument and criticism. Without this two-part strategy, the deconstructive approach to identity advocated by Connolly risks amounting to a hyperliberalism, available only to that narrow class of citizens theoretically and socially advanced enough to have "transcended" more closed, ungenerous practices of identity.

The Antidemocratic Effects of Moralism and Cynicism

We have seen above how Sandel's valuable critique of liberalism's "virtue deficit" is severely weakened both theoretically and politically by his assumption that virtue is primarily a matter of following the correct set of rules, an assumption tied closely to his unduly restricted conception of identity. Connolly's critique of Sandel and the alternatives he proposes under the banner of "civic pluralism" and "postfundamentalism" aims to challenge the same basic tendencies in Sandel — and in the reigning orthodoxies of American liberalism and conservatism. What Connolly names as fundamentalism is very close to the "moralism" that I explore and criticize in the following section. However, to exploit more fully the democratic possibilities of the open and contested practice of identity and faith that Connolly recommends, the more generous relation to difference and political conflict he begins to sketch out needs to be developed into a more fully and effectively nonmoralistic mode (and language) of political engagement and responsibility. The closing section of the chapter offers a tentative sketch of what such a language of political engagement and responsibility would look like, the specific vision of the democratic "we" it works with, and how it might help cultivate a form of civic virtue better able to negotiate the series of dilemmas and burdens that haunt democratic political action today. First, however, we need to investigate more thoroughly the nature of moralism and the precise ways in which it undermines sustainable forms of democratic politics, especially in the context of the vicious circle of public disinvestment.

By *moralism*, I mean, most generally, the rigid attachment to, investment in, and overconfidence in rules as means of handling or solving social and political problems. In its stronger forms, moralism refers to that type of discourse that speaks, acts, and calls others to act, from a presumed, or desired, position of moral and political purity and unquestionable correctness. Articulating its political claims in an implicit — often explicit — language of guilt and innocence, moralism desires to regulate personal and collective behavior according a preexisting code of right and wrong, the existence of which ideally assures the possibility of clear answers and correct behavior and decisions, based on the possibility of mapping one's actions onto the code without excess or remainder. The code, or moral rule-book, adherence to which acts as the marker of membership in the moral community, is not itself seen as open to interrogation or in need of argumentative defense. Moralism is in this and other senses deeply antipolitical. Its promised purity depends on the possibility of a noninterpretive and fully adequate relationship to a code or set of guiding principles, a relationship in which the subjectivity, peculiarities, interests, and power of the interpreter, together with the context of the action or interpretation, are ideally of no consequence. By promising a clear and complete set of rules — rules by which one can live without ambiguity and without cost to other equally important values — moralism expresses the wish to remain untouched by, and without implication in, those things that one rejects or is working to change (even when that includes much of the world within which one must work). The desire is to purify oneself and others of society's and politics' dirt, rather than to work in and through the dirt to rearrange it — and oneself — in more just and equitable ways.[28]

In the case of the competing moralisms of American "liberals" and "conservatives," we can see not only these basic characteristics at work but also how the paradoxically antipolitical character of their respective projects undermines the sustainability of democratic political culture. Here each side speaks in the name of a political community, a "we, the people," defined by a moral consensus that is assumed to be under attack, even as its fundamental tenets are not seen to be in need of any real argumentative defense. As a result, little effective political dialogue, much less compromise or transformation, is possible. Instead, each side imagines that the way "we" (good liberals, decent Americans, good Christians) do things is simply the way things should be done; there's no point in engaging in real debate about it, especially not with those crazy (intolerant/bigoted, immoral/heathen) people threatening our basic American values. Thus the moralism that tempts many liberal proceduralists, unable to understand how their "neutrality" could impose a particular way of life on anyone, rather than simply letting people be however they want. Why can't others be as tolerant as we liberal proceduralists? Why are they so morally blind? The moralism of conservative virtue politics, in its turn, is unable to see how the actions they recommend, policies they support, or ways of life they promote could have any role in, or parallels with, the immoral behavior and social problems they attack.

In both cases, a crucial role in the antidialogic character of their inter-actions is played by another characteristic assumption of moralism: that holding the correct position or following the right set of rules is proof of the essential goodness of the believer, and that any resistance from others to those rules and beliefs can result only from ignorance or from essential, and irremediable, moral corruption.[29] Moralism in this sense is often motivated as much by the moralizer's desire to reassure himself about his own moral worth as it is directed toward changing another self for the better; it's an act of self-judgment and reassurance *through* the judgment of another, and it relies on a particular understanding of the moral, or ethical, nature of the self. Moralism is thus deeply apolitical, not just because it denies both the contestability of its own code and any involve-ment in power or in the ethically questionable, but also in having aban-doned the work of identity transformation necessary to establishing iden-tifications with a larger, more inclusive, political community. Far from working to reverse the vicious circle of public disinvestment, its mode of politicization aims at the victory of one "we" over another, and in this way to help shore up fragile selves through identification with the moral community destined to triumph.

At the heart of the self-perpetuating cycle of competing moralisms, then, is a resistance to democratic openness and to the fundamental ambi-guity and uncertainty that, as we have seen in the preceding chapters, characterize the democratic "we." Refusing to accept that there can be no prepolitical definition of the terms on which each of us is to be included in the political community, moralism frequently tries to *answer* the dem-ocratic question through the assertion of a particular version of the "we." In denying that such uncertainty is constitutive of democratic politics, moralism ultimately makes the condition more, rather than less, danger-ous. For the moralism of one side in the competition between liberal and conservative partisans provokes the cynicism of the other. Each side all too easily sees the other as hypocritical, as speaking in the name of a neu-tral, already accepted, moral consensus, which in fact they are attempting to impose on their fellow citizens without their agreement or meaningful input. Moralism and the cynicism it carries with it are thus twin aspects of a cycle that is a constant threat to democratic politics.

Much of the difficulty here is that although moralism and the cynicism it so easily brings in its wake are particularly damaging to liberal-demo-cratic politics, they are also especially easily provoked by precisely this mode of politics, given the way in which liberal democratic argument rests on normative values that are at once particularly demanding and yet so abstract as to be essentially ambiguous, often even in tension with each other. The lack of any single, shared definitions of what the crucial words of democracy mean, while an essential source of democratic freedom, is thus also a constant source of confusion, disappointment, and cynicism for many citizens, especially many of those political partisans, liberal, conservative, or radical, who are strongly committed to a particular vision of the democratic "we." As we have seen in the previous chapters, for claims about the common good, or the basic terms of the democratic "we," to be democratic, they must be submitted to a process of debate and discussion and constructed in and through politics and rhetoric. Yet as a result, claims must be made about what "is" the common good before everyone, or even a majority, accepts that as what is truly in their common interest. Any claim in the name of the people, their will, the common good, or the general interest can thus only be shown to be "correct" after the fact, once it has been ratified by the people (and even then the ratification is never final or complete). Without a single agreed-upon definition, the act of speaking in the name of "the people" or "equality" or "freedom" or "the common good" can thus always seem to those with a different definition of the relationship of freedom and equality, or of the proper bounds of the political community, to be cynical, self-interested, merely a means of achieving power. This rhetorical move is particularly easy to make given that any definition of the "common good" or "general interest" necessarily limits someone's "private" good, or individual freedom, without it being possible to prove that such a good is truly common or its interest truly general. In the face of the kinds of ideological disagreement that are constitutive of democratic politics — and that are particularly characteristic of contemporary American politics — one person's "general" or "common" can always appear to be "special" or private to another, given that it inevitably benefits and burdens (at least in the short term) some people differently than others.[30]

This is not to argue that one should abandon making claims in the name of the democratic "we," or democracy's other central principles, or that one cannot or should not argue that one's preferred policies respect democratic principles more fully, or more accurately, than those of one's opponents. My argument here, instead, is less epistemological than psychological and rhetorical, pointing to the necessity of recognizing and responding to the tendency of democratic politics to produce its own self-defeating attitudes and practices, especially the mutually reinforcing cycles of moralism and cynicism. As I have argued in the previous chapters, the democratic "we" is not something that can ever simply be *found*; its essential openness means that it must instead constantly be formed through political, legal, and rhetorical means. In the absence of existing consensus, this "formative" process, as Sandel accepts, must to varying degrees and in various ways be a forceful one, drawing the boundaries between individual and community in ways that impose, at least initially, unequal burdens and opportunities on citizens, even when done in the name of equality. Constructing the "we" in which democratic citizens ultimately share, that is, requires reshaping individuals, their identities, and possibilities in differential ways. The forcefulness and contestability of such attempts to call into being something more than today's atomized and minimalist "we" will obviously be felt with special sharpness under conditions of weak collective identifications and the vicious circle of public disinvestment, in which much work must be done not only to produce collective identifications but also to lay the practical and institutional groundwork that makes them possible. The uncertainty of democracy's central principles, in turn, is more likely to produce cynicism and moralistic attacks on one's political opponents, the more unequal, ideologically polarized, and/or socially divided the community becomes. The less plausible the idea of the common good, the weaker common democratic attachments, or the less a consensus exists on the definition of equality and freedom, the more likely one will encounter the cynicism of polarized, bad faith dialogue, in which partisans convert *political* disagreements over the meaning of abstract principles into evidence of the *dishonesty* and bad faith of their opponents.

Indeed, under conditions of such deep democratic disenchantment, cynical unmasking isn't a tempting recourse only for political partisans. For those spectator-citizens not directly involved in partisan battles, the cycle of moralistic and cynical politics is decidedly depoliticizing: seeing through the self-righteous claims on both sides to be free of moral and political impurities, the spectator-citizen is given further reason to cynically dismiss the practice of politics as never amounting to anything *but* the veiled assertion of power. The cynico-moralism of liberal and conservative partisans, then, takes on a particularly destructive power in a political context, like today's, in which there is a large pool of disengaged citizens, for whom the discourse of cynical detachment is both readily available and a comforting palliative for their feelings of political disempowerment. For many spectator citizens, the unmasking of the hypocrisy of the politically engaged and powerful acts not only as a way to justify their own political inactivity but also as a means of claiming a small amount of apparent power: to write off the entire field of political action as hopelessly contaminated with power and self-interest is to assert that at least one isn't a sucker; one has seen through the illusions of the powerful and now knows the score. One won't be so stupid as to be taken in by the system *or* by the naive dream of thinking it can be fundamentally transformed.[31] The same holds, more generally, for moralism's willful reduction of the world's complexity: simply too many people know that the world is more complicated than any single code or set of codes can manage. In a society as saturated with everyday cynicism as ours, where the thought of remaining uncontaminated by unfairness, power, or self-interest is an impossible one for many, the pretense to purity of any form of moralizing discourse is a ripe target for cynical unmasking.[32]

Efforts to resist today's democratic closures by overcoming the vicious circle of public disinvestment and installing more effective democratic identifications therefore require rhetorical and psychological strategies to disarm the mutually reinforcing cynicisms of both partisans and specta-tors, a cycle that moralistic virtue talk helps produce. For calls to civic virtue that continue to base their appeals on strong and clear moral rules will inevitably prove inadequate to the actual experience of liberal dem-ocratic politics, whose essential openness, as the examples above reveal, necessitates forms of action that can never be ethically pure. Given the uncertainty and ambiguity that haunt democracy's central principles — whether "equal liberty," "the common good," or the need to respect the central contestability of these and other principles — no democratic action can be performed in a way that *fully* respects its own principles. This openness of democratic incompletion means that one must always fail to respect some values in order to honor others, and thus, as we have just seen, one will be open to the criticism of hypocrisy or bad faith.[33] Equally important, though, are the dilemmas and difficulties this poses for the democratic actor herself. For as we saw in the first chapter, she is faced with the task of effectively defining, in and through practice, the meaning of democracy's principles, yet in ways that can never satisfy all of democ-racy's ends — much less fully achieve "democracy" itself — and that can-not be grounded in or defended by reference to any more general theory or rule. Similar difficulties arise from the multiple allegiances, identifica-tions, or "identities," of which all contemporary democratic citizens are composed, and the hard choices that their openness and conflicts con-stantly force upon us. (For the democratic actor, like the democratic "we," is always in formation, continually reworking — under the pressure of particular contexts and the need for decisions — the multiple forces and identifications that at any given point define her, though without ever exhausting her.) For these and other reasons, as we've seen throughout the preceding chapters, democratic openness produces a necessarily impure form of politics, imposing demands on its citizens and politicians that have no solutions, only better or worse negotiations, the exact dem-ocratic nature of which cannot be known in advance and whose results are inevitably ambiguous.[34] Sandel's call for a form of civic virtue better able to handle the dilemmas and difficult choices that democratic action imposes on us today is thus an urgent one. Yet as we have begun to see, cultivating such virtue requires resources that his mode of civic republicanism is unable to provide.

The Burdens of Democratic Responsibility

Moralism, then, or any call to responsibility and political engagement based in adherence to strong, clear, simple rules, is fundamentally inadequate to the uncertain, ambiguous, "unruly" experience of liberal democratic politics. In the context of the vicious circle of public disinvestment and its associated democratic deficits, both structural and psychological, even the simplest calls to liberal-democratic virtue — to be concerned with the political world, to follow political events and debates, to express one's opinions, to vote — will often feel burdensome, even aggressive, to many would-be citizens. This is all the more true for broader, more *radical* democratizing projects, with stronger, or more participatory, visions of civic virtue, and more systemic critiques of the closures of existing political practices and institutions. Any such call to others to be actively engaged in making the world a more just, fair, egalitarian, and democratically managed world, immediately confronts — and helps activate — what might be called the excessive, because ungrounded, nature of responsibility. For such appeals are always to a large degree *performative*: claims about what one owes to whom are attempts at once to describe *and* to call into being a contestable vision of community, a "we" (the neighborhood, the nation, the world, all living beings) whose borders could always be — and are always being — drawn differently.[35] To stop the endless chain of actions and consequences that *is* the life of community (of being-with-others), and to say "there, *you* shall be held responsible for [fixing the effects of] action x," is thus to impose a burden on others that, however unavoidable in political and social life, cannot ultimately be grounded in any preexisting logic, rule, or necessity. The burden of political responsibility, that is, is not something one ever "deserves," in the sense of something one already "owes" to the world or to others as through some calculable act of exchange or contract. This is not to deny that each of us is fundamentally in debt to — in the sense of dependent on — those others and those institutions that constitute our social world. Rather, precisely because, in a sense, we owe everything we are to everybody else, what action(s) could possibly be enough to repay our debt? How could such a debt even be calculated?[36]

The difficulties facing calls to political and social responsibility thus grow more severe, the more numerous, complex, and unpredictable people's social and political relationships become, as the always somewhat arbitrary act of locating a truly "responsible" agent among a problem's multiple causes becomes more pronounced. When it comes to the question of one's responsibility to improve the community and the world, in other words, the absence of direct, one-to-one connections between one's previous actions and the bad state of the world, or between one's possible actions and an improved state of the world, is more easily and powerfully experienced. The more complicated, contingent, and unpredictable the world shows itself to be, especially in the absence of effective political resources with which to respond, the more political responsibility comes to be felt as an unfair and undeserved burden.

Radical democratic calls to political engagement that attempt to generate awareness of, and a willingness to work to change, democratic closures, systemic inequalities, and dangers, face an even more daunting obstacle in the fact that there are virtually no spaces *outside* of the "system" one is trying to change. Indeed, this is an additional, but fundamental, meaning of political "closure" today: whether the "system" under critique is understood as capitalism, or bureaucratic rationality, or the society of the spectacle, or consumerism, or modernity, there is virtually no point from which one could effectively articulate or receive its critique that does not deeply implicate one in the suffering, danger, injustice, or antidemocratic characteristics one is criticizing. We are (almost) all stockholders now, and if not stockholders, then homeowners, polluters, overconsumers, racists, sexists, and/or homophobes, enjoying consciously or unconsciously the benefits of American, or first-world, hegemony. We are all now like those whom Rousseau describes in the *Discourse on the Origin of Inequality*, caught in a system in which we are forced to violate our own best instincts and intentions merely to keep our head above water.[37] Yet at the same time, the precise ways in which we are implicated in systemic suffering and injustice are generally quite difficult to know without a large amount of often emotionally painful work — work that easily seems beside the point, given the democratic deficits that such calls to political engagement are meant to address.[38] Indeed, this is often the unintended message of radically democratic, systemic, political critique: that we are all just tiny cogs in huge systems we can't control and that render our personal preferences and good intentions largely irrelevant.[39]

Calls to "systemic" responsibility grounded in democratic values, then, run the risk of undermining the democratic energies of their intended audience in multiple ways.[40] Even if they avoid aggravating the very sense of powerlessness and hopelessness that they are aiming to challenge and overcome, the kinds of political and social self-analysis such critique requires are by their very nature less than pleasant. It is no surprise that so many people refuse to search out critical political and social perspectives, given the disagreeable experience of learning yet again how their own shopping habits, or investments, or employment practices, or taste in film or books, implicate them in forms of suffering and injustice about which they were previously unaware.[41] Or take the critiques of the closures of American political system characteristic of much left political analysis, especially those critiques of the many issues excised from mainstream American political debate as a result of corporate sponsorship of the two major parties and of all major media outlets. Absent great care in the language one uses to articulate it, such systemic critique all too easily sends the moralistic message that anyone who doesn't already see the truth of the critique — which in this case would be most of those one is talking with, since one must enter into mainstream institutions and assumptions in order to have one's critique of them heard — are either naive fools or more or less conscious collaborators with the corrupt system under critique. This is obviously not a message too many people like to hear — which helps explain, at least in part, why such left, democratic, moralizing voices are so rarely invited to take part in mainstream public debate today.[42]

The ways in which radical, systemic, critique can take on a moralistic and ultimately antipolitical cast were vividly on display in a series of posters that appeared on the campus of the University of California at Berkeley after the passage of California's Proposition 187 in the fall of 1994, a measure that cut off virtually all state social services to undocumented immigrants. Rather than setting out even a minimal argument for the unjust and socially harmful nature of Proposition 187, or suggesting ways that the reader could learn more about its likely ill effects, the (nonetheless quite lengthy and detailed) posters contented themselves with the moral gesture of denouncing the "racist" nature of 187's "attack" on immigrants and calling on the reader to "resist" its implementation. Rather than being the opening salvo in a campaign of political persuasion, recruitment, and education, the posters were merely a call to arms on the basis of the *assumed* immorality of a particular political position (and, what follows, the moral correctness of its opposition). By simply assuming the readers' agreement, though, as opposed to appealing for it (with reasons), the poster paradoxically helps drive them away. On the basis of the underlying assumption that everyone rational *already* knows that such restrictions on illegal immigrants are racist and unjust, the poster makes it seem like the very consideration of the opposing position is evil and reactionary. It thus drives the undecided (or simply uninformed) toward its opponents' camp — not merely by the aggressive and insulting nature of an appeal without reasons, but more importantly by implying that they must themselves be racist if they are not *already* convinced of Proposition 187's racism.

Given the magnitude of the problems confronting democratic activists, even of the liberal-democratic variety, such radical democratic critiques are especially prone to produce these kinds of counterproductive effects. The feeling of being overwhelmed by forces beyond one's control can easily provoke rage as one's will to do good is consistently frustrated. What were originally feelings of public concern, commitment to democratic values, or sympathy for others who are suffering are quickly transformed into angry and resentful moralism at a system that loudly proclaims its democratic achievements even as its effective democratic spaces grow ever smaller. The anger and resentment at the world not fitting one's ethical designs, which is almost always to some degree involved in any adherence to high ethical standards, here takes on greater strength and often is displaced onto those one is appealing to for having failed to live up to their political and moral obligations.[43] The burdens that the moralizer's rules impose on those being asked to take responsibility for the world's problems are likely to provoke defensive reactions even in the best of scenarios. Here, though, they are likely to produce their own reactive anger and resentment at the self-righteousness of such criticisms, for the basic impurity of democratic action and the "structural guilt" we all have simply from being part of "the system" make it all too easy to show how the moralizers' themselves fail to meet the high standards they ask of others.

Toward a Nonmoralistic Language and Practice of the Democratic "We"

Moralistic forms of virtue talk, then, only help weaken the democratic spirit of engagement and responsibility they aim to encourage. To be effectively politicizing under present conditions, our appeals to civic virtue would need instead to be as nonmoralistic as possible. That is, for languages of democratic responsibility to assist in efforts to resist democratic closures and open up more space for citizen participation and more democratic public policies and institutions, they need to embrace the democratic openness of uncertainty and incompletion. They would need to incorporate into the very language of their critique and their calls to responsibility an acceptance of the dilemmas and difficulties that the openness of democratic politics imposes on its actors: the fact that democracy's various principles can never fully be satisfied; that one never knows for sure what the most democratic course of action is; that any political action brings with it unintended consequences, ones that can undermine the very principles it is meant to respect; indeed, that we are *all* to various degrees implicated in practices and institutions that violate the principles of equality and freedom.

What would it mean for such a basically *compromising* — never fully democratic — political condition to be acknowledged in one's calls to responsibility? First of all, it would mean not treating the inevitable implication in political and ethical impurities as evidence of the corruption of one's own or another's moral or political character. Rather than appealing to others to change their behavior in order to remove the stain or guilt of their present implication in suffering, or injustice, or unfairness, one would appeal to the positive possibilities of constructing a more just, or democratic, community, possibilities that actually reside in the very fact of our being situated within systems and relations of power. That is, a moralistic appeal says something to the effect of "how can you possibly be involved in 'X,' or supporting 'Y,' or doing 'Z,' when you know the suffering or injustice or immorality this implicates you in? You must instead adapt your behavior to the following rules so that you can redeem and purify yourself." A nonmoralistic appeal, on the other hand, would say something more, such as, "Look, the world is a messy and dirty place and we all are caught up in its injustices and suffering. Becoming more aware of our precise situation within these impurities, though, should allow us to act together more effectively to bring into being a better community, enhancing our own lives and the lives of our fellow citizens. It will take some hard work, but look at the possibilities available to us through shared political action."

A moralistic language, then, tends to speak to others as relatively static and clearly defined persons whose basic moral character is already largely defined by the content of their past actions and thus must often be wholly transformed for them to act more justly or democratically. A nonmoralistic practice of political engagement, on the other hand, not being content simply with taking the "correct" stand for the sake of the democratic actor's own sense of purity, is especially careful to consider the effects of its appeals on its audience and to make them in a way that makes it easier for political opponents and the unconvinced to change their minds. It thus speaks to others as *sites of possibility*. It asks what each of us can do with the power and potential granted us by the specific way we are presently situated, rather than asking us to be adequate to an abstract, contextless set of rules. It thus wagers, in an apparent paradox, that a fuller acceptance of where we are at the present moment can help open up space in which *new* political and ethical arrangements — a new "we" —

become imaginable and seem worth struggling for. It begins from the assumption that accepting the call to political responsibility involves a leap of faith, an act grounded in that capacity of "natality" so important to Arendt. Unable to be grounded in any rational calculation of what one already owes the community, the acceptance of political responsibility depends instead on a willingness to invest oneself in the possibility or promise of a different, better, community to come. Rather than being backward-looking and focused on the calculation and rectification of past injustices and "sins," a democratic language of responsibility must be future-oriented, appealing to the positive possibilities that reside in those who still need to be convinced.[44]

For this sense of possibility, openness, and responsibility to the future to be successfully cultivated, though, it must be accompanied by strong identifications and the sense of *commonality* these can build. These would not, however, be the classic identifications of republican theories of democratic politics like those of Sandel or Taylor. An effective nonmoralistic language of political engagement would involve, instead, our identification with others as *fellow sufferers* from the fundamental burdens and impurities of identity. That is, the language of democratic responsibility takes on transformative powers to the extent that "good democrats" acknowledge not only that they, too, are implicated in their share of injustice and messy political and ethical compromises, but also that they share in the same underlying patterns of greed, insecurity, defensiveness, and anger that they are trying to change or limit in those they are appealing to. It would explicitly acknowledge that the seeds of resentment, anger, aggression, and dogmatism are built into the very experience of "identity" and the deeply felt need to secure one's sense of self against threats to its value or stability. Recognizing the way in which the negativity of identity often informs and affects even one's own democratic actions, especially when combined with an awareness of how easily political discourse today can activate such negativity in others, opens up the possibility of more compassionate and self-critical, and thus more effective, modes of political appeal and critique. This form of identification in turn opens the way for (and is strengthened by) a vision of democratic community that sees the fate of each tied to the fate of others, acknowledging our deep interdependence and commonalities, yet without seeing each as *identical* parts of a homogenous whole.

In other words, a more fully, "radically," democratic practice of "identity" could emerge from abandoning the belief that we are essential — separate, persisting, and autonomous — selves, a belief that characterizes so much moral and political discourse.[45] Challenging the standard liberal-democratic imaginary, this practice of identity would treat the "individual" self instead as a bundle of contradictory habits, resistances, gaps, tendencies, and possible developments that can with more or less difficulty be transformed by skillful rhetorical and environmental interventions. It would see the democratic self as one "formed" and reformed through the constant and never fully coherent influences of those around us, by the "community" in the sense of the aggregate effects of those others who exist with and around and inside us (as well as "natural" forces not always in our control or even known to us). By definition, then, and in contrast with much of the civic republican and "communitarian" tradition, community in this sense isn't something one can ever fit into seamlessly, for it never succeeds in closing in on itself. Nor can it ever constitute a collective essence with which one could merge or to which one would owe specific obligations. "Obligation," in this vision of community, emerges from the self's fundamental indebtedness and secondariness to those others who make the self possible. It is, as Sandel suggests at points, a radical and multiply *encumbered* self. Yet such encumbrances don't mean the self is ever identical with, or subsumable into, or simply determined by, these others or the community, given that there is no center or ground or beginning to this process of constant collective formation and reformation.

The kind of nonmoralistic language of critique and responsibility I am briefly sketching out here would, then, work its *democratic* effects on multiple levels. In the most obvious and pragmatic sense, the more compassionate and self-critical language that emerges from the identification with others as fellow sufferers from identity's burdens could, by loosening attachments to entrenched political positions and identities on all sides, help open up more space for democratic engagement and debate, and possibly even agreement. Its compassion and generosity arise from the recognition of the *shared suffering* we all experience as fluid, open, internally complex beings inevitably trapped (although to different degrees) in more or less fixed identity "scripts" or self-images.[46] It recognizes that suffering comes both from the constraints of identity *and* from our being radically open and indebted to each other even in our mutual otherness. We depend on each other, both materially and for the stories that tell us who we are — even as we don't naturally fit together and are constantly called into question by each other's differences. A democratic, nonmoralistic, language and practice of civic virtue, then, recognize that we all share both a desire for strong personal identities, grounded, when available, in clear collective identities, as well as the experience of the burdensome nature of such desire, especially given the ultimately unattainable nature of its object. Such recognition, and the compassion built into it, then, offers the possibility of negotiating at least somewhat more easily the essential — and irresolvable — democratic tension between the "we" understood as a set of common needs, rights, and duties, and the "we" understood as perpetually uncertain and open to reformulation.

At a more general level, then, such "second-order," or "nonsubstantive," identification and the nonmoralistic language of responsibility it supports are democratic in that they help establish a *common ground* with one's fellow citizens without threatening the kinds of reified, unduly closed, practices of the "we" that postfundamentalist theorists like Connolly rightly worry about. Indeed, it is a more richly democratic practice of identification and language of responsibility in the paradoxical sense that it explicitly acknowledges that for the "we" to be truly *shared*, it will and must always remain uncertain, contested, shifting, open. By abandoning any extrapolitical grounds of authority or certainty and by making us together the equal (non)masters of our collective fate, democratic openness brings this nonsovereign but free experience of politics to the fore: in our radical indebtedness to and dependence on one another, we share a space of mutual appearance and need. The precise nature of what we "have" in common — what Arendt writes of as our shared "inter-est" — however, or the exact way in which we are in debt to each other, the responsibilities we owe each other, remain to be collectively determined.[47] "We" form a *public* perhaps, but not a community that *is* us, or that exhausts our being. For the other who is before and within us, in her simultaneous commonality and otherness, constantly questions us, and questions our "we": what exactly *do* we share, other than the burdens of identity and the experience of this space and the encounter that it allows?[48] Democratic politics, by establishing equal freedom and the process of collective identity-formation as its central principles, brings out more clearly the basically questionable nature of our being-together, together with the additional principle of resisting the inevitable attempt to put an end to this experience. Thus even as it is necessarily and relentlessly oriented toward equality, reciprocity, and commonality, democratic politics can never offer the experience of reconciliation or harmony, but only of sharing the fractures between and within us all. By actively resisting the reification of our being-together into a collective identity to be identified with, a nonmoralistic language of civic virtue, and the relation to identity it supports, would simultaneously affirm this experience and, in the compassion it helps generate, make it easier to bear.[49]

Yet any language and practice of civic virtue, even as it struggles to remain true to this radically open experience of democratic politics, must also work to generate support for more traditionally recognized forms of democratic control. Indeed, as we saw earlier, the democratic possibilities of a compassionate, nonmoralistic, language of responsibility are themselves ultimately sustainable only on the basis of effective public spaces and institutions in which robust democratic debate and discussion are possible, and through which democratic ideas have some possibility of being translated into action. The prospects for achieving any meaningful democratic control over the state, the market, or disciplinary powers of other sorts, any time soon, however, certainly appear less than encouraging. The final, and perhaps most serious, dilemma a compassionate, nonmoralistic language of democratic responsibility faces, then, is how to maintain its generous and self-critical spirit, and its openness to the uncertain, contested status of the "we," even while struggling against overwhelming odds to assert the value and possibility of greater popular participation and control. Can one respect the value of democratic openness under present conditions while also being politically savvy, even relentless, in naming and struggling against those forces and constituencies that presently block most meaningful forms of democratic accountability and participation? What, in particular, do good democrats do today with the rage so many of them feel at such deeply entrenched injustice, inequality, and unaccountable power, and the silence about them in our most basic public spaces? How can *these* closures be challenged in ways that nonetheless respect the fundamentally nonharmonious, incomplete, inadequate, nature of the democratic "we"? The wager that a nonmoralistic language of responsibility makes is to believe that it is only by affirming this difficult and disappointing character of democratic politics that any more traditional democratizing projects have any chance, however remote, of making headway. But it is, in the end, a wager.

Notes

Introduction

1. Anthony Arblaster, *Democracy* (Minneapolis: University of Minnesota Press, 1987), offers a brief but helpful discussion of the historical transformation of the democratic ideal from the radical and threatening idea of popular power — the rule of the demos, of the common people — to one that political and class elites could ultimately come to embrace.

2. For a convincing argument to this effect, which places such developments in the context of economic "globalization" and its social effects, see Claude Ake, "Dangerous Liaisons: The Interface of Globalization and Democracy," in *Democracy's Victory and Crisis*, ed. Axel Hadenius (Cambridge: Cambridge University Press, 1997), 282–96. As my introduction makes clear, however, I disagree with Ake's claim that democracy has a "precise and non-controversial definition," confusions over which are merely a matter of deliberate, and interested, political "manipulation." For an illuminating argument, for instance, for why the restraints and limitations of liberal constitutionalism are not so much antidemocratic as *enabling* of a certain kind of popular power, see Stephen Holmes, *Passions and Constraints: On the Theory of Liberal Democracy* (Chicago: University of Chicago Press, 1995), esp. chap. 5, "Precommitment and the Paradox of Democracy."

3. For a helpful analysis of the practical problems facing today's liberal democracies and the limited ability of dominant conceptions of democracy to make sense of them, see Jeffrey C. Isaac, "The Return of the Repressed: Or, the Limits of 'Democratic Theory,'" in *Democracy in Dark Times* (Ithaca, N.Y.: Cornell University Press, 1998). As he puts it: "This form of government promises civil liberty, political stability, and accountable government. It is also endemically prone to bureaucratization, corruption, and sclerosis. While it claims to stand for equality before the law, it permits and indeed promotes extensive and dramatic social and economic inequalities. While it claims to embody the will of the people, it lacks channels of healthy civic participation, and thus tends to promote — or at least is perpetually vulnerable to the emergence of — political alienation and resentment" (24). See also his discussion of the "crisis" of liberal representative democracy (35–38).

4. For an interesting argument about the "constitutionalization" of democracy, which renders the demos a spectator rather than an actor, see Sheldon Wolin, "Fugitive Democracy," in *Democracy and Difference: Contesting the Boundaries of the Political*, ed. Seyla Benhabib (Princeton: Princeton University Press, 1996). See also Wolin's essay "Norm and Form: The Constitutionalizing of Democracy," in *Athenian Political Thought and the Reconstruction of American Democracy*, ed. J. Peter Euben, John R. Wallach, and Josiah Ober (Ithaca, N.Y.: Cornell University Press, 1994), 29–58. For a less politically radical but nonetheless sobering analysis of the more general decline in rates of public participation by Americans across all spheres of social life, see Robert Putnam, *Bowling Alone: The Collapse and Revival of American Community* (New York: Simon and Schuster, 2001). An earlier version of Putnam's analysis of this issue appeared as "The Strange Disappearance of Civic America," in *Ticking Time Bombs*, ed. Robert Kuttner (New York: New Press, 1996), 263–86.

5. The percentage of eligible voters who vote in U.S. presidential elections has declined steadily since 1960, when it was 63 percent, to 60.2 percent in 1968, to 53.1 percent in 1984, to the record low of 49 percent in 1996 (according to the 2001 edition of the *New York Times Almanac*). Rates of participation are much lower for off-year U.S. congressional elections: in 1994 only 38 percent of the eligible voters cast ballots. The result is that victorious candidates are elected by only about 25–30 percent of eligible voters in presidential elections and 15–20 percent of eligible voters in off-year congressional elections. Participation rates are often much lower in local and state elections. In a further sign that this phenomenon is not limited to the United States, the election returns from the 2001 British parliamentary elections brought with them the disturbing news of a precipitous drop in the percentage of eligible voters who cast ballots, down to a mere 58 percent from the already historically low 71 percent in 1997.

6. An illuminating analysis of the antidemocratic effects of recent changes in the technologies, strategies, and organization of U.S. political campaigns can be found in Marshall Ganz, "Voters in the Crosshairs: How Technology and the Market Are Destroying Politics," in Kuttner, *Ticking Time Bombs*, 245–59.

7. For a brief but powerful analysis of the closed nature of the U.S. political system that results from the particular system of campaign financing enshrined in its laws, see William Pfaff, "The Power of Money in America Has a Stranglehold on Democracy," *International Herald Tribune*, July 15, 1999, 9.

8. This is in part the natural, if self-fulfilling, reaction to the fact that wealthy citizens vote in disproportionately high numbers compared with less wealthy citizens. See the analysis completed by the journal *Left Business Observer*, no. 95 (November 2000), based on U.S. Census Bureau statistics. For details, see Chapter 4, n. 2. For a sophisticated analysis of the complex meanings and forms of political "apathy" in the contemporary United States, see Tom DeLuca, *The Two Faces of Political Apathy* (Philadelphia: Temple University Press, 1995). A more journalistic but still informative reading of political alienation can be found in Susan Tolchin, *The Angry American* (New York: Westview Press, 1996).

9. According to Edward N. Wolff, "Recent Trends in Wealth Ownership, 1983–1998," April 2000 (available at www.levy.org/docs/wrkpap/papers/300.

html), the top 1 percent of the U.S. population owns 38.1 percent of the total net worth, whereas the bottom 40 percent owns only 0.2 percent. Indeed, the top 1 percent has greater wealth than the combined bottom 90 percent. The top 10 percent of the population owns 70.9 percent of the wealth, whereas the bottom 60 percent only owns 4.7 percent. These ratios have been growing more skewed over the past two decades, with average household net worth increasing 42.2 percent for the top 1 percent of the population and *falling* 76.3 percent for the bottom 40 percent. The concentration of wealth in the United States is now the most skewed since the 1920s and, according to the United Nations Human Development Report of 1998, is about three times greater than that of our nearest competitor, Germany. The often-heard phrase that the rich are getting richer and the poor are getting poorer is a simple statistical fact. These inequalities in wealth also have a racial aspect to them: according to Edward Wolff, as quoted in the *New York Times*, January 4, 1999, the typical black household in 1995 had only 12 percent of the wealth of the typical white household; if the value of housing were excluded, the figure would be a mere 1 percent. More than 30 percent of black households, versus 15 percent of white households, have no net worth at all. All statistics cited are available on the website http://www.inequality.org.

10. For a now classic historical study that links an overly ambitious rhetoric and ideal of participatory democracy to disappointment and political disenchantment, see James Miller, *Democracy Is in the Streets* (Cambridge: Harvard University Press, 1987), esp. the final chapter.

11. Schumpeter's minimalist conception of democracy — defined as "that institutional arrangement for arriving at political decisions in which individuals acquire the power to decide by means of a competitive struggle for the people's vote" — is found in Joseph Schumpeter, *Capitalism, Socialism, and Democracy* (London: George Allen and Unwin, 1943), 269. See also Max Weber, "Parliament and Government in a Reconstructed Germany," Appendix II in *Economy and Society* (Berkeley: University of California Press, 1978), 2:1381–469. Jean-François Lyotard offers a more recent, and quite different, argument that equates modern democracy with the *absence* of "the people," in *Postmodern Fables* (Minneapolis: University of Minnesota Press, 1997).

12. Alexis de Tocqueville, *Democracy in America*, ed. Phillips Bradley, trans. Henry Reeve (New York: Vintage, 1990), 1:3. Further references to this volume are in parentheses in the text.

13. Claude Lefort, "The Image of the Body and Totalitarianism," in *Political Forms of Modern Society* (Cambridge: Cambridge University Press, 1986), 303. In this chapter, further references to this essay are abbreviated BT and included in parentheses in the text.

14. Claude Lefort, "Human Rights and the Welfare State," in *Democracy and Political Theory* (Minneapolis: University of Minnesota Press, 1988), 34. In this chapter, further references to this essay are abbreviated HR and included in parentheses in the text.

15. Claude Lefort, "The Question of Democracy," in *Democracy and Political Theory*, 17. In this chapter, further references to this essay are abbreviated QD and included in parentheses in the text.

16. Wolin, "Fugitive Democracy," 31.

17. Such debates have been extensive and have by this point ranged across most disciplines in the humanities and social sciences. My point here is not to intervene in any particular debate or aspect of the debate so much as it is simply to mark the fact that this book in part emerges out of and then enters back into this ongoing intellectual conversation.

18. For a theory of democratic law and politics that places this sort of revisability of decisions and flexibility of institutions, see the work of Roberto Unger, especially *Critical Legal Studies* (Cambridge: Harvard University Press, 1986). I discuss Unger's work and the critique of it offered by Stanley Fish, in my work "The Democratic Question: On the Rule of the People and the Paradoxes of Political Freedom," Ph.D. dissertation, Johns Hopkins University, 1995, chap. 4.

19. This phrase is taken from Wolin, "Fugitive Democracy." For a similar understanding of democracy, in which an overly optimistic ideal produces an overly pessimistic diagnosis that democracy is fated to live only a sporadic, occasional existence, see C. Douglas Lummis, *Radical Democracy* (Ithaca, N.Y.: Cornell University Press, 1996). For my own more extensive critique of Lummis's understanding of radical democracy, as well as a critical treatment of the diversity of radical democratic visions found in David Trend, ed., *Radical Democracy: Identity, Citizenship and the State* (New York: Routledge, 1996), see Alan Keenan, "The Beautiful Enigma of Radical Democracy," *Theory & Event* 1, 3 (1997), at http://muse.jhu.edu/journals/theory_&_event.

20. For an excellent critique of the formalist dead ends to which Derrida's political and ethical arguments lead if they have no ethical or psychological supplement, see Timothy Bewes, *Cynicism and Postmodernity* (New York: Verso, 1997).

21. For an essay that examines some of the most important contemporary obstacles to radical forms of democratic practice in an especially helpful and rigorous way, see Mark Warren, "What Should We Expect from More Democracy? Radically Democratic Responses to Politics," *Political Theory* 24, 2 (May 1996): 241–70.

Chapter 1

1. Cornelius Castoriadis, "The Greek Polis and the Creation of Democracy," *Graduate Faculty Philosophy Journal* 9, 2 (fall 1983): 98. Further references are given in parentheses in the body of the text.

2. Greek democracy thus has what Castoriadis calls "its essential precondition" in an even more fundamental openness, or more accurately, in the Greek vision of the essential disjunction "between our desires and decisions, on the one hand, and the world, the nature of being, on the other" (95). It is only because the human world has no ultimate order or truth and human laws are not given by God or determined by the laws of nature or history, that there is any room for political action, creation, and judgment. Politics and democracy are possible because the world can be known and ordered only partially. As Castoriadis puts it: "If a full and certain knowledge (*episteme*) of the human domain were possi-

ble, politics would immediately come to an end, and democracy would be both impossible and absurd: democracy implies that all citizens have the possibility of attaining a correct *doxa and* that nobody possesses an *episteme* of things political" (96). With the recognition that there is no science of politics and no "law of laws" — no extra-social standard that can be discovered so as to determine "proper" political action and judgment — the questions of justice and of political judgment open up as "genuine, that is, interminable, question[s]" (105).

3. For this same reason there is no role in democracy for "experts," and there can be no expertise in political affairs. Political issues concern the community as a whole and are to be decided by the community as a whole — there are no "specialists of the universal" or "technicians of the totality" (100).

4. For an interesting and very thorough treatment of a wide variety of ways in which this problem affects democratic politics and democratic theory, see Frederick Whelan, "Prologue: Democratic Theory and the Boundary Problem," in *Liberal Democracy: Nomos 25,* ed. J. Roland Pennock and John W. Chapman (New York: New York University Press, 1983), 13–47.

5. In modern liberal democratic societies, of course, it is the constitution that is the imperfectly democratic means by which the people is created so as to be able to rule itself. For an excellent argument in defense of liberal constitutionalism as a democracy-enhancing practice, see Stephen Holmes, *Passions and Constraints: On the Theory of Liberal Democracy* (Chicago: Chicago University Press, 1995), esp. chap. 5.

6. As Castoriadis himself makes clear, "the exclusion of women, foreigners, and slaves from citizenship is a limitation we do not accept" (98). As I suggest later, however, one of the many paradoxes Castoriadis's analysis falls into is that the failure to accept the non-autonomy of the people and their always less than fully general existence in fact makes it more difficult to resist more radically exclusive political projects (such as contemporary nationalisms and racisms).

7. What "being a good citizen" and thinking about the general will means, in other words, cannot be entirely formal or procedural (as we see again when we consider Benhabib's theory of deliberative democracy): it requires some similarity and shared sense of who the community is in order to know what is general (and thus to know who is being too particular). In fact, the very possibility of knowing what is common to a group or what is of general concern to it depends on the existence (real or ideal) of some outside entity, or alternate form of living together, against which the community is defined. "We" can know who we are, and thus what is general to us, only in relation to what we are not. Castoriadis suggests as much himself with one of his prime examples of the Athenian cultivation of "the unity of the body politic." Citing Aristotle's *Politics,* he writes that "when the *ecclesia* deliberates on matters entailing the possibility of *a conflict such as a war* with a neighboring *polis,* the inhabitants of the frontier zone are excluded from the vote. For they could not vote without their particular interests overwhelming their motives, while the decision must be made on general grounds only" (102, emphasis added). In this case, the outside threat to the continued existence of the polis helps determine the clear distinction between general and particular grounds for judgment.

8. The people exist in the space "between past and future," to use Hannah Arendt's phrase. Castoriadis's account of the Greek polis owes much to Arendt's reflections on Greece and on political action and political freedom. The essay "The Greek *Polis* and the Invention of Democracy" was, in fact, given as part of a lecture series in honor of Arendt at the New School for Social Research in the early 1980s. For an extended treatment of Arendt's work on the temporality of political foundation and the community it brings into being, see Chapter 2.

9. My point here is not that Castoriadis actually does in fact assume that "the people" already exist prior to politics. Given his arguments about the status of grounds in democracy and the nature of the self-institution of the polis, Castoriadis obviously would never make such a claim. The point is more that his refusal to engage with the paradox of the heteronomous closure necessary to democratic openness necessarily implies that the people can ultimately be fully formed, made into a completely autonomous entity. This achievement would be possible only if the people did somehow, ideally, already exist in such a form.

10. I am in broad agreement here with Jane Mansbridge and her argument that since democracies need coercive power to achieve their democratic ends, and since "no coercion can be either incontestably fair or predictably just, democracies must find ways of fighting, while they use it, the very coercion that they need." See her essay "Using Power/Fighting Power: The Polity," in *Democracy and Difference: Contesting the Boundaries of the Political*, ed. Seyla Benhabib (Princeton: Princeton University Press, 1996), 46. Mansbridge's own suggestion for handling this dilemma is that democracies ensure the existence of "protected enclaves" of deliberation "in which the relatively like-minded," and especially those who have been on the receiving end of democratic coercion, can "consider in their deliberations not only what is good for the whole polity but also what is good for themselves individually . . . and for their group," thus "facilitating opposition" to democratic coercion in particular cases (57, 59). At the end of this chapter and then again in the final chapter, I offer my own ideas about "ways to recognize, store, and rethink our understandings" of "the injustices we commit as we act collectively" (60).

11. Throughout, quotations from Jean-Jacques Rousseau, *On the Social Contract*, come from *On the Social Contract, with Geneva Manuscript and Political Economy*, ed. Roger D. Masters, trans. Judith R. Masters (New York: St. Martin's Press, 1978). In-text page references are to the book, chapter, and page (e.g., II/iv/85) of the Masters edition. Occasional references to the French original are to volume 3 of the Pleiade edition of Rousseau's *Oeuvres complètes*, ed. Robert Derathe (Paris: Editions de Gallimard, 1964).

12. Whether one chooses to see the social contract as a mutual promise or a collective self-naming, it is clearly a "performative" speech act. Rather than *describing* an entity or state of affairs that already exists, a performative is a use of language, or a "speech act," that calls a new state of affairs into being. Classic examples include christening a baby or a ship and the ceremony of marriage. Not being a statement that can be judged as true or false, performatives are judged instead on the basis of their success or failure. The "felicitous" character of a performative — to use the words of J. L. Austin, whose *How to Do Things with*

Words (Cambridge: Harvard University Press, 1975) first codified performatives as a distinct species of speech acts — depends on how well it satisfies certain conventional requirements: For instance, was it a properly ordained minister, or certified justice of the peace, who performed the marriage? Was it the duly appointed official who swung the bottle against the ship and proclaimed it in service? In other words, a performative can only be successful if there are already established conventions and authorities in place, whose criteria it then meets. One way of understanding the difficulties that this chapter traces with respect to Rousseau's social contract and the foundation of "the people" is to say that the social contract is plagued by the necessity of establishing its own such conventions and the authority that will then be used in judging its own "felicity." Whether such a performative can ever be said to be successful, and a new entity actually brought into being, is a question that, strictly speaking, cannot be answered definitively. The chapter seeks to uncover some of the more important of the effects of that uncertainty on democratic politics, and the constitutively questionable nature of "the people" that follows from it. For further discussion of these issues, especially in relation to the act of promising, see Chapter 2, an earlier version of which was published as "Promises, Promises: On the Abyss of Freedom and the Loss of the Political in the Work of Hannah Arendt," *Political Theory* 22, 2 (April 1994): 297–322.

For other important texts that use the category of the performative to analyze the social contract or other moments of political foundation, see Jacques Derrida, "Declarations of Independence," *New Political Science* 15 (summer 1986): 7–13; Paul de Man, "Promises (*Social Contract*)," in *Allegories of Reading: Figural Language in Rousseau, Nietzsche, Rilke and Proust* (New Haven: Yale University Press, 1979), 246–78; Bonnie Honig, "Declarations of Independence: Arendt and Derrida on the Problem of Founding a Republic," *American Political Science Review* 85 (winter 1991): 97–113. See also David Ingram's impressive critique of this line of argument in his "Novus Ordo Seclorum: The Trial of (Post)Modernity or the Tale of Two Revolutions," in *Hannah Arendt: Twenty Years Later*, ed. Larry May and Jerome Kohn (Cambridge: MIT Press, 1996), 221–50.

13. The precise relationship between a common *interest* — based perhaps in a similarity of material conditions, or shared religious or cultural beliefs, to name just two possibilities — and common *standards* — for judging how members of the community are or should be the same, or what makes them all part of the same community — is complex. For our purposes, it is enough to say that Rousseau needs the social contract to produce *both*. Their relation, however, is structured by the very paradox they try to solve: each needs the other in order for itself to be possible.

14. In the terms of speech act theory this would amount to the claim that a performative (the social contract) cannot supply its own standards for judging its success, or felicity. Those standards must already exist, in the form of commonly accepted conventions. The paradox of the social contract, therefore, is that it must provide those standards, even as it can at best do so only retroactively.

15. Rousseau acknowledges something like this point himself, in a footnote to the final sentence of book 1. Elaborating on the claim that through the social con-

tract naturally unequal men "all become equal through convention and right," Rousseau adds the following: "Under bad governments, this equality is only apparent and illusory. It serves merely to maintain the poor man in his misery and the rich in his usurpation. In fact, laws are always useful to those who have possessions and harmful to those who have nothing. It follows from this that the social state is only advantageous to men insofar as they all have something and none of them has anything superfluous" (I/ix/58).

16. I owe the idea of looking to the Geneva Manuscript, as well as some of my analysis of it, to de Man, "Promises (*Social Contract*)." Also helpful along these lines in working out my reading of *On the Social Contract* have been Robert Bernasconi, "Rousseau and the Supplement to *The Social Contract*," *Cardozo Law Review* (Deconstruction and the Possibility of Democracy) 11, 5–6 (July/August 1990): 1539–64; and Samuel Weber, "In the Name of the Law," ibid., 1515–38.

17. It is worth noting that in book 1, chap. 5, which immediately precedes the description of the social contract, Rousseau distinguishes between "subjugating a multitude" (which is a matter of slavery) and "governing a society" (which requires the legitimacy of the laws). To call the people a "blind multitude," then, is to suggest quite directly that the people have not yet fully come into being.

18. As part of this shift, Rousseau spends much of the following chapters arguing that the legislator and political theorist must take into account a people's particular characteristics in order to frame laws and institutions that have some hope of granting the people a lasting, autonomous, foundation. As Rousseau explains, "just as an architect, before putting up a big building, observes and tests the ground to see whether it can bear the weight, so the wise founder does not start by drafting laws that are good in themselves, but first examines whether the people for whom he intends them is suited to bear them" (II/viii/70). This suggests a basic limit to the reach of formal, theoretical analyses of political legitimacy. As Rousseau puts it, the "general objects of all good institutions should be modified in each country according to the relationships that arise as much from the local situation as from the character of the inhabitants, and it is on the basis of these relationships that each people must be assigned a particular system of institutions that is the best, not perhaps in itself, but for the State for which it is intended" (II/xi/75). Because a people necessarily exists in a particular, not perfectly general, form before its properly political (generalizing) foundation, the strategies designed to transform it into generality must themselves be particular to the situation, adapted to the specific conditions of the situation at hand. Unfortunately, Rousseau argues, only certain peoples satisfy the prepolitical "conditions for founding a people" (II/x/74) — such as size, age, history, opinion, temperament, wealth, and so forth — that must be in place for them to be able to be transformed into a self-ruling people. Thus Rousseau's famously outrageous claim that at the time of writing *On the Social Contract*, only the island of Corsica met enough of the criteria to be "capable of legislation" (II/x/75).

19. Some such strategies, I am arguing, are needed in any form of democratic politics, even those that do not aim to achieve the difficult standards of Rousseau's general will. Indeed, one thing I suggest in the concluding section of

the chapter is that to the extent that they remain democratic, and thus oriented toward ideals of equality and reciprocity, more pluralist forms of politics, precisely by opening up new spaces of freedom, also produce new forms of conflict and uncertainty that require their own strategies of negotiation.

20. Thus the claim that in the social contract "one gives himself to no one" is strictly speaking not true: for better or worse one gives oneself to whatever segment of the community most effectively speaks in the name of the people.

21. This is not to deny that there are particular situations of political crisis and/or massive inequality—for instance, Haiti in 1994—where it seems fairly unquestionable who the people are and who their enemies are. Yet even here questions remain. For once the moment of crisis passes and the work begins of defining the terms on which all will be members of the community—which is to say, defining the people in practice—sharp ideological differences inevitably reemerge, in particular with respect to the proper treatment of, and role for, those who had previously opposed "the people." In what way are they now part of the people? Indeed, the experience of political instability and violence in Haiti after the U.S. intervention to reinstate President Aristide has shown just how fleeting the people's clear identity can be—and how dangerous the continuing desire for it can be.

22. It is possible, that is, to read the legislator not just as an allegory for the difficult efforts that *democratic* actors must go through in order to bring into being an autonomous community of political equals but also as a figure for a variety of forms of *non*democratic efforts to generate attachments to political institutions and laws. In this latter reading, the forceful and non-autonomous nature of "the people's" foundation would be less paradoxical—since the people being constructed would not effectively be a democratic people—yet also something that the lawgiver would work publicly to cover over or deny. For a fascinating article that argues that American politics is best characterized as being such a "representation of democracy," rather than a "representative democracy," see Sheldon Wolin, "Fugitive Democracy," in Benhabib, *Democracy and Difference*, esp. 34.

23. Seyla Benhabib, "Deliberative Rationality and Models of Democratic Legitimacy," *Constellations* 1, 1 (April 1994): 29. In this chapter, further references to this article are given as DR in parentheses in the body of the text. A revised version of Benhabib's essay, without the discussion of Rousseau but with more detailed analysis of deliberative democracy, was published as "Toward a Deliberative Model of Democratic Legitimacy," in Benhabib, *Democracy and Difference*, 67–94. In this chapter, further references to this article are given as TDM in parentheses in the body of the text.

24. For a good discussion of how central are contestation and questioning to the Habermasian notion of deliberative democracy, see Patchen Markell, "Contesting Consensus: Rereading Habermas on the Public Sphere," *Constellations* 3, 3 (1997): 377–400.

25. For an excellent argument in favor of liberal constitutions as means that are necessary to democratic self-rule even as they impose constraints on that same rule, see Holmes, *Passions and Constraints*, esp. chap. 5. Arguing for liberal democracy as a paradoxical but *not* self-contradictory form of politics, Holmes does an admirable job of describing the many ways in which "the rule of the peo-

ple" is actually enabled, rather than disabled, by liberal constitutions. As Holmes argues in a different version of one of the central points I make in this chapter, "autonomy in some respects requires heteronomy in others" (160). Indeed, as he shows, the people only become a people *through* the rules and institutions laid down by the constitution. In his words, "the constitution is an instrument of self-government, a technique whereby the citizenry rules itself. How else could a large democratic community manage its own affairs? A collectivity cannot formulate coherent purposes apart from all decision-making procedures. 'The people' cannot act as an amorphous blob" (167). Despite his cogent, almost encyclopedic, arguments for the necessarily paradoxical — and necessarily liberal — nature of democratic self-rule, Holmes pays little attention to the particular experience of political action that such constraints produce. That is, rather than attending to the difficulties and dilemmas that such a politics involves, and the need to formulate responses to them, Holmes tends to present the institutions and practices established by constitutions as if they were themselves naturally self-sustaining. My argument in Chapter 4 in particular suggests the need for supplementary forms of "civic virtues" that would make the difficulties and paradoxes of liberal democratic politics more easily accepted and endured by democratic citizens. For a very different view from that of Holmes on the democratic nature of liberal constitutionalism, one that emphasizes the costs that constitutional constraints impose on democracy as popular power and collective action, see Sheldon Wolin, *The Presence of the Past* (Baltimore: Johns Hopkins University Press, 1989).

26. I turn now to the most recently published version of Benhabib's essay, "Toward a Deliberative Model of Democratic Legitimacy" (TDM), since it contains a much more extensive discussion of how deliberative democracy relates to liberal rights than does the earlier essay cited above.

27. But, asks Benhabib, doesn't this land us in a vicious circle? On the one hand, "discourses, even to get started, presuppose the recognition of one another's moral rights among discourse participants; on the other hand, such rights are said to be specified as a result of the discursive situation." Benhabib's answer is no: we are caught not in a vicious circle but in the hermeneutic circle. This is, in fact, the only place such judgments can ever be made, whether in moral and political theory or in practice, for "we are always situated within a horizon of presuppositions, assumptions, and power relations, the totality of which can never become wholly transparent to us" (TDM 78–79). Discourse ethics, then, and the theory of deliberative democracy built upon it, "presupposes the reciprocal moral recognition of one another's claims to be participants in the moral-political dialogue," even as Benhabib accepts that such reciprocal recognition is the result of a world-historical process of political struggle.

28. For a brief discussion of how this works, see DR 38.

29. Benhabib's guiding vision of theory's role is captured well in an endnote in which she writes: "What moral and political theory should not do is freeze the historical and essentially contestable outcomes of democratic discourses into some immutable catalog of rights; rather moral and political theory should provide us with general principles to guide our moral intuitions and concrete deliberations when we are confronted with such controversial cases as domestic violence, child

abuse, and marital rape, or using the sex of an unborn baby as a basis for aborting that fetus" (TDM 93 n. 41).

30. It is difficult to know what to do with this claim, however, not only because it is tucked away in an endnote but also because, along with the reference to the "wager" of deliberative democracy, it disappears from the second, revised, version of the essay. Once again, the exact status of Benhabib's model of deliberative democracy remains ambiguous: Is it an improved description of actual practice? Is it a model toward which present practices should be transformed, and if so, to what extent? Nonetheless, the tensions and risks that I am arguing exist between rights and deliberation would exist regardless of how Benhabib, or any other deliberative democrat, resolved these ambiguities.

31. I call this an un-Benhabibian reading since there seems to be an assumption throughout her essays that democratic actions *necessarily* require respecting a specific set of procedures and rights. Thus, in a passage cited above, she writes that democratic contestation requires respecting the set of rules and rights one is trying to change, whereas "when basic rights and liberties are violated the game of democracy is suspended and becomes either martial rule, civil war, or dictatorship." Although this is true in one sense, there are all too frequent occasions (of grave social crisis and division) when a plausible argument can be made that the preservation of democracy (at least in the long run) requires the temporary suspension of certain rights (in order to respond to a more serious threat to democracy). In such cases, can such actions simply be ruled out (in a positivistic fashion) as necessarily undemocratic?

32. To avoid these kinds of tensions between (the deliberative) process and (the) substance (of rights or of justice), one would have to assume either that there exists a teleology of progressively increasing rationality, or else that the practice of deliberation itself, whether in general or under conditions of liberal-democratic constitutionalism, makes people systematically more rational, perhaps because there is some universal tendency toward full deliberative rationality. And even this general process wouldn't be enough to avoid frequent cases of my dilemmas in the transitional period along the way, given the existence of serious constraints on rational deliberation in the present and the foreseeable future.

33. This is a point also made by Michael Walzer, "Deliberation . . . and What Else?" in *Deliberative Politics: Essays on Democracy and Disagreement*, ed. Stephen Macedo (Oxford: Oxford University Press, 1999).

34. I would argue that a similar limitation faces the deliberative democracy advocated by Amy Gutman and Dennis Thompson. In the essay "The Disharmony of Democracy," in *Democratic Community: Nomos 35*, ed. John W. Chapman and Ian Shapiro (New York: New York University Press, 1993), 126–60, Gutman proposes a variety of deliberative democracy that promises to avoid the paradoxes of "populist democracy," bedeviled as it is by an inevitable conflict between the actual outcomes of popular rule and those conditions necessary to maintaining popular rule over time. A populist democrat, Gutman argues, will frequently be faced with having to respect one or another, but not both, of her most basic principles, being forced to choose between accepting the outcomes of public debate in a given situation and limiting or refashioning such decisions so

as to respect those conditions necessary for collective decisions to be legitimate. Gutman's preferred form of deliberative democracy, on the other hand, would avoid such dilemmas by placing the ideal of autonomy, as expressed through reasoned debate and deliberation, at the core of democratic legitimacy. Doing so gives one a single and more fundamental principle that underlies and justifies both the practice of popular rule and the practice of individual liberties that can temper or restrict such rule. Autonomy thus gives one a ground for choosing in particular cases between the otherwise competing sides of the democratic ideal without facing an inherent paradox. Because "the aim of deliberative democracy is not popular rule, but autonomy, . . . no inherent tension exists between popular rule and those conditions necessary to support autonomy as long as it is possible to design recognizably democratic political institutions that further autonomy" (144). Gutman is convinced that is possible to do so. Thus, while even decisions that emerge out of the robust public deliberation that is an expression of autonomy may frequently limit personal freedom, the demands of autonomy itself are not violated so long as the limitations do not either undermine the fundamental identity and self-governability of individuals or "deprive citizens of their share in making decisions that demand deliberation and in holding their authorized decision makers accountable" (155).

Yet while the principle of autonomy may in its abstract form offer a common ground for democracy's otherwise competing demands (popular, majoritarian decision-making and the conditions of equal freedom that legitimate such decision-making), in practice the tensions of democratic politics will return, even in the most deliberative situations. As Jeffrey Rosen argues in a review of the revised and expanded version of deliberative democracy offered in Gutman and Thompson's *Democracy and Disagreement* (Cambridge: Harvard University Press, 1996), their argument that public debate should be restricted to "moral arguments that 'are shared, or could be shared' by all citizens — ones which would respect the fundamental principle of autonomy" — means that "they must pitch their fundamental principles at such a high level of generality that the principles are, in the end, empty. By manipulating these easily manipulated abstractions, they are able to argue throughout *Democracy and Disagreement* that 'deliberative democracy' requires the adoption of public policies that American citizens, in actual democratic debates, have decisively rejected" (Rosen, "In Search of Common Ground," *New York Times Book Review*, December 29, 1996, 21). Far from having avoided populist democracy's paradoxes, deliberative democracy thus merely displaces them onto the meaning of autonomy itself. For deciding on the meaning of autonomy in concrete cases — whether those of reproductive choice, or fair educational and employment opportunities, or welfare policies — goes to the heart of the most divisive contemporary American political debates. The tension between establishing the conditions of democratic legitimacy and respecting the outcomes of popular deliberation in the here and now thus remains as strong as before — even if one accepts the values of widespread deliberation and of some version of autonomy. And a deliberative democrat of Gutman and Thompson's variety will thus be faced with the same basic dilemma I argue faces Benhabib's citizen: establishing in practice the principle of democratic deliberation, and of the autonomy that makes it valuable, will itself often require the use of means — including force of various kinds — that don't themselves fully respect those same principles. For a closely related critique of Gutman and Thompson, see Stanley Fish, "A Wolf in Reason's Clothing," in *The Trouble with Principle* (Cambridge: Harvard University Press, 1999), 187–210.

35. For a related critique of Benhabib's notion of deliberative democracy, see Chantal Mouffe, *The Democratic Paradox* (New York: Verso, 2000), 46–49.

36. One problem this constraint raises is that the formally recognized public space — the one that people have the right of equal access to — may not in any particular case be where the most important political decisions are taken. The "real" public space — or space of power and decision — might not, in other words, be public. It is hard not to believe that this has largely become the case in the contemporary United States, and indeed throughout most reportedly democratic states.

37. For a helpful argument to this effect, see Lynn Sanders, "Against Deliberation," *Political Theory* 25, 3 (June 1997): 347–76. Relying in part on social scientific and social psychological analyses of deliberative practices on American juries, Sanders argues that many voices and perspectives are effectively excluded from having real influence over most deliberative outcomes — either because "material prerequisites for deliberation are unequally distributed" (349) or because the existence of status hierarchies, especially of race, class, and gender, means that certain modes of address or argumentation within deliberative fora are often not recognized as properly rational, or deliberative. Thus there is often much work of democratization that needs to be done before deliberation can in practice be a legitimately — and legitimating — democratic procedure: work ranging from the equalization of resources and access to deliberative fora, to the equalization of deliberative skills, to the various forms of transformation and "interventions in the structure of group deliberations" (366) necessary for socially marginalized voices to be heard and respected as equal partners in democratic debate and discussion.

38. Seyla Benhabib, "Lyotard, Democracy and Difference: Reflections on Rationality, Democracy and Postmodernism," paper delivered at the 1992 Meetings of the American Political Science Association, 13. A slightly revised version was later published as "Democracy and Difference: Reflections on the Metapolitics of Lyotard and Derrida," *Journal of Political Philosophy* 2, 1 (1994): 1–23.

39. To be "public" the space must be open to all and on equal terms, yet this "openness" and equality of access require institutionalization; it is possible only if certain specific rights are established, enforced, and effectively practiced. One can understand these rights and their practice as constituting a minimal definition of the people: "the people" are those who, on certain terms and to a particular extent, have a right of access to the debate over their shared identity. It is, then, only on the basis of an already established version of the people that the people can question and be questioned. As we have seen, this is the dilemma that Benhabib unsuccessfully tries to circumvent with the idea of "recursive validation."

40. For a very interesting argument to this effect with respect to voting rights, see Lani Guinier, *The Tyranny of the Majority: Fundamental Fairness in Representative Democracy* (New York: Free Press, 1994).

41. This is a point made forcefully by Sanders in "Against Deliberation."

42. Claude Lefort, "Human Rights and the Welfare State," in *Democracy and Political Theory* (Minneapolis: University of Minnesota Press, 1988), 31.

43. For an argument on the necessity of coercive, frequently unjust, power to achieve democracy's own ends, see Mansbridge, "Using Power/Fighting Power." My argument here is that theories of democracy and deliberation need to begin from the acceptance of these forms of power and closure as *essential* to democratic politics, not as *in principle* accidental.

44. Walzer, "Deliberation . . . and What Else?" Among the specific examples Walzer cites: the need to educate citizens and activists in the history of democracy and democratic struggles and to foster the identifications with these particular traditions and forms of political life; the crucial role of political bargaining, which depends on the strength of organizing and mobilization, rather than on having the better argument; the important role of leadership in such organizing and of many learning to act in unison (rather than questioning) when necessary; the power of public demonstrations, designed to pressure those in power through displays of political strength and the depth of commitment, rather than by offering rational arguments; political debates that aim not to achieve the rational agreement of those debating but instead to persuade an audience and win over converts to one's side; lobbying, which requires charm, networking, and dealing-making skills; and the many talents necessary to successful electoral campaigns, including the personal appeal of candidates and their public images.

45. This is not meant to downplay the constraints on debate and questioning that result from *unstated*, often unconscious assumptions and beliefs. Even as democratic debate should be structured to make it possible to challenge such assumptions, they too will always place limits on their own interrogation. For an argument that the questioning and critique are always limited by the very assumptions necessary for them to take place, see virtually any of the chapters in Stanley Fish, *Doing What Comes Naturally* (Durham, N.C.: Duke University Press, 1989). See also Sanders, "Against Deliberation."

46. When such action is appropriate, of course, requires judgment. There is no rule, in other words, about when a competing sense of the people is a plausible, if flawed, conception — worthy of discussion and victory if a majority accepts it — and when what claims to be a version of "the people" is in fact effectively undemocratic and thus worth excluding as a practical option, by force if necessary. Such a rule would be available only if there were a neutral, noncontestable "concept" of the people, or of democracy. To adopt the distinction between "concept" and "conception" often used in legal philosophy, one finds there is no clear rule for when a competing "conception" becomes so different from one's own that it is transformed into a different "concept" all together. Any answer can only be a strategic, contextual one. Michael Sandel makes a similar point in his critique of liberal proceduralism in *Democracy's Discontent: America in Search of a Public Philosophy* (Cambridge: Harvard University Press, 1996). See in particular his discussion of abortion and slavery in chapter 1 (esp. 19–21). I offer a detailed analysis of Sandel's critique of proceduralism in the final chapter.

47. An obvious American example of shielding certain fundamental principles

from the play of politics is the requirement of a two-thirds majority of the states to amend the Constitution. The role granted the legal system to review the constitutionality of legislation is a more general example of this practice. This is not, however, meant as an endorsement of judicial review as it is presently practiced, only a claim that it, too, can be defended as a democratic practice. For an argument to this effect, see Ronald Dworkin, "Equality, Democracy, and Constitution: We the People in Court," *Alberta Law Review* 28, 2 (1990): 324–46.

48. In short, however important procedure and process (in particular, that of questioning) are to democracy, democracy still demands the *rule* of some particular version of the people, even in the absence of consensus about who the people are. Democratic conflict can always exceed its institutional boundaries, as the potential for violence that resides in the people's non-autonomous foundation is realized in the struggle between mutually exclusive political programs (each of which may plausibly be said to represent, or desire to institutionalize, "the people"). Although the democratic values of both full inclusion and questionability argue for efforts to avoid polarized, warlike situations, where one's opponents are made into enemies, such situations cannot simply be understood as evidence of the absence of democracy, despite the obvious dangers they pose to democratic openness and freedom. The "democratic" thing to do may well be, in certain cases, to shut down debate, perhaps violently, so as to protect the possibility of "the people" ruling.

49. As I argue at length in Chapter 3, the central flaw in the theories of radical and plural democracy offered by Laclau and Mouffe is precisely their implicit attempt to make the questionability and ungroundedness of democracy into an *answer* to the practical demands of democratic politics.

50. For a more detailed discussion of the democratic possibilities to be found in the recognition of the contingency of identity, see my analysis of Laclau and Mouffe in Chapter 3. See also the work of William E. Connolly, especially *Identity/Difference: Democratic Negotiations of Political Paradox* (Ithaca, N.Y.: Cornell University Press, 1991); and idem, *The Ethos of Pluralization* (Minneapolis: University of Minnesota Press, 1995). I consider some of Connolly's arguments on this topic in the final chapter.

51. Indeed, within the experience of any deliberation and questioning, there is the conflict and ambivalence within the self as it first entertains and then begins to adopt and act on a new belief. In the midst of such transformations (which in various ways are happening all the time), one is more or less at odds with oneself, either in one's consciousness or in practice, as one's emerging beliefs and commitments call into question and make more precarious one's present mode of life, identifications, promises, investments, and so forth.

52. Democratic openness, in other words, does not work by reason alone; the successful exchange of reasons, especially under conditions of democracy, requires a particular set of relationships to self and other, mediated by linguistic and bodily capacities, to be in place.

53. Hannah Arendt, *The Human Condition* (Chicago: University of Chicago Press, 1958), 240–41.

54. I consider the complex relation of cynicism and democracy at greater length in the final chapter.

Chapter 2

1. Hannah Arendt, "What Is Freedom," in *Between Past and Future: Eight Exercises in Political Thought* (New York: Penguin, 1961), 169. In this chapter, further references to this volume are abbreviated WF and included in parentheses in the text. Other cited texts are idem, *On Revolution* (New York: Penguin, 1963), abbreviated as *OR*; idem, *The Life of the Mind*, vol. 2, *Willing* (New York: Harcourt, Brace, Jovanovich, 1978), abbreviated *LM*; and idem, *The Human Condition* (Chicago: University of Chicago Press, 1958), abbreviated *THC*.

2. One of the most recent, and most thorough, arguments that Arendt offers a democratic conception of politics is found in Jeffrey C. Isaac, "Oases in the Desert: Hannah Arendt on Democratic Politics," *American Political Science Review* 88, 1 (March 1994): 156–68. This essay was published in a revised version as chapter 5 of Isaac, *Democracy in Dark Times* (Ithaca, N.Y.: Cornell University Press, 1998), which also features other excellent essays that draw out the radically democratic elements in Arendt's work.

3. For a fascinating article that begins as a forceful critique of Arendt's preference for "the political" over democracy (as the regime of *social* equality and of "the people" as the homogenous mass), only to endorse at the end a sense of democracy that is strikingly indebted to Arendt's notion of the political, see Sheldon Wolin, "Hannah Arendt: Democracy and the Political," *Salmagundi* 60 (spring/summer 1983): 3–19. For two helpful critiques of Arendt's disinterest in modern democracy that grow out of very different interpretations of her work, see George Kateb, *Hannah Arendt: Politics, Conscience, Evil* (Totowa, N.J.: Rowman and Allanheld, 1983), esp. 115–48; and Claude Lefort, "Hannah Arendt and the Question of the Political," in *Democracy and Political Theory* (Minneapolis: University of Minnesota Press, 1988), 45–55.

4. To some extent, of course, the uncertainty of Arendt's relation to democracy is simply a result of the inherent uncertainty in the meaning of democracy. There are, however, numerous other difficulties. To elaborate an adequately detailed picture of Arendt's relation to democratic politics would at the very least require a direct engagement with Arendt's distinction between "the political" and "the social." For an all too brief attempt to suggest some of the issues this would raise, see n. 18. For one possible "democratic" critique of the distinction, see Wolin, "Hannah Arendt: Democracy and the Political."

5. For a helpful discussion of this and other aspects of Arendt's account of political action — one that, like the present chapter, emphasizes the importance of contingency, plurality, and nonsovereignty — see Dana Villa, "Beyond Good and Evil: Arendt, Nietzsche and the Aestheticization of Political Action," *Political Theory* 20, 2: 274–308, esp. 277–81. Villa's argument *for* the deep connections between Arendt's project of revaluing political action and Nietzsche's critique of Platonism and *against* Arendt's "colonization" by either Habermasian or poststructuralist readings is both convincing and useful. My chapter, however, takes a very different approach: by exploring the nature and effects of the tension between freedom and foundation within Arendt's own texts, I argue for the

inevitable failure of any project aimed at recovering an experience of politics purified of "unfree" or "nonpolitical" elements.

6. Melvyn A. Hill, ed., *Hannah Arendt* (New York: St. Martin's Press, 1979), 317.

7. One of the central concerns of the present chapter is to complicate Arendt's argument that violence is "essentially nonpolitical." Arendt's most extensive treatment of violence and its relation to power can be found in "On Violence," in *Crises of the Republic* (New York: Harcourt, Brace, Jovanovich, 1972), 105–98; see esp. sec. 2 and Appendix 11. She argues there that power is, in its *essence*, distinct from violence. Generated and maintained by the joint action and support of many people, power has no purpose other than itself; indeed, power is "the very condition enabling a group of people to think and act in terms of the means–end category" (150). Violence, on the other hand, is purely instrumental; it can command obedience, but it can never generate power; at best it is a temporary, and inessential, supplement for a lack of power. It thus follows that Arendt holds that laws are not essentially commands, which rest in the final analysis on coercion, but rather merely "direct human intercourse as the rules direct the game" (193). Although Arendt is right that violence alone cannot *replace* power as the foundational source for political communities, I argue in the concluding section of this chapter that because the foundation that power itself turns out to need inevitably has particular, nonneutral *purposes* attached to it, instrumentality and violence are not essentially separable from the political realm. Or, in other words, although laws are not *merely* commands, it is nonetheless of the essence of law that it be able at times to act as a command. For further thoughts on the inevitable role that force and violence play in political freedom, see the concluding section, particularly n. 18.

8. It is worth noting the obvious here, however, which is that Rousseau's "sovereignty" is itself built on a moment of mutual promising — that is, the social contract. The distinction between Arendt's promising and Rousseau's contracting may not, in the end, be so great.

9. For an illuminating account of the importance of speech to Arendt's conception of political action, see Kateb, *Hannah Arendt: Politics, Conscience, Evil*, 15. As he writes: "Arendt frequently distinguishes between words and deeds, or between talking and doing, as the basic modes of action. But given all that she excludes as not properly political, the distinction cannot stand. It must collapse, with the result that there is only one true mode of political action, and that is speech, in the form of talking or occasionally writing, as with the Declaration of Independence and other manifestoes or addresses to the world, writing that should be read aloud." I argue in the closing section that the *written* nature of "speech-action" plays a larger, more essential role in Arendt's version of political action than something "occasional" might be expected to, with substantial consequences for the rest of Arendt's understanding of political freedom and foundation.

10. Central to Arendt's claim for the effectiveness of promising as a foundation for freedom is the fact that it acknowledges the plurality of those who make up the political community. Promising resists the violent, totalizing pretensions of a sovereign and general will, and thus the vicious circles of foundation as well, in

part because it does not claim to be the expression of a singular will; it is, rather, no more than a temporary, always revisable, agreement of many different wills and intentions. Although from this point on I concentrate on Arendt's description of the *temporality* of the act of promising, it is important to note this additional argument of hers for the free nature of promising. I return to the issue of promising's relation to plurality at the end of the chapter.

11. I take this to be the meaning of a very difficult passage at the conclusion of "What Is Freedom." A few paragraphs from the end of the essay, Arendt writes that "what usually remains intact in the epochs of petrification and foreordained doom is the faculty of freedom itself, the sheer capacity to begin, which animates and inspires all human activities and is the hidden source of production of all great and beautiful things. But so long as this source remains hidden, freedom is not a worldly, tangible reality; that is, it is not political." Arendt goes on to argue that although "the source of freedom remains present even when political life has become petrified and political action impotent to interrupt automatic processes," freedom "develops *fully* only when action has created its own worldly space where it can come out of hiding, as it were, and make its appearance" (WF 169, emphasis added).

12. This solution is the only one that does not violate Arendt's understanding of the distinctively non-instrumental nature of political action. Unlike labor, which struggles with the necessities of life, and work, which produces "products" designed to achieve a preexisting end, political action has only itself as an end. Action has no other purpose than the continuation of action and the preservation of the conditions for future action. For a sympathetic treatment of the difficulties that this conception of political action raises, see the first chapter of Kateb, *Hannah Arendt: Politics, Conscience, Evil*, esp. 10, 12–13, and 16–22. See also Villa, "Beyond Good and Evil," 277–81. As evidence, however, that Arendt also maintained a more purposive understanding of political action, there is this passage from "On Violence": "What makes man a political being is his faculty of action; it enables him to get together with his peers, to act in concert, and to *reach out for goals and enterprises* that would never enter his mind, let alone the desires of his heart, had he not been given this gift — to embark on something new" (179, emphasis added; see also 150).

13. The force of promising is, in other words, the force of the *performative*. As we have seen in Chapter 1, however, and as I argue in the concluding section of this chapter, this force is effective, and the promise a "felicitous" one, only to the extent that certain other conditions, themselves in part the product of different kinds of "force," are already established.

14. It is important to note at this point that Arendt's argument about the ability of the American Revolution to avoid the vicious circles and violence that destroyed the French Revolution consists, in fact, of a number of related, but separate, claims. One claim, just detailed, is that the Americans were able to avoid the unsolvable dilemma of having to constitute the power necessary to constitute themselves as a political body because *power was already there* — the people were able to avoid the vicious circle of foundation because they had already been formed. It was not enough, however, that the American people already existed;

they had to exist in a particular form. The fact that they did so constituted what Arendt calls their "great good fortune." Hence Arendt's two related claims: first, that the conditions of relative social equality in the colonies allowed the Americans to avoid the instability associated with "the social question," provoked when the violence necessary to *liberate* the masses from poverty and the realm of necessity invades the properly political sphere and is confused with political *freedom*; and second, that the *multiplicity* of the sites of power/promising in revolutionary America allowed the revolution to avoid the trap of imagining there had to be a single, indivisible national will that would be the locus of both power and authority, with the violent repression of the plurality of political action which that brings. Indeed, "the word people retained for [the Americans] the meaning of manyness, of the endless variety of a multitude whose majesty resided in its very plurality" (*OR* 93). To the extent that the American Revolution succeeded in finding a stable foundation for freedom, then, it was able to do so only because a particular kind of people and political practice, supported by specific material conditions, was already established. The "new beginning" of the revolution, in other words, was itself a *re*-foundation. Indeed, as I argue in the concluding section, it is in the very nature of performatives of political foundation to be refoundations. This helps explain why, as Arendt complains, even the Founding Fathers were forced to "renege" on the experience of freedom when faced with "the perplexities inherent in every beginning." The particular conditions of the prerevolutionary American "people" also help explain how Arendt is able to avoid recognizing the various forms of force, and even violence, that are necessary to the formation of political communities.

15. This separation of power from law and authority, Arendt argues, follows the lines of the distinction between a democracy and a republic. The republican form was expressly chosen by the American Founders, Arendt argues, to "prevent the procedures of majority decisions from generating into the 'elective despotism' of majority rule" (*OR* 163–64), which, along with the theory of the general will, imagines political society in the image of a single body, thus threatening the plurality that is essential to the political realm. Unlike in a democracy, where the decisions of the majority are taken for the expression of the will of the whole, "in the republican form of government such decisions are made, and this life [of the nation] is conducted, within the framework and according to the regulations of a constitution which, in turn, is no more the expression of a national will or subject to the will of a majority than a building is the expression of the will of its architect or subject to the will of the inhabitants" (*OR* 163). The hope is that the foundational law will set down principles that will place limits on the freedom of the majority, thus preserving a place for all members of the community, even those in the minority on any particular issue. This republican aspect of Arendt's argument, which arises directly from her conviction that freedom must take place within definite walls and be supported by a firm foundation, is not always taken seriously enough by readers who too quickly see in Arendt's ideal of political action the basis for a radical and participatory democracy. Yet Arendt's distinction between a republican and a democratic form of government is not necessarily the most helpful one either. As we have seen in the previous chapter, the distinction is

better understood as a tension *within* democracy between "the people" understood as today's majority and that sense of "the people" defined by the set of
rights and guarantees necessary to full and equal membership in the political
community. The people of today must, in this sense — precisely in order to respect
the imperative that the people rule — be restricted by some form of the people
instituted in the past. Reframing the issue in terms of this central democratic tension makes clear what is at stake for Arendt's argument: freedom itself is torn
between its need for lasting foundations (in part to protect plurality) and the possibility of radically new beginnings. Freedom cannot simply be identified with just
one or the other: freedom is always possible only on the basis of some closure,
including the requirement that certain new beginnings be ruled out if they
threaten the conditions of future freedom. It is because the apparent separation of
power from law and authority reveals such a fundamental tension within freedom
itself that what is described here as "separation" soon turns out to be a much
more complicated relation.

   16. As we have seen in the previous chapter, the interpretive nature of the distinction between "augmenting" (or following) and "rejecting" poses one of the
central problems for democratic theory and practice.

   17. To argue this is not to disregard the status of a promise as a performative
speech-act or to ignore the distinction between performatives and constatives. It
is meant to suggest, instead, that because, according to Arendt, the act of mutual
promising creates a monument or mark to which a group is bound into the future,
the performative immediately becomes a text in need of interpretation, about
which claims are made and around which arguments and disputes circulate. Without denying its status as a performative, one can recognize that it also becomes the
site for constative speech-acts, and with them, a whole set of possible conflicts as
well. For a helpful and provocative discussion of the relevance of speech-act
analysis to the study of Arendt's texts, see Bonnie Honig, "Declarations of Independence: Arendt and Derrida on the Problem of Founding a Republic," *American Political Science Review* 85 (winter 1991): 97–113. For a critique similar to
the one I propose of Arendt's need for the meaning of the promise to be "relatively
unproblematic," see especially 104. And for Derrida's argument that the strict
separation of performative and constative is impossible to maintain at the
moment of political foundation, see Derrida, "Declarations of Independence,"
New Political Science 15 (summer 1986): 7–15.

   David Ingram offers a powerful critique of Derrida's and Honig's deconstruc-
tions of the performative-constative distinction in his "Novus Ordo Seclorum:
The Trial of (Post)Modernity or the Tale of Two Revolutions," in *Hannah
Arendt: Twenty Years Later*, ed. Larry May and Jerome Kohn (Cambridge: MIT
Press, 1996), 221–50. For Ingram, the vicious circles of foundation that Honig
and Derrida see as involved in performatives of political foundations are better
understood on the model of hermeneutic circles, so long as the founding principles they establish consist of "procedural rule[s] for agreeing on rights rather than
as a direct prescription of them." "*If* the 'higher law' that binds the activity of
consenting is a *procedural condition* for its possibility," Ingram writes, "and *if*,
moreover, such a law is constituted in turn as a *meaningful and determinate pre-*

scription (or set of rights) within this very same activity, then it need no longer confront the contractors as an *external* constraint on their autonomy" (223–24). Ingram's juxtaposition of Derrida's reading of the American founding with that of Arendt illuminates the issues of political legitimacy and collective autonomy in powerful ways. Yet his Habermasian reading of Arendt, like Benhabib's defense of deliberative democracy that we saw in the preceding chapter, rests more weight on the process of "recursive validation" than it can bear. I agree with Ingram that the freedom and legitimacy of a political community have a greater claim to being respected the more closely the basic procedural discursive rules of mutuality, equality, inclusiveness, and so forth are followed in practice. I would nonetheless argue that to the extent those principles themselves are open to interpretation and must frequently be established against political, and nonpolitical, resistance, no practice of democratic politics can entirely avoid the vicious circles and difficult dilemmas to which a deconstructive approach to political foundings calls our attention. Ingram's and Benhabib's otherwise valuable arguments fall silent when faced with these sorts of difficulties. One purpose of this chapter, and the book as a whole, is to argue that the inevitable existence of such difficulties suggests not so much the logic of nihilistic resignation as the need to work to fashion more effective ways of negotiating and living with their burdens.

18. However integral such work is to political freedom — both in itself and as what makes possible the acts of explicit foundation — Arendt nonetheless expresses little or no interest in analyzing it. To do so, of course, would require directly confronting the role that violence plays in the formation of political communities, in particular, the violence involved in the liberation from the realm of necessity, a liberation that is, for Arendt, a necessary (although insufficient) condition of political freedom. As Arendt herself points out, the relative unimportance of "the social question" in the American Revolution, which allowed it to avoid the violence that derailed the French Revolution, was due in part to the institution of slavery. The ability of the Americans to achieve political freedom required the relative liberation from necessity that was to a significant degree bought with the radical *unfreedom* of African slaves (see *OR* 70–71). Thus even as political freedom cannot be achieved *simply* through violence, Arendt's own argument accepts that violence is necessary to the formation of free political communities — whether in the form of forcefully relegating some to unfreedom so as to liberate others, or in the form of the violence necessary to overcome that unfreedom. Although there is not enough space here to go into the issue in detail, it is by itself enough to suggest the necessity of rejecting the *essential* distinction that Arendt draws between violence and the political. It should also suggest that the sharp line between "the political" and "the social" needs to be rethought as well. For at the very least, the social (understood as the realm of need and necessity from which one must be liberated in order to experience political freedom) will be in some necessary relation to the political realm — either as those issues and persons that must be violently excluded for political freedom to be possible, *or, if one accepts the democratic imperative of full inclusion,* as what must be negotiated when considering the level of social equality necessary to equal membership in the political community. In either case, setting the terms of membership

is a fundamentally *political* question. Indeed, it raises what is perhaps the central question of democratic legitimacy: who has the right to define the terms of membership of the political community, and what should they be? As the previous chapter should have made clear, there is no final answer to this question; since no perfectly equal terms will be found, it will always remain a question. Whatever one's response, however, thinking seriously about the status of "the political," not to mention accepting the burdens of its practice, requires some engagement with the question. One cannot, that is, endorse an experience of freedom without accepting freedom's implication in force and violence, and the necessity of negotiating its dangers. This is not to say that Arendt was or should have been a theorist of legitimacy (or of democracy). Nor is it to say that she did not, or could not, have responded to the condition of freedom's implication in violence by arguing it should simply be accepted, and that the relegation of some to unfreedom is a price worth paying for freedom's preservation. Indeed, it is to Arendt's credit that she points out so clearly the dangers that the quest for social equality poses to political freedom, especially in democratic cultures that accept the necessity of some such equality to the possibility of expanding the realm of political freedom. Thinking through how to respect her warnings about the violent and antipolitical resentments that the drive for social equality can produce, while nonetheless respecting the democratic imperative of full inclusion, is one of the central tasks facing democratic thought today. It is, in any case, where any extensive investigation of Arendt's relation to democratic politics would have to begin.

19. As we have seen earlier, the American Revolution was able to avoid the violence that plagued the French search for a foundation in large part because power and promising were already established in the colonies. For this reason, whatever force was necessary to achieve the prerevolutionary American people is more easily hidden from view in Arendt's account.

20. Arendt's effective silence on this aspect of foundation is a particular problem in her treatment of the American founding, involving as it did the violent displacement of an entire civilization. (I say "effective" silence because Arendt does accept that the European conquering of the American continent was violent, even "criminal"; she simply refuses to see this violence as in any essential relation to the "properly" political activities of establishing law and authority [see *OR* 92–93].) It is a trait that Arendt's work shares with the tradition of social contract theory, whose practitioners were fascinated in their own ways with the "emptiness" of the "new world" as a model for the "state of nature." It is consistent with this logic that her favorite act of promising — the Mayflower Compact — was actually agreed to at sea on the way to "the new world," thus adding to the illusion that it displaced no existing forms of community. For additional, complementary, reflections on the location of the drafting and signing of Mayflower Compact, see Honig, "Declarations of Independence," nn. 6 and 12.

21. This equation of politics with the act of "resisting" foundation is the debatable conclusion to Honig's excellent "Declarations of Independence." Despite her critique of Arendt's tendency to equate political freedom too easily with performance and "performatives" and her neglect of the inevitable role of "constatives" in political action and foundations, Honig's concluding attempt to

find some common ground between Derrida's political "strategy of intervention" and Arendt's theory of political authority as augmentation ends up sounding remarkably Arendtian in its faith in "practices of augmentation and amendment [that] make [the] beginning our own — not merely our own legacy but our own construction and performative" (111). The suggestion that political action and authority consist in the constant renewal of the beginning as one's *own*, in a process whereby "we treat the absolute [or antipolitical constative] as an invitation for intervention, . . . declare ourselves resistant to it, [and] refuse its claim to irresistibility by deauthorizing it" (112), still equates the political with only the first side of the performative/constative (or freedom/foundation) division. Even though Honig accepts Derrida's point that the performative necessarily involves a constative moment (or the support of something whose existence and authority is not questioned), she still sees the essentially *political* act as the resistance to and deauthorization of "the constative," in order to prevent us from forgetting the free, and thus revisable, nature of our political foundations or institutions. Although such resistance is certainly political, so too is its apparent opposite, the "constative" insistence that certain things *have been decided* and are no longer to be debated or resisted (however debatable such decisions might soon become).

22. For a related critique of Arendt's overly purified vision of political action, see William Connolly, *Why I Am Not a Secularist* (Minneapolis: University of Minnesota Press, 2001), chap. 7.

23. Defining compassion as an attempt to abolish the distance between people so as to feel and respond to the suffering of others, Arendt sees compassion as having no need for the words and speech-action that are essential to the practice of politics. Indeed, Arendt argues that when compassion does enter the political world, it is likely to take a violent form, demanding swift action to do away with suffering and inequality. The particular character of compassion, she argues, helps explain some of the violence and cruelty of the pity-inspired "virtue" of Robespierre and much of the French Revolution, about which Arendt has such powerful analyses to offer in *On Revolution* (see esp. 75, 81, and 85–88). For a helpful discussion of Arendt's understanding of compassion, see Kimberly Curtis, *Our Sense of the Real: Aesthetic Experience and Arendtian Politics* (Ithaca, N.Y.: Cornell University Press, 1999), 85–92. For a fascinating and Arendtian discussion of forgiveness in democratic politics, see Melissa Orlie, *Living Ethically, Acting Politically* (Ithaca, N.Y.: Cornell University Press, 1998), chap. 7, esp. 177–85.

Chapter 3

1. Ernesto Laclau and Chantal Mouffe, *Hegemony and Socialist Strategy: Towards a Radical Democratic Politics* (London: Verso, 1985), 193. In this chapter, further references to this volume are abbreviated *HSS* and included in parentheses in the text.

2. Ernesto Laclau, "New Reflections on the Revolution of Our Time," in *New Reflections on the Revolution of our Time* (New York: Verso, 1990), 78. In this chapter, further references to this essay are abbreviated *NR* and included in parentheses in the text.

3. Rather than lamenting "the generalization of dislocatory relations," Laclau argues that "the accelerated tempo of social transformation and the continual rearticulatory interventions the latter demands lead to a higher awareness of historicity" (NR 39) and of the political nature of the world: the space of freedom and politics is increasing all the time. Because "the world is less 'given' and must increasingly be constructed," "a much more optimistic vision is gained of the prospects opening up for contemporary social struggles" (NR 40, 52).

4. There are obvious connections between this aspect of Laclau and Mouffe's argument and the work of Claude Lefort, which was briefly discussed in the Introduction. His analysis of the "democratic revolution" and of the importance of rights within democratic politics has clearly been of great influence on their notion of radical and plural democracy. See *HSS* 186–88 for an explicit discussion of his arguments.

5. It is worth noting at this point an interesting doubleness in the democratic revolution as Tocqueville describes it. In Tocqueville's account, the critique of the natural and the hierarchical went together, since the hierarchies of the predemocratic era were defended on the basis of their supposedly natural, if not divinely inspired, status. But there are nonetheless two potentially separable critiques at work there: the critique of the inequality, and the critique of the supposed givenness of the category itself and of the political closure this entails. One important connection of radical and plural democracy to this latter aspect of the democratic revolution — its critique of closure — is explored in the final section of the chapter.

6. I address the fragmented and multiply-indebted nature of the democratic self, and the need for rhetorical strategies able to speak to the burdens such multiplicity brings with it, in the closing section of the final chapter. For a very helpful discussion of Laclau and Mouffe's theory of the discursive nature of "subject positions" and identity formation, see Anna Marie Smith, *Laclau and Mouffe: The Radical Democratic Imaginary* (New York: Routledge, 2000), 55–74.

7. It should be noted that Laclau and Mouffe are not always consistent in their definition (whether implied or explicit) of democracy. At certain moments in their writings (for example, in the concluding pages of *Hegemony and Socialist Strategy*), they restrict democracy to the extension of the egalitarian principle and its critique of subordination. At other moments, democracy is described as involving equality *and* liberty for all (although these are also at certain points, especially in Mouffe's essays, each associated with the different logics of democracy and of liberalism). Finally, democracy is also defined at some points as the realm of politicality itself — of freedom, self-creation, openness, and so forth, which is often associated with the *tension between* the democratic principles of liberty and equality for all, and the need to preserve that tension.

8. Linda Zerilli argues that Laclau's work on the idea of the "empty signifiers" — defined as a "particular" that, by standing in for the "universal," allows for the hegemonic articulation of a democratic chain of equivalences — makes possible a useful reworking of recent debates over the relation of the particularity and universality in feminist political struggles. See Zerilli, "This Universalism Which Is Not One," *Diacritics* 28, 2 (1998): 3–20.

9. A social relation can itself only become an antagonism through the dis-

placement of an equivalential logic, which redescribes the relation as an inequality and a matter of subordination (see, e.g., *HSS* 154). This helps explain how they can argue for the compatibility of a multiplicity of antagonisms in the midst of a single hegemonic articulation.

10. Although Laclau and Mouffe make "liberty" one of the essential values of radical and plural democracy and argue that such democracy is radically "libertarian," their notion of liberty is primarily that of "positive liberty," or autonomy — the value of having control over one's own life in all the various spheres or subject positions that involve them. This helps explain why they consider liberty and equality to be essentially compatible: autonomy combines both values.

11. The deconstruction that Laclau and Mouffe advocate of the traditional public/private division (and its corollary of individual rights as prepolitical) has from their perspective the additional benefit of expanding the field of the political and the number of relations that are considered open to struggle and negotiation, which brings with it an increase in the possibilities for a hegemonic rearticulation of the dominant patterns of power and subordination.

12. It might seem at first glance that the specificity of radical and plural democracy rests in the set of struggles, issues, and identities that make up the "new social movements." As Laclau and Mouffe themselves argue, however, such struggles carry no inherent political valence. They can be articulated by any political program at all. At particular moments in their work — for instance, in their presentation of the character of "democratic" rights — the force of their argument relies in part on the implied existence of a more decided sense of what constitutes the specificity of radical and plural democracy — a more specific sense, for instance, of what the demands of equality might mean in particular political situations. To enunciate such a program, however, even in very general terms, would threaten to sever the close connection they wish to establish between radical and plural democracy and the constitutive conditions of contingency, plurality, antagonism, and so forth. Instead of choosing between the two levels of analysis — between, for instance, the general "democratic" *form* of rights and the particular definition a right would have to have in order to be "compatible" with other rights — Laclau and Mouffe choose to work at both levels simultaneously. Part of the effort of this chapter is to explore the difficulties for their position that result from this argumentative strategy.

13. Chantal Mouffe, "Democratic Citizenship and Political Community," in *Community at Loose Ends*, ed. Miami Theory Collective (Minneapolis: University of Minnesota Press, 1991), 70–82; reprinted in Chantal Mouffe, ed., *Dimensions of Radical Democracy* (New York: Verso, 1992), 225–39. In this chapter, further references to this essay are abbreviated DC and included in parentheses in the text. Other essays by Mouffe that cover similar terrain, and that have been republished as part of her collection *The Return of the Political* (New York: Verso, 1993), include "American Liberalism and Its Critics: Rawls, Taylor, Sandel and Walzer," "Citizenship and Political Identity," "Feminism, Citizenship and Radical Democratic Politics," "Liberal Socialism and Pluralism: Which Citizenship?" "Radical Democracy: Modern or Postmodern?" and "Radical Democracy or Liberal Democracy?" See especially "Preface: Democratic Politics Today," in

Dimensions of Radical Democracy. A more recent collection of essays that expands Mouffe's arguments in interesting ways, most of which, however, appeared too late to be taken fully into account in this chapter, is *The Democratic Paradox* (New York: Verso, 2000).

14. I offer my own extended analysis of the limitations of the civic republican understanding of pluralism and the democratic "we" in the final chapter.

15. Mouffe is quoting from Michael Oakeshott, *On Human Conduct* (Oxford: Oxford University Press, 1975), 175.

16. There are obvious parallels here between the interpretation of Oakeshott offered by Mouffe and the attempt by Arendt to articulate the plurality characteristic of freedom with the necessity of foundation, which was analyzed at length in Chapter 2. Although Mouffe's analysis of the structure of freedom has clear connections to Arendt's understanding of freedom and political action, Mouffe nonetheless accepts — in a way that we have seen Arendt resist — the antagonism, division, and violence that the contingency and plurality essential to freedom necessarily bring with it.

17. There is thus an isomorphic and mutually supportive relation between the form and the content of the *respublica*: the form of our commonality is a set of principles, which, because they do not constitute a single substantive good, can preserve plurality; what they protect or allow, in turn, are the twin ideals of liberty (plurality) and equality (commonality).

18. Mouffe's model here, once again, is Oakeshott, who writes that in his *societas*, "every situation is an encounter between 'private' and 'public,' between an action or an utterance to procure an imagined and wished-for substantive satisfaction and the conditions of civility to be subscribed to in performing it; and no situation is the one to the exclusion of the other" (*On Human Conduct*, 183; quoted in DC 81).

19. Depending on the perspective one adopts, Mouffe's goal of a single communal bond that would preserve and protect diversity/plurality is either impossible, to the extent that the diversity will always be challenging the singularity of the bond, or impossible *not* to achieve, given that some degree of diversity and commonality is constitutive. To put this point another way, when Mouffe writes that the "common" can be "compatible with the recognition of conflict, division and antagonism" ("Preface: Democratic Politics Today," 12), the meaning of "compatible" remains ambiguous. For Mouffe's argument to be more than a *theoretical* claim (and it is certainly a theoretical advance over the Rawls–Sandel debate), it would have to provide more specifics about how the problem of their compatibility is to be dealt with.

20. As Mouffe puts it in "Preface: Democratic Politics Today," democracy is not relativist: it proposes and imposes a single set of values: "there can be never be pure, neutral procedures without reference to normative concerns" (11–12).

21. It would seem, then, that what characterizes the specifically "modern" form of democracy, for Mouffe, is the *recognition* of the "permanent" tension between liberty and equality.

22. Any commonality produced out of the shared experience of *subordination* or oppression would itself, according to Mouffe's own theory of discourse, be fully

a *product* of discursive articulation and political struggle and thus cannot by itself act as the *ground* for the construction of a new democratic common concern.

23. This is not, however, to deny that there will always be existing standards, lodged both explicitly and implicitly in political and legal discourse, which will *in practice* help shape and place limits on what "equality and liberty for all" can mean. Such standards themselves, however, are fully contingent and discursive, and can never be definitive, or act as the ground, of the meaning of radical and plural democracy's principles.

24. Laclau offers a very similar analysis in an interview included in *New Reflections*. He mentions in particular the failure of San Francisco's diverse constituencies to articulate their "popular" demands in a complementary rather than a contradictory fashion. He argues in general that "social conflictiveness is so widespread and has taken on such new forms in today's world, that it has more than surpassed the hegemonic capacity of the old left" (NR 228). Unfortunately he offers nothing in the way of an analysis of how such an impasse might be overcome and a "new" left imaginary constructed other than to say that it is likely to "revolve around the themes implicit in the concepts of 'democratic revolution' and 'radical and plural democracy'," and that this will have the advantage of "creat[ing] a horizon . . . that enables a whole multitude of social and political demands . . . to be equated" (NR 228). Which brings us back to square one. Nor, unfortunately, does Laclau offer any suggestions for how better to negotiate the inevitable conflict, disappointment, and anger arising from the fact that the diverse identities and positions don't yet fit together.

25. In other words, the notion of autonomy that is at the basis of Laclau and Mouffe's notion of freedom and democracy (and which is itself the reconciliation of liberty and equality) doesn't by itself solve any of the political difficulties a politics of radical democratic hegemony will face. The whole problem is the degree or range of the different autonom*ies* and how to balance them, given the nonnatural, non-essential definition of the self who seeks autonomy. In other words, one is left with the rather classic liberal dilemma: since I can't control the entirety of my world and must respect the autonomy of those others with whom I share it, what and where are the limits to be imposed on my actions? People will necessarily be within the hold of their present identities and some sense of what is necessary to their controlling their lives and being full and equal members of the community; their inevitable conflicts with those of others must be negotiated. But in the absence of a neutral, essential notion of the "self," this will be difficult and conflictual. Laclau and Mouffe offer nothing in the way of suggestions about how to negotiate this process in a way that is consistent, rather than at odds, with radical and plural democracy.

One consequence of this is that there will be a tension between the autonomy of the various struggles that make up the movement for radical democracy and the necessity of a hegemonic articulation of them: at particular moments, some of the demands will have to be privileged over others for reasons either of justice or strategy. This also means that the emphasis Laclau and Mouffe give to contingency does not mean necessarily that issues of class and the economy need in any way to be downplayed: although they cannot be given any *necessary* or *essential* priority over other spheres and identities, there is also no reason that they won't or shouldn't be given a provisional priority. That decision depends on strategic and analytical reasons, not theoretical or ontological ones.

This, in turn, helps explain the disappointing quality of Laclau and Mouffe's debate with the Marxist theorist Norman Geras. (Originally published in *New Left Review*, the two sides of the debate were reprinted separately in Laclau's *New Reflections* and Geras's *Discourses of Extremity: Radical Ethics and Post-Marxist Extravagances* [London: Verson, 1990].) There were, in effect, two simultaneous but one-sided arguments taking place, with each side talking past the other. On the one hand, Laclau and Mouffe defended the claim that radical democratic political positions could still be taken after accepting post-structural and Wittgensteinian philosophical argument. Geras, on the other hand, defended Marxism against the charge that it was essentialist, all the while attacking their anti-essentialist arguments. Neither side addressed the possibility that the *theoretical* critique of anti-essentialism (and of those versions of Marxism that rely on it) in no way rules out the *contingent* — strategic, provisional, political — privileging of class and the class struggle as the primary focus of hegemonic politics, over and above other democratic struggles. Although Laclau and Mouffe's anti-essentialist theory can describe the conditions of such political decisions, it says nothing about the relative weights to be given to the different democratic struggles.

26. For an excellent sense of the difficulties that attempts to forge a democratic politics of identity face from the attachments people have to their identities as grounded in past suffering and injustice, see Wendy Brown, "Wounded Attachments," *Political Theory* 21, 3 (August 1993): 390–410. This topic also raises the crucial issue of the material and institutional nature of discourse and articulation and the identities they constitute. The equality to be achieved by articulating an ever larger chain of equivalences has to be "paid for" — in economic, cultural, and psychic resources — and by some more than others. These constraints need to be "theorized." (To the extent that Laclau and Mouffe neglect to do so, they leave themselves open to the charge of being concerned "merely" with issues of discourse and rhetoric, despite their protestations that the discursive cannot simply be opposed to the material.) For a recent attempt to think through such constraints, see William Connolly, *Identity/Difference: Democratic Negotiations of Political Paradox* (Ithaca, N.Y.: Cornell University Press, 1991), especially his discussion of the idea of "branded" contingency. For my still rather preliminary attempt to work out a specific mode of democratic rhetoric that would make it easier for people to accept the risks and burdens of "identity reconfiguration," see the closing sections of the final chapter.

27. Laclau and Mouffe describe this relation as the "maximum autonomization of spheres on the basis of the generalization of the equivalential-egalitarian logic" (*HSS* 167).

28. The disturbingly formal character of their analysis that I am drawing attention to here might have been mitigated were they to offer a more extensive analysis of *subordination*, for the *democratic* nature of the various struggles that a radical and plural form of democratic politics would bring together hegemonically is defined by their challenging distinct forms of subordination. Unfortu-

nately, what counts as subordination is left tantalizingly vague—no doubt so as to respect the contingent and contextual nature of its meaning. For an interesting argument to the effect that Laclau and Mouffe's understanding of radical and plural democracy actually implies a stronger, even Kantian, ethics of universality and equality than what they explicitly endorse, see Vincent P. Pecora, "Ethics, Politics, and the Middle Voice," *Yale French Studies* 79 (1991): 203–30.

29. Mouffe, "Preface: Democratic Politics Today," 14. For an earlier, virtually identical formulation of this problematic by both Laclau and Mouffe, see *HSS* 188.

30. Chantal Mouffe, "Democracy, Power, and 'the Political,'" in *The Democratic Paradox* (New York: Verso, 2000), 21. In this chapter, further references to this essay are abbreviated DP and included in parentheses in the text.

31. For a more extended analysis of the incompletion and antagonistic "ground" of every identity, see Laclau's "New Reflections on the Revolution of Our Time," esp. 17–26.

32. I quote here from the original, unpublished version of Mouffe, "Democracy, Power, and 'the Political,'" delivered at the annual meeting of the Conference on Social Thought, Yale University, March 1993, 4. This set of arguments returns one to the tension encountered in Rousseau between the present "people" and the past "people" who rule in their name, and the paradoxical structure whereby the necessity of protecting freedom through some institutional form for the expression of the people's will sets limits on the present and future freedom of that "same" people. Although Laclau and Mouffe rarely invoke the category of the people in their treatment of democracy, an analysis of how democracy demands the rule of *today's* people helps explain in part why they argue that no political arrangement (or "universal") can be immune from critique and revision: it is always immediately out of date.

33. Although Mouffe clearly intends this as a critique of the role that the concepts of the ideal speech situation and "communicative action oriented to consensus" play in Habermas's and others' visions of "deliberative democracy," it is not so clear just how far Mouffe's democratic politics would be *in practice* from a Habermas-inspired one. For an excellent argument that shows the centrality of active contestation and nonconsensus to the Habermasian notion of deliberative democracy, see Patchen Markell, "Contesting Consensus: Rereading Habermas on the Public Sphere," *Constellations* 3, 3 (1997): 377–400. For Mouffe's own engagement with Habermas and deliberative democratic theorists such as Seyla Benhabib, see *Democratic Paradox*, esp. 45–49 and 83–94. For a capsule version of what Mouffe sees as the difference between her approach and those of Habermasians, see 137.

34. This is central to the argument that Stanley Fish makes against Roberto Unger and other "antifoundationalist" theories in *Doing What Comes Naturally* (Durham, N.C.: Duke University Press, 1989). For Laclau's own argument to the same effect (which is why, strictly speaking, his and Mouffe's positions are not *anti*foundationalist), see NR 43–44. See also my discussion of his argument below.

35. Even the most "universalist" or "neutralist" versions of liberalism, for

instance, accept that politics is always a matter of choices, of analyzing benefits and costs.

36. To a large extent, the close association that Laclau and Mouffe make between radical and plural democracy and "openness" emerges out of their appropriation of the democratic critique of totalitarianism formulated by, among others, Lefort and Castoriadis. Some of the uncertainty in the meaning of their radical and plural democracy stems from the attempt to employ those same characteristics that set democracy off from totalitarianism — plurality, contest, questioning, openness — as those that also distinguish a new, more radical, democracy from other forms of democracy, the implication being that somehow openness is the *essence* of democracy and radical and plural democracy the most democratic of all democratic political forms. The problems with this argument, which I am trying to suggest in the rest of the chapter, are as follows: (1) this seems to give undue privilege to the "open" side of the open/closed dialectic that constitutes democracy; and (2) whatever is truly distinctive about radical and plural democracy will have to be found in the specific character of the openness it practices, and not in its status as a general demand — but these specifics are what Laclau and Mouffe do not provide.

37. Mouffe, "Democracy, Power, and 'the Political,'" unpublished version, 4.

38. William Connolly begins to explore this terrain in some of his more recent writing. See in particular his discussions of "the ethos of critical responsiveness" in *The Ethos of Pluralization* (Minneapolis: University of Minnesota Press, 1995), esp. 178–88.

39. A very interesting borderline case is the discourse of the "free market," which can be understood either as a political scheme designed to achieve certain goals and exclude others or instead as a natural, or at least "neutral," and thus nonpolitical form of social relations. Whether such a discourse was antidemocratic, then, would depend on the particular uses to which it was put in particular situations. For a very different analysis of the ways in which "culture" can stand in for "race," an analysis that is intended as a *critique* of "anti-essentialism," see Walter Benn Michaels, "Race into Culture: A Critical Genealogy of Cultural Identity," *Critical Inquiry* 18, 4 (summer 1992): 655–85. See also idem, "Posthistoricism," *Transition* 70:4–19; and idem, "Autobiography of an Ex-White Man," *Transition* 73:122–43.

40. For a fascinating discussion of how this can work, see Etienne Balibar, "Is There a Neo-Racism," in Etienne Balibar and Immanuel Wallerstein, *Race, Nation, Class: Ambiguous Identities* (New York: Verso, 1991), 1–28; see esp. 21–23.

41. As Laclau puts it at the conclusion to "New Reflections," "the recognition of our limitation and contingency, of the precarious and pragmatic construction of the universality of our values . . . is the very condition for a democratic society" (NR 83).

42. "It is in our pure condition of event, which is shown at the edges of all representation and in the traces of temporality corrupting all space, where we find our most essential being, which is our contingency and the intrinsic dignity of our transitory nature" (NR 84).

43. The exploration of the tension *within* freedom between openness and closure is, of course, a central motif of my discussion of Rousseau in Chapter 1 and of Arendt's analysis of freedom in Chapter 2.

44. In his more recent writings — see especially his collection of essays *Emancipation(s)* (New York: Verso, 1996) — Laclau seems to go even further: he argues that the constitutive lack and instability of human subjectivity are such that subjects always desire the imaginary resources of the Law or Authority to provide order and a phantasmatically complete collectivity, or primal unity, with which they can identify. Politics, then, is always oriented toward closure: the very experience of openness and uncertainty that it offers us also provokes desires for and promises of completion and stability. For a helpful analysis of the influence of Lacanian theory on Laclau's recent writings, see Smith, *Laclau and Mouffe*, 76–83. My analysis of Laclau is not based on a close reading of these more recent writings.

45. My critique of the role of openness in Laclau and Mouffe's notion of radical and plural democracy, then, is distinct from Stanley Fish's critique of "antifoundationalist theory hope," which recognizes no such possible consequences, since it gives no consideration to the demands of democratic legitimacy. Nonetheless, my criticisms of Laclau and Mouffe owe a major debt to Fish's work. See his essays collected in *Doing What Comes Naturally*, esp. chaps. 14–19; and idem, *There's No Such Thing as Free Speech* (New York: Oxford University Press, 1994). For my critique of the democratic deficits of Fish's pragmatism, see Alan Keenan, "The Democratic Question: On the Rule of the People and the Paradoxes of Political Freedom," Ph.D. dissertation, Johns Hopkins University, 1994.

46. This risk could be dismissed if one held a Mill-like faith that the correct opinion or decision would ultimately result from a truly open and fair decision-making process, in which all possible questions could be asked. But to hold that belief is dangerously close to the "rationalist" dream of universality and a coercion-free process of communication, which is one of the chief targets of Laclau and Mouffe's critique of closure.

47. There is the following possible explanation of the equation Mouffe draws between conflict and democracy: conflicts and confrontations would be here understood as signs of the unsettled, not yet determined, open character of the social situation. An increase in conflict would mean an increase in politics and freedom, both understood as the experience of openness. Since democracy, especially in its radical and plural version, is the mode of political community in which politics and freedom are most directly experienced and highly valued, there would indeed be a direct relation between the existence of conflict and democracy.

48. As I have suggested at various points in this chapter, a basic ambiguity surfaces at various moments in Laclau and Mouffe's argument (the most pronounced such moment being in their debate with Norman Geras). They sometimes move from the argument that the deconstructive theoretical analysis does not *rule out* effective political action to the more difficult claim that the recognition of our ontological and existential condition should, or at least can be used to, *lead to* new radical politics. It is this latter argument that still needs to be *argued* convincingly.

49. Strictly speaking, this is true of all rules, given that they are always interpreted on the basis of other principles, values, and assumptions, which limit their
extension. Democracy is, then, a particularly clear example of the unruly nature
of all rules and all political action. In this respect, democracy may indeed be the
experience of politics "itself" (though not as a principle of openness and critique,
as Laclau and Mouffe often would have it, but rather as the tension *between*
openness and closure).

50. My argument here is that the *negativity* involved in democracy's irresolvable tensions and fundamental incompletion must first be recognized and
accepted in order for the affirmation of contingency and openness to hold out any
positive democratic possibilities. Laclau and Mouffe, on the other hand, are so
determined to prove that the recognition of contingency and lack of any rational
ground for politics are good things for democratic politics that they consistently
downplay such negativity (except in the most abstract affirmation of the necessity
of conflict and power). Thus one of Laclau and Mouffe's repeated, and mislead-
ing, argumentative tropes: democracy's constitutive tensions — whether between
liberty and equality, or pluralism and hegemonic articulation — are not in fact lia-
bilities or limitations, but rather democratic "resources" or "values" to be
affirmed, since by ruling out the full completion or realization of democracy, they
prevent totalitarian closure and the end of democratic contestation. The problem
here is that the acceptance of this lack of closure is good only *because* democracy's
basic principles can't be fully realized; if they *could* be — if liberty and equality
were both available to all citizens fully and simultaneously, or if the autonomy of
the various democratic struggles could be maintained fully even while achieving
an effective hegemonic bloc, or if contestation could be institutionalized without
endangering democracy's own achievements — in what way would democracy's
tensions and incompletion be politically positive? My preferred formulation,
which is both more true to the experience of democratic politics and more useful
for responding to it, is to say that while the tensions and incompletion that are
basic to democracy make politics difficult, it is *more dangerous* to deny them than
to accept them and try to work with them. Laclau and Mouffe's somewhat forced
theoretical optimism makes it harder for them — and their readers — to see the
crucial need to theorize and develop rhetorical and *ethical* strategies that enable
citizens to bear more effectively the very real burdens of democratic politics. I
should note here that Mouffe's most recent writings, especially *Democratic Paradox*, give much greater emphasis to the negative aspect of democratic incompletion and the violence and antagonism lodged at the heart of democratic politics.
She is, in turn, critical of what she calls "'postmodern' ethical approaches." "The
kind of pluralism they celebrate," she writes, "implies the possibility of plurality
without antagonism, of a friend without an enemy, an agonism without antagonism. As if once we had been able to take responsibility for the other and to
engage with its difference, violence and exclusion could disappear" (DP 134).
Although I heartily agree with the basic point being made here, it remains unclear
just which theorists this critique is meant to refer to, or what might be the practical content of the alternate "ethics of the Real" that Mouffe endorses in the concluding paragraphs of *Democratic Paradox*. What is still missing from Mouffe's

"negative" ethical turn is the recognition that for a political practice of radical and plural democracy to be sustainable, rhetorically and psychologically aware "ethical" practices are needed to make the experience of uncertainty and conflict more bearable for political actors. Without such practices, the burdensome politicization of daily life that democratic demands for justice and equality bring with them is bound to further turn people *away* from politics. I try to work out in the final chapter in a very preliminary way what such practices might look like.

51. Here I am echoing criticisms of Laclau and Mouffe made by both Romand Coles and William Connolly. See Coles, *Rethinking Generosity: Critical Theory and the Politics of Caritas* (Ithaca, N.Y.: Cornell University Press, 1997), 190, in which he argues that Laclau and Mouffe's vision of radical and plural democracy suffers from the lack of an *ethical* sensibility of generosity toward "the other." A similar criticism is made by William Connolly in a review of Mouffe's *The Return of the Political* in "Twilight of the Idols," *Philosophy and Social Criticism* (winter 1995): 127–37. In the final chapter I begin to sketch out what a language of democratic engagement might look like that was infused with a nonmoralistic ethical spirit of generosity and acceptance of otherness, both in "others" and in one's "self." It remains unclear whether Connolly's and Coles's theories of ethics are included in those "postmodern ethical approaches" that Mouffe criticizes in *Democratic Paradox*.

Chapter 4

1. According to the 2001 edition of the *New York Times Almanac* (New York: New York Times Books, 2000), the percentage of eligible voters who cast ballots in presidential elections reached its low point in the 1996 election, with a turnout rate of only 49 percent. The rate has been declining steadily since 1960, when it was 63 percent. In 1968 the rate was down to 60.2 percent, and in 1984 it was down to 53.1 percent. For off-year congressional elections, the rates of electoral participation in the United States are much lower: in 1994 only 38 percent of eligible voters cast ballots. As a result, victorious candidates generally receive votes from approximately 25–30 percent of the possible electorate in presidential elections and only 15–20 percent of eligible citizens in off-year elections for Congress. Participation rates are generally even lower in local and state elections. For the now classic, and disturbing, analysis of the more general decline in rates of public participation by Americans across all spheres of social life, see Robert Putnam, *Bowling Alone: The Collapse and Revival of American Community* (New York: Simon and Schuster, 2001). An earlier version of Putnam's analysis of this issue was published as "The Strange Disappearance of Civic America," in *Ticking Time Bombs*, ed. Robert Kuttner (New York: New Press, 1996), 263–86.

2. As evidence of widespread political ignorance among U.S. citizens, one can note the results of a survey conducted jointly by the *Washington Post*, the Kaiser Foundation, and Harvard University in late 1995. For example, only 22 percent of those surveyed knew the names of both of their U.S. senators, and whereas 54 percent knew that it is the U.S. Supreme Court that has final responsibility for deciding the constitutionality of laws, only 6 percent knew the name of the Supreme

Court's chief justice. For more examples, see the *Washington Post*, January 28–February 2, 1996. The surveys also reveal the not-so-surprising correlation between income and education levels, as well as that between the likelihood a person will vote and other forms of involvement in political campaigns (including making financial contributions). The journal *Left Business Observer*, no. 95 (November 2000), uses U.S. Census Bureau statistics to calculate the disproportionate rates at which high-income citizens voted in the 2000 election relative to their lower-income counterparts. For example, although only 12 percent of the voting population have incomes over $100,000, 16 percent of voters came from this income bracket. The ratios for the other income brackets are as follows: $75,000–$100,000: 10 percent of the population vs. 13 percent of voters; $50,000–$75,000: 18 percent of the population vs. 25 percent of voters; $15,000–$49,999: 43 percent of the population vs. 40 percent of voters; and those earning less than $15,000: 17 percent of the population but only 7 percent of voters. Thus among income earners, those in the lowest 60 percent accounted for only 47 percent of the actual votes cast. According to the *Left Business Observer*'s calculations, "had the income mix of the electorate matched the population, and assuming preferences within the brackets stayed the same, the popular vote would have been 50% for Gore and 46% for Bush, instead of 48–48%" (1).

3. For an excellent essay that explains many of the democratic failings of the U.S. electoral system through reference to recent changes in the technologies, strategies, and organization of American political campaigns, see Marshall Ganz, "Voters in the Crosshairs: How Technology and the Market are Destroying Politics," in Kuttner, *Ticking Time Bombs*, 245–59.

4. According to Nancy Folbre, James Heintz, and the Center for Popular Economics, *The Field Guide to the U.S. Economy* (New York: New Press, 2000), economic inequality in the United States has increased significantly over the last three decades to reach dangerously undemocratic proportions. In 1983 the richest 1 percent of U.S. households owned 43 percent of the country's financial wealth. By 1997, their share had increased to 49 percent, whereas the share of the bottom 90 percent of households had dropped from 20 percent to 17 percent over the same period. Whereas in the 1970s the inequalities in the distribution of wealth in the United States were roughly on a par with those of other industrialized countries, by the late 1990s the inequalities in the United States had surpassed even the historical leader in inequality, Great Britain. For more statistics on economic inequality in the United States, see the Introduction, n. 9.

5. Charles Taylor, "Living with Difference," in *Debating Democracy's Discontent: Essays on American Politics, Law, and Public Philosophy*, ed. Anita L. Allen and Milton C. Regan, Jr. (New York: Oxford University Press, 1998), 220.

6. Charles Taylor, *The Ethics of Authenticity* (Cambridge: Harvard University Press, 1991), 112–13.

7. Ibid., 113.

8. Michael Sandel, *Democracy's Discontent: America in Search of a Public Philosophy* (Cambridge: Harvard University Press, 1996), 331. Further page references are given in parentheses in the body of the text.

9. My thanks to Steve Rubenstein for helping me clarify this point. For a par-

ticularly good treatment of what I am calling the vicious circles of public disinvestment that connects the appeal of market and individualist logic to the defeat of the Democratic party in the 1994 congressional elections, see Michael Walzer, "What's Going On," *Dissent*, winter 1996, 5–11. I have discussed these issues at greater length in "Twilight of the Political? A Contribution to the Democratic Critique of Cynicism," *Theory & Event* 2:1 (http://muse.jhu.edu/journals/theory_&_event).

10. It is worth noting here that Sandel is noticeably more Tocquevillean in his formulation of this practice of civic virtue than is Taylor. For Sandel, the collective identification that he advocates is not so much with the nation or with the people as a whole as it is with the local community and local associations, understood as training grounds for the habit of caring about concerns larger than one's own private interest — ones that can then extend farther afield when necessary.

11. The public discourse on the American public's cynicism reached its recent height in 1995 and 1996 (later, at least temporarily, displaced by the discourse of economic and technological euphoria that accompanied continuing economic growth, the rise of the stock market, and the burst of Internet-related wealth). Most frequently lamented as signs of American's "cynicism" were the declining rates of participation in national and local elections, growing displeasure with the negativity and "incivility" of American political discourse, especially during election campaigns, anger at the broken promises and undeserved "perks" of professional politicians, lack of faith in the efficiency and effectiveness of the federal government, and high levels of economic insecurity — even in apparently good economic times — that feed widespread doubts that the nation's social problems can be solved or mitigated anytime soon. In a particularly lengthy and serious treatment published in the *Washington Post* in early 1996, all of the above attitudes were analyzed in detail, based on the results of extensive public surveys done in 1995. Although the week-long series of articles, titled "Reality Check: The Politics of Mistrust," failed to present a coherent interpretation of Americans' political disenchantment, it offered evidence that levels of mistrust, alienation, anger, ignorance, and pessimism with respect to the country's governing political institutions had reached unprecedented highs. For instance, the opinion polls on which the articles were based revealed the following as evidence of Americans' mistrust and cynicism: the percentage of Americans questioned who stated that "most people can be trusted" fell from 54 percent in 1964 to 35 percent in 1995, whereas the percentages of those who thought the federal government could be trusted to do the right thing most of the time fell from 76 percent to 25 percent over the same period. Of those questioned, 48 percent believed that most of the time people are mainly looking out for themselves; when offered the choice between "most people can be trusted" and "you can't be too careful" dealing with others, 63 percent agreed with the latter. In a sign of Americans' pessimism, 54 percent said they were not at all confident that their children's lives would be better than theirs (*Washington Post*, January 28–February 2, 1996). The articles were based on surveys conducted jointly by the *Post*, the Kaiser Foundation, and Harvard University. A more coherent analysis of the results than was offered in the articles themselves can be found in Robert J. Blendon, Richard Morin, Drew

E. Altman, Mollyann Brodie, Mario Brossard, and Matt James, "Changing Attitudes in America," in *Why People Don't Trust Government*, ed. Joseph S. Nye, Jr. (Cambridge: Harvard University Press, 1997), 205–16.

12. For an excellent critique of the way this sort of "voluntarist" illusion characterizes so much of the political activity of the American left, see Jeffrey C. Isaac, "The Poverty of Progressivism," in *Democracy in Dark Times* (Ithaca, N.Y.: Cornell University Press, 1998), 123–49.

13. There are, of course, many other forces at work in our (post)modern, hyper-mediated, culture that explain this turn, too, although liberalism is plausibly one factor among others. Both because liberalism does not offer citizens any language of systemic analysis and because, as Sandel suggests, this absence of moral language opens space for nonliberal moralizing voices, liberalism ends up encouraging systemic problems to be read as personal moral failings, with responsibility laid more on bad, corrupt politicians than on a basically corrupt*ing* system.

14. Taylor, "Living with Difference," 222, 223.

15. One could argue that the political alienation of both American liberals and conservatives is a negative reaction to different aspects of *modernity*. This reading would be consistent with the central argument in Taylor, *Ethics of Authenticity*.

16. This sense of alienation — of not being heard — is obviously heightened by the various voting fiascos in the Florida presidential election of 2000, given that many black Americans votes literally were not counted or were not able to be cast.

17. William E. Connolly, "Fundamentalism in America," in *The Ethos of Pluralization* (Minneapolis: University of Minnesota Press, 1995), 111. In this chapter, further references to this essay are abbreviated FA and included in parentheses in the text.

18. Connolly's argument here is consistent in many ways with those of Thomas and Mary Edsall in *Chain Reaction: The Impact of Race, Rights, and Taxes on American Politics* (New York: Norton, 1992). See also E. J. Dionne, Jr., *Why Americans Hate Politics* (New York: Simon and Schuster, 1991), 31–97. For earlier attempts by Connolly to understand the problems facing American liberalism and the Democratic Party during the early 1980s, see "The Politics of Reindustrialization," and "Civic Disaffection and the Democratic Party," in William E. Connolly, *Politics and Ambiguity* (Madison: University of Wisconsin Press, 1987), 17–41. For a very different reading of this same historical change in white working- and middle-class attitudes toward the Democratic Party and liberalism, see Felicia Kornbluh, "Political Arithmetic and Racial Division in the Democratic Party," *Social Policy* (spring 1996): 49–63. In Kornbluh's interpretation, the view of the Democratic Party and liberalism as catering to the excessive demands of African Americans and other racial minorities was the result of fundamentally racist reactions to attempts in the 1960s to democratize and make more inclusive a welfare state that in its New Deal version distributed its benefits in racially exclusionary ways,

19. It is also not clear how exactly the retrieval of civic virtue that Sandel

advocates here will be able to reverse the vicious circle of public disinvestment. There would, at least at first glance, seem to be ample grounds for skepticism. For such a reversal would seem to face the kind of paradox that Rousseau articulates in his discussion of the legislator in *On the Social Contract*: the effect — in this case, the sense of civic virtue and collective identification that *depends on* vibrant and egalitarian public institutions — would have to become the *cause of* those institutions.

20. For a very helpful — although very different — analysis of the many unanswered questions provoked by Sandel's reliance on the category of "virtue," see Thomas Pangle, "The Retrieval of Civic Virtue: A Critical Appreciation of Sandel's *Democracy's Discontent*," in Allen and Regan, *Debating Democracy's Discontent*, 17–31.

21. It is interesting to wonder to what extent the policies of enforced "good citizenship" that Sandel endorses are the product of the phenomenon that Sandel himself bemoans, and whose dangers he highlights: the decline of public spaces in which citizens from diverse social, economic, and ethnic backgrounds can meet and learn from each other. In the absence of such spaces and of healthy, egalitarian public institutions, not only are a whole host of social problems likely to emerge, but so, too, are reactive and moralistic attempts of more privileged and resource-rich segments of society to impose their moral standards through undemocratic forms of social control. My thanks to Karen Werner for drawing my attention to this connection.

22. There is, in other words, a worrying tendency in Sandel to slide from arguing for the situated character of human selves to supporting the use of highly contested moral and religious arguments to determine law and public policy. For example, Sandel proposes quite plausibly that to master today's global political forces, we need to turn to "the places and stories, memories and meanings, incidents and identities, that situate us in the world and give our lives their moral particularity" (349). For Sandel, the weakness of liberalism in this context is that it asks us to "bracket these attachments, to set them aside for political purposes, to conduct our political debates without reference to them. But a procedural republic that banishes moral and religious argument from political discourse makes for an impoverished civic life" (349). Without making an explicit argument for the overlap, Sandel here simply equates *situatedness* and *particularity* with "moral and religious argument." While religious and moral arguments certainly draw on and produce particular attachments, they by no means exhaust such attachments, stories, memories, or identifications. Recognizing the importance of the stories and attachments that situate us in no way requires accepting that the majority's moral and religious beliefs are appropriate legal standards for all. Yet this is the leap Sandel repeatedly makes, without ever offering any theoretical defense for it.

23. Amartya Sen, "Other People: Beyond Identity," *New Republic*, December 18, 2000, 26–27.

24. This reading of Sandel would bring it fairly close to the definition offered by William Connolly: "My identity is what I am and how I am recognized rather than what I choose, want, or consent to. It is the dense self from which choosing, wanting, and consenting proceed. Without that density, these acts could not

occur; with it, they are recognized to be mine"; Connolly, *Identity/Difference: Democratic Negotiations of Political Paradox* (Ithaca, N.Y.: Cornell University Press, 1991), 64.

25. William E. Connolly, "Civic Republicanism and Civic Pluralism: The Silent Struggle of Michael Sandel," in Allen and Regan, *Debating Democracy's Discontent*, 205–11. In this chapter, further references to this essay are abbreviated CR and included in parentheses in the text.

26. That Connolly is well aware of the vicious circle of public disinvestment and the need to escape it is made clear in the following passage: "These civic virtues — each of which offers support and sustenance to the others — provide enabling conditions for a cultural pluralism of democratic governance appropriate to contemporary life. When they find expression in family life, schools, churches, military organizations, political speeches, public elections, corporate structures, and city politics, they enable cultural pluralism to be. When such a pluralism is in place it creates the most impressive possibilities obtainable in contemporary life to build general political coalitions in support of its own economic and educational conditions of existence" (CR 210). My point is simply that we need first to figure out what the "enabling conditions" of the civic virtues might be, especially given what Connolly gestures toward in his final sentence — the fact that such civic pluralism and the virtues it is based on are themselves in need of "economic and educational conditions of existence" that are not yet in place.

27. My argument here is sympathetic with and influenced by Taylor's *Ethics of Authenticity* and his warning about the dangers of "soft relativism," in which a number of the most powerful and constitutive threads come together to threaten to undermine the possibility of making value judgments that can be meaningful across diverse social groups and political constituencies. Although I do not share Taylor's harsh opinion of Nietzsche and contemporary "Nietzscheans," who take much of the philosophical blame for this tendency, and although I do not think that Connolly's own argument is a relativist one, I do think that unless proper precautions are taken, arguments like Connolly's can easily appear to be, especially to social conservatives desirous of clear moral answers. The risk I am pointing to is, I think, very close to what worries Sandel in his brief and inadequate response to Connolly's criticisms in his "Reply to Critics" in Allen and Regan, *Debating Democracy's Discontent*. Sandel worries that "as a matter of moral psychology, decentering or disrupting people's sense of who they are doesn't necessarily inspire greater openness toward the practices and convictions of others" (332). Although I agree with Sandel that "the best response to the intolerance that fuels the culture wars is not [simply] to deconstruct the identities of the combatants," I don't believe this is *all* that Connolly is arguing for. Nor does Sandel's alternative — "to challenge the economic forces and cultural tendencies that enervate citizenship and erode the dispositions that equip us for self-rule" — give adequate consideration to the kinds of psychological and rhetorical resources that both Connolly's "postfundamentalism" and my "nonmoralistic" approach to civic virtue attempt to activate.

28. For one of the best accounts of the role and dangers of the moralistic political discourse, especially on the left, see Wendy Brown, *Politics out of History*

(Princeton: Princeton University Press, 2001). Although I don't use the term exactly as Brown does, my discussion of moralism is indebted to her critique. Particularly insightful is Brown's argument that moralism's antipolitical stance toward the world can be understood at least in part as a reaction to how difficult and discouraging the political world can be. In its promises of moral purity and certainty, moralism offers a sense of reassurance, able at least in part to make up for the experience of political powerlessness. Thus the particular appeal — across the political spectrum — of the position of the victim, whose "purity" resides in its distance from power. Out of a fear and resentment of power, moralism withdraws morality from the world.

29. My reflections on moralism and the cynical reactions it generates have learned much from Hannah Arendt's devastating critique of the antipolitical logic of the virtue politics characteristic of the French Revolution. To the extent that the point of political action became that of purifying one's heart through compassionate responses to the sufferings of the masses, a vicious logic of suspicion and hypocrisy was unleashed, ultimately fueling the antipolitics of the Terror. Although my focus here is not specifically on the politics of the heart, whose hidden motives Arendt argued could never be known and were thus a perennial source of suspicion, the kind of "virtue" that contemporary moralism tries to establish has much the same, if less severe, kinds of antipolitical effects. See Arendt, "The Social Question," in *On Revolution* (New York: Penguin, 1963), chap. 2, esp. 96ff.

30. The same basic openness and uncertainty of democratic politics and argumentation also manifest themselves in the never-ending process of determining the meaning of the democratic principle of "equal liberty for all" — and with the same risk of provoking cynical critique. These twin principles of equality and liberty are presented in this phrase as compatible, as they are in many cases. Yet the fact that in a variety of other ways they prove to place limitations on each other can be a source of much frustration and doubt about the legitimacy of the system, or about the good faith of those who speak in the name of its principles. Thus, although democracy promises "equal freedom for all," in practice it simultaneously offers many apparently legitimate examples of people who have things (power, property, wealth, opportunities) that others do not. So, too, from the opposite direction, the goal of guaranteeing the equal freedom of some citizens constantly requires restrictions on the freedom of others. These might take the form of limits placed on the use of one's property in order to ensure others' basic human dignity (e.g., regulation of working conditions, labor rights, etc.) or to ensure others' equal right to clean air and water. So, too, with the limitations, through taxation, placed on how much wealth people are free to control, in order to ensure the good of the community (schools, highways, etc.) or others' equal freedom (a decent education or basic needs). In these and other cases, policies designed to achieve equality also require restricting someone else's freedom, yet *without any obvious or agreed upon way to calculate or balance* different kinds of freedom or the two goals of liberty and freedom. The "same" principle can thus be invoked to argue for widely divergent policies — indeed, "equal liberty" can even be used to defend those de facto *restrictions* on people's equality and potential due to the fact that

some are *free* to use their wealth and power as they see fit, thus depriving others of resources. In these cases, too, then, democratic argumentation can easily bring with it charges of cynicism. For a brief but powerful set of examples of how American conservatives today invoke the basic principles of liberal democracy — individual rights, equality, nondiscrimination — in ways that are diametrically opposed to political liberals, see Stanley Fish, "Epilogue: How the Right Hijacked the Magic Words," in *The Trouble with Principle* (Cambridge: Harvard University Press, 1999), 309–12. Fish argues that American liberalism is severely weakened by its general inability to notice and accept that there is no inherently liberal, or good, meaning to its own cherished principles and that they can thus be put to political purposes that liberals abhor.

31. For an analysis of attitudes about voting written prior to the 1992 presidential election that makes this basic point, see Joe Sartelle, "Cynicism and the Election," *Bad Subjects* 2 (October 1992); also available on line at http://eserver.org/bs/02/Sartelle.html.

32. For helpful analyses of the huge reservoirs of cynicism to be found in contemporary "popular," advertising, and media culture, see Mark Crispin Miller, *Boxed In: The Culture of TV* (Evanston, Ill.: Northwestern University Press, 1987), especially the essays "Hipness unto Death" and "A Viewer's Campaign Diary, 1984"; Todd Gitlin, "Television's Anti-Politics," *Dissent*, winter 1996, 76–85; and idem, "The Culture of Celebrity," *Dissent*, summer 1998, 81–83. More generally, my thinking on the politics and discourse of cynicism has been influenced by Peter Sloterdijk's impressive and encyclopedic *Critique of Cynical Reason* (Minneapolis: University of Minnesota Press, 1987). Also helpful is Timothy Bewes, *Cynicism and Postmodernity* (New York: Verso, 1997).

33. For a fascinating analysis of the centrality of this process to American politics over the past two centuries, see Samuel Huntington, *American Politics: The Promise of Disharmony* (Cambridge: Harvard University Press, 1981). For Huntington, the proper response to the perpetual disappointment of democratic politics and the threat it can pose to the legitimacy and stability of the state is to reduce the spaces for popular participation and restrict the democratizing demands that average citizens can make on the state. The value of the kind of nonmoralistic language of political engagement I am advocating resides, instead, in its potential to make it easier to sustain the inevitable disappointments and difficulties of democratic politics, thus allowing for *more* popular participation and democratizing projects.

34. For a helpful analysis of the "dilemmatic" character of contemporary politics, especially with respect to issues of "identity," see Bonnie Honig, "Difference, Dilemmas, and the Politics of Home," *Social Research* 61, 3 (fall 1994): 563–97.

35. This problem, in essence, is the one we saw bedevil Rousseau's attempts to construct a seamless ground for political legitimacy, which ultimately brought him face to face with the paradox of effect and cause.

36. For an excellent recent discussion of the difficulty of drawing boundaries to political and social responsibility and the problems this poses for attempts to formulate more generous democratic practices of responsibility, see Marion Smiley's review essay "Reconstructing the Generous Public," *Political Theory* 29, 1 (February 2001): 127–44.

37. My use of the term *system* here is deliberately meant to echo the uses Habermas makes of the same term, especially in his *Theory of Communicative Action*, vols. 1 and 2 (Boston: Beacon Press, 1984 and 1987). For a very different analysis of the present closures of "the system," see Jean-François Lyotard, *Postmodern Fables* (Minneapolis: University of Minnesota Press, 1997), especially the essays "The Wall, the Gulf, the System" and "A Postmodern Fable." Habermas and Lyotard, of course, disagree profoundly over whether *in principle* there are ways of rationally stepping outside the confines of the system so as to offer a moral and political critique. I argue, however, that both would agree with my point here: that in practice, even in the best of situations, democratic actors today are forced to a large extent to use the system's own tools against it, and thus they are caught up, to varying degrees, in the suffering and injustice of the system, even as they try to change it.

38. Kim Curtis, *Our Sense of the Real: Aesthetic Experience and Arendtian Politics* (Ithaca, N.Y.: Cornell University Press, 1999), offers an excellent analysis of how difficult it is to break out of the political ignorance that prevents us from seeing, and then responding democratically to, our implication in a whole variety of forms of suffering and injustice. Indeed, she argues that the central thrust of Arendt's political philosophy was to analyze and work against the radical forgetfulness that modernity forces on us and the suffering of oblivion that many others are forced to endure. For Curtis's particularly powerful reflections on different forms of political oblivion and "enclaving," in which citizens more easily forget and are forgotten, losing touch with the political reality of plurality and mutual indebtedness, see her first chapter, esp. 1–5.

39. This suggests the need for an understanding and practice of civic virtue that takes this condition into account. For an interesting critique of Sandel's failure to articulate such a vision of civic virtue, one that would be appropriate to modern conditions of mass society, in which few citizens can have confidence that their individual political action makes a difference, see Jeremy Waldron, "Virtue *en Masse*," in Allen and Regan, *Debating Democracy's Discontent*, 32–39.

40. For a brief but very interesting discussion of the role of emotions in democratic deliberation, and the need to formulate rhetorical and discursive strategies for effectively coping with the burdens and risks they pose, see Ricardo Blaug, *Democracy Real and Ideal: Discourse Ethics and Radical Politics* (Albany: State University of New York Press, 1999), 153–54.

41. One example of such an unpleasant discovery was a recent magazine exposé of the international flower industry, which detailed the massive environmental destruction, labor abuses, and outrageous surplus value that goes into most of the flowers found at the local florist. See Niala Maharaj and Donovan Hohn, "Fleurs du Mal," *Harper's Magazine*, February 2001, 66–67.

42. For an analysis of the self-defeating character of the moralizing rhetoric of the New Left in the 1960s, and of the Students for a Democratic Society in particular, see James Miller, *Democracy Is in the Streets* (Cambridge: Harvard University Press, 1987).

43. Charles Taylor discusses the ways in which high ethical standards of justice and benevolence can provoke and be provoked by less-than-appealing atti-

tudes such as resentment, guilt, anger, self-satisfaction, and self-condemnation, in the closing pages of Taylor, *Sources of the Self* (Cambridge: Harvard University Press, 1989), esp. 515–16. For Taylor, however, it seems that such difficulties are primarily the result of the disjunction between the high standards and the lack of moral sources strong enough to sustain, or ground, them. With the proper spiritual and/or religious beliefs supporting them, he argues, the language and practice of high ethical standards would not run the risks both he and I see it running today. How those beliefs could be awakened today in democratically friendly ways is not a question Taylor answers.

44. This is not to say that there is no room in democratic discourse for backward-looking responsibility or accountability for past injustices or violations of democratic principles. It is to say, though, that this juridical inclination runs much greater risks to democratic politics when used in appeals to one's fellow citizens, as opposed to the treatment of large institutions and powerful interests and actors who would otherwise tend to escape democratic accountability. It should thus be kept to a minimum within specifically political, as opposed to legal, discourse — and one should generally resist treating political issues *as* legal questions. More generally, of course, political pragmatism demands that one be aware of the past actions and tendencies of one's opponents as well as those of the unconvinced and of one's supporters — but only as evidence for what they might *become* and how they might be appealed to, not as telling us anything about an essential character or personality they might have. My argument here has been influenced by Max Weber's powerful analysis of the political irresponsibility of backward-looking searches for the guilty party. See Max Weber, "Politics as a Vocation," in *From Max Weber: Essays in Sociology*, ed. H. H. Gerth and C. Wright Mills (New York: Oxford University Press, 1946), esp. 117–28.

45. For a particularly helpful discussion — and deconstruction — of the central features of our everyday notions of the self, see Guy Claxton, "Meditation in Buddhist Psychology," in *The Psychology of Meditation*, ed. Michael A. West (Oxford: Clarendon Press, 1987), 29–31.

46. K. Anthony Appiah offers an excellent analysis of the damage done by restrictive identity "scripts" in his essay "Identity, Authenticity, Survival: Multicultural Societies and Social Reproduction," in Charles Taylor, *Multiculturalism: Examining the Politics of Recognition*, ed. Amy Gutman (Princeton: Princeton University Press, 1994), 149–63.

47. For a helpful analysis of Arendt's notion of "inter-est" as that which literally "is between" or "in-between," see Lisa Disch, "'Please Sit Down, but Don't Make Yourself at Home': Arendtian 'Visiting' and the Prefigurative Politics of Consciousness-Raising," in *Hannah Arendt and the Meaning of Politics*, ed. Craig Calhoun and John McGowan (Minneapolis: University of Minnesota Press, 1997), 142–43. Disch's essay also contains an excellent discussion of the dangers of political moralism in radical democratic critique and offers an appealing attempt to use Arendt, and the experience of feminist practices of consciousness-raising, to theorize a nonmoralistic language of democratic critique and engagement. For a fascinatingly similar theory of "inter-being," one that also aims to "ground" a compassionate language and practice of political and social respon-

sibility, although written from the very different intellectual tradition of Mahayana Buddhism, see the work of Thich Nhat Hanh, especially *Peace Is Every Step* (New York: Bantam, 1992); and idem, *Being Peace* (Berkeley: Parallax Press, 1987). For an example of a related practice of Buddhist nonmoralism and compassion as a form of democratic politics, see the writing of the Burmese democracy leader Aung San Suu Kyi, *Freedom from Fear and Other Writings* (New York: Penguin, 1995); and idem, *The Voice of Hope* (New York: Seven Stories Press, 1997).

48. On the crucial role played in a democracy by the other as "stranger," who questions us and calls our certainties into question, the artist, architect, and activist-theoretician of public space Krzysztof Wodiczko has much to say. For a particularly illuminating discussion of his ideas and public interventions with respect to the necessity of the stranger to democracy, see the interview of Wodiczko by Bruce Robbins, "The Science of Strangers," *Alphabet City*, no. 6 ("Open City") (1998): 134–47.

49. The Arendtian echoes in my discussion here are deliberate. It may seem counterintuitive to invoke Arendt in support of a theory of democratic compassion, given the convincing argument she offers in *On Revolution* for the antipolitical nature of compassion. Nonetheless, my vision of a nonmoralistic, compassionate mode of democratic language and responsibility is actually highly indebted to Arendt's work, particularly in its emphasis on the possibilities of new political beginnings supported by a forward-looking language of responsibility and other forms of "forgiveness." My reflections here can be understood as a beginning attempt to theorize more fully the role of "forgiveness" in politics, which Arendt argues is an essential companion to democratic founding and promising, and yet which she herself wrote very little about. Melissa Orlie offers a fascinating, and consciously Arendtian, discussion of forgiveness and its relation to promises, resentment, and radical democracy, in chapter 7 of her *Living Ethically, Acting Politically* (Ithaca, N.Y.: Cornell University Press, 1998), esp. 177–85. For an interesting discussion of Arendt's understanding of compassion, see Curtis, *Our Sense of the Real*, 85–92.

Index